A TRUE STORY

FORWARD

The first time that I saw John Swanger, I have to admit, I was a bit intimidated. It wasn't because he looked scary or anything. It was his confidence. It was the way he walked. It was the way he would look at you when you talked to him—like he was sizing you up for truthfulness and sincerity. In other words, his bullshit meter was running and you could see it registering any time he thought you slipped up.

He does look tough. I've always thought of him as a cross between a biker and a cowboy. His gray hair can be tied back into a ponytail or hang loosely on his shoulders. His gray beard can be close-cropped or long. He's even taken gigs working as a Santa Claus character during the Christmas season. Never before had I thought that Kris Kringle could ride a Harley during the off-season. The irony is not lost on Swanger and his sly sense of humor.

He's a man of integrity. In other words, he's integrated. He is the same on the outside as he is on the inside. He's a what-you-see-is-what-you-get kind of a guy. In all the time I've known him, he's never lied to me about anything. And there was plenty to lie about to a pastor. I was leading a young, punk-rock church (even though I'm John's age). We needed a place to meet, and he was sure he had just the right place. John had been working with homeless people for twenty years — feeding them, listening to their stories, helping them out of addictions, clothing them, and just being a friend. He had a place he called, *The Tollgate Coffeehouse*. It was a drop-in center for street people, a coffeehouse for those who slept outside, it was daycare for down-and-out adults. They could come eat a hot meal, wash their clothes and dry them, talk on the telephone, and use that address when they filled out job applications. It was the perfect meeting place for a church we named, ***Scum of the Earth***, and John knew that. He also knew that his building's neighbors would have as difficult a time accepting us as they did the homeless. John didn't care what the neighbors thought of him or the rest of us.

Over the years, I have listened to many of the vignettes from John's past. I've listened to them on occasion, two or three times, while watching the reactions of people who have never heard them before. There is no one else who can hold a room so spellbound just by telling stories from his varied and colorful life. From the difficult childhood, to the orphanage, to the petty crime, to the grand theft auto, to the many bank robberies, to prison, to the guitar-slinging, harmonica-ringing Country Rock band tours of Canada, to the strip-club bouncing, to the drug dealing (and that's not even the half of it), to his own hilarious and miraculous conversion to follow Jesus, to the present day, John's journey is nothing short of amazing. All of these episodes piece together the mosaic of a man searching for love, significance, and belonging; and then finding them in the most unlikely people and places.

So, dear reader, get ready for a wild ride. Strap on your life jacket. Put on your crash helmet. Make sure that your seat backs and tray tables are in their upright and locked positions. You're about to enter the life of one John Swanger.

Mike Sares

DEDICATION

BILLY JAMES HEADRICK
JANUARY 29, 1927 - MARCH 8, 1989

He taught me how to love others.
I consider him one of the best men I have ever met. He
taught me what unconditional love is. He showed me how to
respect others and to give to those in need.
He was a father figure and a man of integrity.
Unfortunately, he was also a Bank Robber.
We all have our faults and we all struggle with sin.
Therefore how could I ever judge him for his?

DR. BARBARA ELIZABETH BLISS
SEPTEMBER 29, 1924 - JULY 26, 1998

She taught me how to love myself.
I consider the countless hours she spent listening to me
and genuinely caring about my life, invaluable. Her love and
friendship were instrumental
in putting me on the path to who I have become.

TABLE OF CONTENTS

CHAPTER ONE

······························

CAPTURE

Wednesday - October 6th 1971

Shadows of the Minnesota sun lengthened as daylight gave way to dusk. My little sister Tammy sat tracing raindrops with her fingers as they hit the kitchen window. Dinner dishes had been cleared to make room for Walt and me to play chess. It was a peaceful scene until Tammy jumped up and warned, "There's a man heading for the garage."

My step-father, Walt, got up so fast his chair toppled to the floor. He grabbed the pistol from above the door and ran outside yelling, "Get off my property!"

I was right behind him.

The scene unfolded like an old movie. There were lawmen coming out from behind the barn, the garage, and from around the house. Some were leaning over vehicles with badges in one hand and 357's in the other.

"F.B.I. Throw down the gun!"

Immediately I thought: *wow, the F.B.I. for a deer? How did they know we'd been poaching?* Walt knew right away why the feds were there.

He tossed me the gun and said, "It's your game, how do you want to play it?"

I turned and tossed the gun to Mom who was standing in the doorway with her broom. She'd come out, armed and ready to take on the intruders. The rain had dwindled to a mist as Walt and I walked, with our hands in the air, to the center of the yard. One of the agents approached me.

"John Swanger?"

"No."

"That's a bunch of crap. You match the description to a tee."

Someone brought out a clipboard, examined a paper, and pulled up my shirtsleeve.

"Tattoo upper right arm. It says 'John.' Yep, you're our man, John Swanger."

They leaned me across the hood of a car, searched and cuffed me. Someone read me my rights.

I figured it was time to ask, "What's the charge?"

"Bank robbery."

"Don't you mean suspicion of bank robbery?"

"No, smart ass. The F.B.I. doesn't screw around."

I heard Walt ask if he could speak to me. Permission was granted. He came over and grabbed my Seiko watch, pulling it off my wrist.

"Listen John, you won't be needin' this or that diamond pinky ring." He took them both. "Do you have any cash on you?"

"About10 bucks."

Walt reached into my pocket, pulled out a wrinkled old sawbuck, and relieved me of that, too.

An agent approached and said, "Time to go." He took me by the arm and installed me in the back seat.

As we slowly drove out of the yard, it was raining again. I could see Mom standing on the porch, crying into her apron, with Tammy's arms around her. Mom's broom lay in the mud. Walt was nowhere to be seen.

Less than an hour later we pulled into the Beltrami County Jail in Bemidji, Minnesota. Several mug shots later I was fingerprinted; not just the typical set, but palm prints and the sides of each finger. The whole procedure took about two hours. When they allowed me to use the phone, I called the house. Walt answered.

"Listen John they're gonna put you away for a long time and there ain't nothin' you can do to change that. So listen to me real good. You just became the black sheep of the family. Most will disown and talk bad about you. And your Mom'll probably spend forever makin' excuses for you. Someday they'll let you out, but no one will be waiting for you. Count us all as dead. Understand?"

"Are you and Mom coming down here?"

"You're not listening. Let it go John, let us all go. You hear me?"

"But, are you and Mom coming down?"

The answer I got was the obnoxious sound of a dial tone blaring in my ear. I tried to convince myself Walt didn't mean what he said, and that he hadn't just hung up on me. My heart was broken.

I spent the next few hours going over every word Walt had said. I was doing what I could to keep my emotions in check. It was nearly morning before I accepted the fact that Mom and Walt weren't coming.

I had stayed awake all night thinking about the one thing I knew for certain. I was at a crossroad and the choice of which direction to take was no longer mine.

CHAPTER TWO

FREEDOM LOST

Thursday - October 7th 1971

By sunrise I was rolling down the highway with two of the F.B.I. agents who had arrested me. Destination: Duluth, Minnesota. The rocking motion in the back seat was more than I could handle. When I woke up, we were pulling into the sally port of Saint Lewis County Jail.

"How long have we been on the road?"

"Just over four hours. It's about a 200 mile trip."

Sleeping upright, in handcuffs had been brutal. I was both physically and emotionally drained. After being booked, I was taken to a doctor who examined me. I must have looked like a wreck because he gave me a couple Librium. Within an hour I was out cold.

Friday - October 8th 1971

I asked for more Librium. He told me, "No. You're on today's transport list." I had no idea what that meant.

After a breakfast of scrambled eggs, soggy toast and the worst coffee ever, I spent the morning staring out at Lake Superior through a wall of glass and bars. I bet they put this glass here on purpose, so inmates would reflect on what they're missing. The beautiful view that otherwise would have been a blessing was somehow an additional punishment.

What in the world had I gotten myself into? Not wanting to show any signs of weakness, I fought to keep my composure.

"Swanger."

Did I just hear my name? Guess not. I continued staring across the lake.

"Swanger!"

I turned as the jailer called out, "Swanger, chains in the hole."

That was my first lesson in jailhouse jargon. "Down and out" means come to the bars, you're headed to court or you have a visitor. "Hat on tight" means you're being released and "chains in the hole" indicates you're being transported.

At the bars I was instructed to turn around and put my hands behind my back. After cuffing me, the guard "racked the bars," meaning the cell doors were opening. He took me to a holding area. Through the glass I saw two familiar faces. The same F.B.I. agents were signing me out.

"Where are we going this time?" I asked.

The taller guy replied, "As soon as the wheels are turning we'll let you know."

When we pulled onto the Interstate the shorter agent turned to me, "We're headed to the Twin Cities."

"What does that mean?"

He snickered, "Minneapolis-Saint Paul, about a 150 mile trip."

Unlike the day before, both agents were very chatty, trying to engage me in conversation. It felt like an interrogation as we cruised down the highway. It was an obvious attempt to extract whatever information they could.

"Look, gentlemen, I had nothing to do with anything and I'm not interested in becoming friends. So we can chitchat about the weather or I'll just take a nap. Either way we're not discussing the bust."

They changed their tactics and stopped talking to me. Instead they were talking about me. Maybe they thought I could be tricked into divulging something. Instead, I went to sleep.

Jail in Minneapolis-Saint Paul was much different than Duluth. I was stripped of my clothes and issued an orange jumpsuit with COUNTY JAIL stenciled across the back in big black letters. I kept to myself, trying not to attract attention. It was a good move. There were frequent fights over card games and television programs. Tobacco was the main fuel for conflict. Every newcomer was pressured for his "straights," "tailor-mades" or "ready rolls" . . . all jailhouse terms for store-bought cigarettes. The guards passed out rolling tobacco every other day. Real cigarettes were a commodity.

Each cellblock was designed to hold 64 men in 16 cells, eight on a side. Each cell was eight feet square, with upper and lower bunks on opposite walls, a toilet and sink between them. Five, sometimes six guys were packed into a four-man cell. Extra mattresses were shoved under the bottom bunks. We were only allowed in the cells at night. The Day Room was where we ate, watched TV, played cards, and hung around . . . waiting.

Monday - October 11th 1971

The Federal Courthouse was only a few blocks away. We drove there in a van with tinted windows. I was parked in a room no bigger than a closet. One hour later, a man in a tan tweed jacket walked in.

"I'm your lawyer."

"That's news to me. I haven't hired anyone. Is this some kind of trick?"

"Not at all."

"I know my rights. I don't have to talk with you."

"But I'm on your side. I represent you."

"I don't believe it."

He showed me his Public Defender's I.D. and gave me one of his business cards. "You'll be appearing before a federal Judge for arraignment. Bail will be set at the same time."

I didn't want to look dumb so I just acted like I knew what he was talking about. He knocked on the door and the guard came in, cuffed me and escorted us to the courtroom.

The judge read the charges against me, "One count of bank robbery in the Western District of Washington. Do you understand the charge?"

"Yes."

"Bail is set at $50,000. Will you be able to post it?

"I don't know."

"The guard will return you to your cell."

The attorney asked permission for more time with me. It was granted. Back in the tiny room, his expression changed to a smirk.

"Well, did you do it?"

"No." I still didn't trust him.

"Do you want me to send a bail bondsman to see you?"

"I don't know what that is."

He explained the process to me then asked, "Can you cover the 50k?"

"It's possible."

"Right, you didn't do it but you can come up with 50k just like that."

I couldn't help it. I smiled.

The bondsman weighed 400 pounds and smelled like soap. He wore a hat like the one Tom Landry wore and looked like he'd been around the block a few times.

"Normally we take 15 percent but I need 25k to get you out."

I thought for a moment before saying, "If you get me out, I'll take you to the money."

"No way kid. Tell me where the money is; then I'll get you out."

I told him Mom's address and he gave me a strong warning. "Don't waive removal until you hear from me."

"What does that mean?"

"I gotta run; your lawyer will explain."

Monday - October 18th 1971

One week went by without hearing from the bondsman. What I did hear was the familiar call, "Swanger, down and out." Once again I was taken to the holding room at the courthouse where my attorney explained the process of removal to Washington State.

"You have the right to fight removal but the Feds have substantial evidence against you. Eventually you'll lose."

"The bondsman said I shouldn't waive removal until he comes back."

"John, he isn't coming back. The farmhouse you sent him to was vacant."

I tried to hold back my tears. The attorney was shocked. I guess he thought bank robbers were tougher than that. My only thought was: *where's my Mom now? Will I ever see her again?*

Once in the courtroom, the judge explained the removal process, and asked, "Do you want to schedule a hearing?"

"Can't I just go to Washington?"

He handed me a bunch of papers. I signed.

CHAPTER THREE

SURPRISES

❖ ❖ ❖

Tuesday - October 26th 1971

One week later I was called to the bars again.

"Swanger, chains in the hole."

I expected to see the same F.B.I. agents. Instead, I was met by two U.S. Marshals, both in their late thirties. They were dressed in suits. One was much taller than me; the other was about my size with bright red hair. I was surprised when they each addressed me as sir. They shook my hand, introduced themselves, and gave me my dirty street clothes. I changed. They cuffed me and led me to their car. The tall one drove. Our destination: Minneapolis-Saint Paul International Airport.

I remember thinking: *these guys are real pros.* We entered the airport and walked to the gate. In a secluded corner, the red-headed marshal turned me around, looked me straight in the eye, and opened his suit coat to reveal a shoulder holster.

"This is a .357 Magnum, a very deadly weapon and I am highly trained to use it. Federal regulations require that we remove your handcuffs before boarding the aircraft. Are we going to have any problems?"

My answer was quick and to the point. "No sir."

"Very well Mr. Swanger, let's have a pleasant trip."

We entered the plane and took the last row. I was in the window seat on the left side with the redhead next to me. The other marshal sat across the aisle.

Once in the air, the stewardess came to our row. "Would you like something to drink?"

My answer was immediate. "I'll take a Vodka Collins."

The redhead glared at me and whispered, "You're not only a prisoner, you're under age."

Red got up and walked back to where the stewardess was pouring drinks in the galley. He returned with a glass and held it out to me. "You do drink orange juice don't you?"

I nodded and took it. One sip later I turned to see him put a finger to his lips. I smiled, sat back and enjoyed the last Screwdriver I would have for several years.

We deplaned at Sea-Tac Airport. Both men shook my hand, thanked me for a pleasant trip, and became marshals again. I was cuffed and handed off to two Seattle agents.

King County Jail was bigger and louder than my previous accommodations. It took nearly two hours just to get booked. The guard briefed me as I followed him down a long hall.

"In the cellblock you'll be on your own. Find a bunk if there is one. That will be your new home."

As I entered the Day Room of cellblock C, I did a double take. There was my best friend and partner in crime, Bill, sitting on a bench reading.

Unbelievable.

He saw me, came over and gripped my arm. "Great to see you John. We need to talk."

He took me to his four-man cell. There was one empty bunk so I threw my jail issue pillow and blanket on top. After a quick peek out the door we sat down.

"Linda and I were arrested in Elk City, Sunday, October 3rd. How about you?"

"They got me three days later, the 6th. Where's Linda?"

"I haven't seen her since the arrest. I don't know if she's up here or still in Oklahoma. How are you fixed for money?"

"I'm dead broke. Walt stripped me of everything."

Bill tossed over a crumpled pack of Marlboros. "I'll get you some more later."

I took the cigarettes, said my thanks and edged closer to Bill. We spoke in hushed tones.

"How do you think they caught us?"

Bill looked surprised. "You didn't hear?"

"Hear what?"

"Remember the bank on Ballinger Road up in Shoreline? The one we were going to hit right before things blew up?"

"Yeah."

"Well, Marty hit it right after we split. Shot three people including a cop and took four bullets himself. He got life. With nothing to lose he started talking, trying to buy back time. They shortened his sentence when he told them about all of us and Irene too."

"That creep turned in his own wife?"

"Marty has no conscience. He never could keep his mouth shut. So here we are."

"What's going to happen to us?"

"I don't know yet. For now, just keep to yourself."

For the next few minutes we sat, saying nothing, just thinking. Bill seemed older. He looked worn down, like he'd been through hell and back. But then again, I was exhausted and probably didn't look so hot either. There were no words for how I was feeling. Only two things were certain: all I owned was this half pack of Marlboros and the only person in the world who cared if I lived or died was Bill.

We'd been talking for an hour when a buzzer went off.

"Come on, John, that's dinner. We'll talk more later."

Salisbury steak and mashed potatoes sounded impressive until I took a mouth full. The steak tasted like rubber and the potatoes could have passed for glue. My plastic knife broke trying to cut the meat. I watched other guys stabbing their beef with a fork and bite off pieces. I did the same.

After the meal, back in our cell, Bill took a Three Musketeers bar, broke it in two, and dropped the pieces into our coffee cups.

"Hot chocolate," he said.

It felt good to laugh again.

As Bill poured hot water from the tap into the cups he said, "Mary is coming to see me tomorrow afternoon. I'll have her put a few bucks on the books for you. Do you have anybody on your visitors list?"

"No."

"Put Donna and Mary down. When the guards figure out we're together, they'll separate us for sure. If we need to talk, we can do it through the girls."

I still had a few questions needing answers. This seemed like a good time.

"Bill, I've always wondered about, well, about you and Mary. She's still your wife, but for as long as I've known you, Linda has been your woman. How does that work?"

Bill stretched and leaned back against the wall. "Mary is a wonderful lady, kind and always forgiving. In the beginning, we had something special. I'm the one who broke my vows. And, of course, our kids are important to me. I love them more than anything. By the way, I noticed you and my youngest hit it off from the start."

"Donna is a pretty girl, but a little young for me.

"But you're only 18 and she's 15."

"Compared to me, she's had a good life and I've been…."

"You've been hanging out with me."

"That's not what I meant. Donna and I are friends."

"Is that all?"

"Yes sir."

We discussed a few more subjects before Bill pulled out a book and began reading. I lay still, acting like I was asleep, but there was no switch to shut off my mind. I kept thinking about Walt's last words. *Was he right? Should I let go of everyone in my family? Count them all as dead?* Somehow, right then, it didn't seem to matter.

I began thinking about my older brother Donnie, when he came home from Nam, how distant and lost he was. Now, I was the one lost.

Wednesday - October 27th 1971

Bill shook my arm. I shot straight up.

"Easy tiger. Hurry or you'll miss breakfast."

I crawled off my rack, mumbling, "If it's anything like dinner last night, missing it might be a good idea."

Bill laughed.

Breakfast turned out to be cartons of milk and boxes of cereal, coffee and orange juice. Not too bad. We spent the next hour reading newspapers.

About mid-morning, I heard, "Swanger, down and out."

I had no one on my visitors list yet. I looked at Bill.

"It's probably your new attorney."

I went to the bars and turned around for the cuffs but the guard said, "Let's go."

They took me to a small room down the hall. I sat and waited. A few minutes later a tall thin man in his early thirties walked in.

"John Swanger?"

"Yes."

The man extended his hand. "I'm Garry Bass, your court appointed attorney."

We shook hands.

"Are they treating you alright?"

"How am I supposed to tell?"

The lawyer chuckled. "Let's get down to business."

I took that as my cue, "What's going to happen to me?"

"It's not complicated. We go to trial and if you're found guilty, you'll go to prison."

"What are the charges?"

"When you were arrested, the charge was robbing the National Bank of Commerce between Kent and Renton, but other banks are showing up. Seems you've been a busy boy."

I felt sick at my stomach.

"Several more states are also looking into filing armed robbery charges against you."

"So what do we do now?"

"That all depends. By the way, do you need anything?"

"I want to put two people on my visitors list."

"I'll take care of it."

"Thanks. But what happens next?"

"A photo show. It's a lineup using photographs. You'll probably face an actual lineup sometime before court. Oh, and if they offer a deal, are you open to pleading guilty for a reduced sentence?"

"I don't know."

He handed me his business card and said, "Keep your head up. I'll be in touch."

The guard came back and took me to a different cellblock, just as Bill predicted. Other than new roommates, everything was the same. Cell number 11 was like the one I'd shared with Bill, except for three thick glass blocks, high on the outside wall behind bars. Sunlight filtered in through them and actually created a tiny bit of warmth.

I flopped down on the lower bunk and stared at the mattress above me. It was being held up by straps, which crossed, leaving spaces that looked like holes. With nothing better to do I began counting the holes and thinking about what my lawyer had said.

Dinner time came and went but I ate a leftover sandwich from my stash. There was plenty of time to gaze at the high window and try to imagine what was on the other side. My guess was a misty gray evening growing bleak in the darkening Seattle sky. I lay there for hours, thinking about being locked up and lonely.

From the hollows of my confinement, I could faintly hear the echo of Janis Joplin singing Bobby McGee on a distant radio.

"Freedom's just another word for nothing left to lose. . . ."

CHAPTER FOUR

BEYOND THE GLASS

❖ ❖ ❖

Thursday - October 28th 1971

In the morning two things came to mind, Kris Kristofferson and black coffee. I caught myself humming Bobby McGee and debating which artist had the better cut . . . Kris or Janis. I poured a cup of mud and determined Janis, by far.

Inconspicuosity was my plan.

Stealth.

I settled down in a corner of the Day Room to listen and observe.

A larger-than-life man was obviously making known his position as dominator of the cage. He asked each man the same question, "Hey, whacha in for?"

One by one, they told their stories, swearing they'd done nothing wrong. They were either framed or some stupid girl ratted on them. However they worded it, each man was innocent. Could it be I was the only guilty one in here?

A deafening silence filled the room as everyone turned to look at me when he said, "How about you? What are you doin' here?"

"Drinking coffee or something vaguely like it," was my gruff reply.

It was the kind of thing you begin to regret almost before it's completely out of your mouth. I figured I could look away and risk his wrath or look them all in the eye and pretend to be confident. I chose the latter. They all watched as I shook out my last Marlboro, lit it and looked dead straight at the big one.

"I robbed a few banks. And now, as a punishment, I'm forced to drink this really bad coffee."

That managed to stir up a few laughs, but more important was a nod of approval from the large one. He sat down at my table and asked, "Did you really do it?"

"Well obviously not. I'm in here aren't I?"

He taught me to play Spades.

That night, dinner was barely over when I heard the familiar call, "Swanger, to the bars." The guard held out two packs of smokes and said, "These are from your father in C-12."

I lay down and once again counted holes on the bunk above. Stupid, but it was something to do. The guard had said, your father; I'd had four, and not one of them worth a shit. Growing up without a father wasn't as bad as growing up with several who didn't give a rip. Bill was more of a Dad than anyone I'd ever known.

I turned to the wall, terrified. *Oh God! I could spend the rest of my life in prison.*

Without warning, a rumble began in my stomach. Grabbing the toilet I puked so violently I thought dying might bring relief. When the worst was over, I used the sink to pull myself upright, twisted the faucet to full force and discovered full force produced a mere dribble. It took a while to wash my face and rinse my mouth. Turning and hoping to find a towel, instead I found my two cellmates standing, watching.

"Back up, I don't think I'm done yet."

At the same moment, "Swanger, down and out," came blaring from the speaker. The guys cleared a path and I walked to the bars. The guard looked at me with concern and said, "You have a visitor if you're up to it."

"No, no I'm good. Let's go."

I found myself thanking God for getting me out of that cell and distracting my thoughts, even if only for a few minutes.

Aware of our echoing footsteps, I decided the worst part of jail wasn't the dingy gray walls, awful food, or even the terrible coffee. It was the harsh clang of cell doors opening and shutting. There is a certain finality about cell doors slamming shut. I wondered if it was by design. Those sounds ricocheting down the halls had a demeaning effect. It made me feel small.

The guard and I eventually reached a long room divided into cubicles occupied by jumpsuit-clad villains. I walked toward my assigned station, passing men who were yelling, some crying and a few just waiting. Each sat facing windows of thick glass. Emotions were as varied as the faces of the inmates, their visiting girlfriends, moms, wives and children. There were only women visitors. That seemed a bit strange.

At cubicle 14, I sat staring at a vacant chair behind the glass. Within minutes a very pregnant version of Donna appeared. I tried to talk, but couldn't keep from staring at her bulging belly. I was totally distracted.

Finally Donna asked, "Are you okay?"

"I'm fine. You're pregnant."

She smiled, "The baby is due sometime after Christmas."

"Who's the father?"

"Just a guy."

"Does he know you're pregnant?"

She almost looked annoyed. "No, I was only with him once; then he left town."

My heart sank. I looked down at the rivets holding the metal frame around the inch thick glass between us. In my mind I began counting the rivets and trying to collect my thoughts. *One, two, three. No one should be without a father. Four, five. Look where I ended up. Six, seven, eight, nine.* My eyes moved to the portion of frame that ran across the top of the window. *Ten, eleven. What would it have been like to live in a normal family? What if I'd known just one father, one dad who cared? Twelve.*

Still staring at the last rivet, I said, "Tell them I'm the baby's father." I looked at Donna. "No one should grow up without a dad. Tell your Mom and Bill, tell everyone I'm the father."

It was like I had no control over my words. A shocked look covered Donna's face. From the corner of my eye, I saw my reflection in the glass. Our expressions matched. We were both scared. Donna looked lost and confused, staring at me without saying a thing. Was she put off by my words?

Over her shoulder I could see the red light signaling our time was up. The guard tapped my arm and barked, "Let's go."

As I rose, Donna did too. Then she looked me in the eyes and simply said, "Okay."

I don't remember walking back to the cell but I can tell you I was a different man. I desperately wanted to be the father I never had. Nothing else mattered.

My cellmates had moved. Who could blame them? The place reeked of vomit. My mind was in turmoil, too many emotions in one day. Alone, scrubbing the toilet and floor, no one was about to interrupt me, I needed time to think.

After changing into a clean jumpsuit, I switched bunks and tossed my pillow on the foot of the bed. Looking up at the high window, again I tried to imagine what was beyond the glass. My thoughts were of Donna, the baby and me. How long before we'd be together?

The King of the Cage had been moved to another cellblock, which brought conflict over a new pecking order. Racial tensions were building. You could feel the stress elevate each day. Staying in my cell writing letters to Donna seemed the best way to avoid the explosion I sensed was coming. I found myself praying, "God protect me."

CHAPTER FIVE

....

FERMENTED FRUIT

Wednesday - November 3rd 1971

I awoke wondering if the other cellblocks were as riled up as ours. Break-fast was worse than usual because the kitchen coolers were down and the cartons of milk were warm, which didn't help an already tense situation. Everyone was cussing and yelling. Two men were taken out for fighting, then everything went quiet. For a moment I thought we were back to normal, but it was quiet without peace. In fact it became a sinister silence.

Lunch was Lasagna without much meat but I liked it. Others didn't and grumbled their discontent. By mid-afternoon I was hungry and reached under my bunk for a Baby Ruth. Cigarettes and candy bars were comforting and held me til dinner.

Bored and needing a change of scene, I grabbed my coffee cup and entered the Day Room. While drawing down a refill, I overheard two men talking.

"There's no sense in us fighting each other."

"Yeah, workin' together maybe we can get 'um ta change a few things around here."

Soon the two guys were canvassing the Day Room giving out orders and making sure everyone was on board.

"Take yer trays, but don't eat."

I didn't think the food was all that bad. Why not eat it?

Then it happened. Dinner arrived and the guards began hand-ing out trays. Spaghetti, salad and garlic flavored rolls. As the last tray came through, the conspirators began throwing food back at the guards. Everything, including the trays, became missiles.

Everyone was chanting, "No more bad food; no more bad food...."

I quickly learned what a hunger strike was and found myself laughing at the guards as they ran the gauntlet of Italian food laden projectiles. The chant was loud enough to infect other cellblocks and we began hearing the same roar from the next one over and then the next. Apparently pasta twice in the same day was grounds for revolt. None of it made sense to me. I was just going along to get along.

Somehow local TV got wind of our demonstration. On the late news, they said mutiny had spread throughout the entire facility. I discovered there's nothing like a hunger strike to restore harmony within the fellowship of felons.

Thursday - November 4th 1971

Morning brought a breakfast of French toast with bacon and scrambled eggs. It's amazing how French toast can derail an uprising. Ironically, the two who started the whole thing were the first to pick up their forks. Within a couple of hours talk of reform had faded.

After finishing my meal, I was taken to meet with Garry Bass. He looked troubled.

"We only have a few minutes. You're scheduled for a lineup across the hall at 10:30.

Yesterday the Feds staged a paper lineup. Witnesses were asked to look at a series of photos and pick out the man who robbed them."

"And they all picked me?"

"No, but I'm concerned with how the whole thing was run. The only detail witnesses could agree on was: the bandit had a southern accent. They described the assailant as anywhere from six feet to six three, 21 to 29 years old, right handed, with blonde, brown or black hair and either brown or blue eyes."

"So what's the big deal? They didn't pick me."

"True, but the photos were five random 2x2 black and white mug shots of inmates, marked King County Jail, Seattle Washington. And there was one 4x5 color photo of you marked Dallas County Jail, Dallas Texas."

"So, if they didn't pick me we're fine. Right?"

"John, think about it, all the other pictures were small black and whites marked Seattle. Your photo was a big colored one marked Dallas,

Texas. And how do Texans talk? This is called 'poisoned fruit.' Images are being planted in the minds of witnesses."

"They're setting me up?"

"You got that right. And at the lineup, you'll have to stand with five others guys and say something like, 'Give me all the money.' You'll be the only one with a southern accent and the only one whose picture was in the photo show. It's definitely a set up. All we can do is hope for the best. Oh, and try not to look guilty."

Garry knocked on the door. The guard came and took us across the hall. One by one, the six of us in the lineup were asked to put on a wig. We were told to step forward, turn to the right and say, "Hand over the cash and no one gets hurt."

Bass was right. Three of the seven witnesses selected me even though none had picked me from the photo show. When the guards returned us to the conference room, Bass finished the briefing.

"John, it gets worse. Most of the witnesses who saw you in the lineup just now and in the photo show, will be convinced you're guilty when they see you in the courtroom."

That wasn't a great thought to leave on. Bass shook my hand and said, "Hang in there."

When he was gone, I heard, "Swanger, step out."

A harsh, unfamiliar voice summoned me into the corridor. I stepped out to find three guards. The shortest one said, "Hands on the wall and spread your feet."

I complied. After being searched and cuffed, they asked me to verify the contents of a bag. "Three packs of Marlboros, a few candy bars, paper, envelopes and stamps. Yeah, those are mine. Why?"

"You'll get them when you're back in gen pop."

"What's gen pop?"

"General population," quipped the short one, then added, "You're goin' to the hole."

"The hole," I learned, was a separate cellblock used for disciplinary purposes and protection. It's the jail within the jail.

Parker, the guard who had escorted me to see my lawyer, told the other two, "I got this."

The others walked off with my stuff. Parker and I headed to the hole.

"We stage random searches for contraband. During a sweep of B-Block, we found a knife on your bunk. You head out for a visit and leave your shank lying around in the open? Not too smart Swanger."

"It's not mine. But I don't expect you to believe me."

To my surprise he replied, "I do believe you. But it's out of my hands. Someone saw us coming and ditched the blade. It happened to land on your bunk. Just be glad they aren't throwing another charge at you."

"How long will I be in the hole?"

"A week, maybe five days. You'll be fine." He waited a moment, then added, "Swanger, you're young and from what I've seen, not a bad kid. Find something you're good at and apply yourself. It's not too late. You can still become an honorable man."

Parker's words stirred something inside me. They were words I would never forget. When we reached the end of our time together, he handed me off to another guard. I watched as Parker disappear into the catacombs.

The guard at the hole was a bulky man with a handlebar moustache. He took me by the arm. "You're not going to be a problem, are you?"

CHAPTER SIX

....

MUSIC

D-Block looked very different from the others. No Day Room, no coffee pot and no TV, just a series of much smaller cells. The guard removed my cuffs and handed me two blankets. I thought, *cool, in B-Block I only got one.* There was no mattress and no pillow in my cell, only a metal slab hanging from the wall. Two blankets? No wonder.

Unlike the sink back in my old cell, this one had plenty of water which ran constantly. There were no handles, no way to turn the roaring river on or off. The toilet was made of stainless steel with no lid. It was bare butt on bare, ice cold metal. For security purposes a light shined in from across the hall. Other than random psychotic screams, the hole was fairly quiet.

I spread out one blanket as my Serta Perfect Sleeper and rolled the other to use as a pillow. I flopped down wishing for something to read. There wasn't even a bunk above me. No holes to inventory. Within two minutes boredom was already threatening.

There was only a slight echo as I observed, out loud, "Crap, this is gonna suck."

I looked at my wrist, for a watch that wasn't there. I had no idea what time it was. With nothing to use as a reference, it was easy to see how a person could lose track. I was startled when an anonymous voice said, "About four p.m. near as I can tell."

The voice came from the next cell. I was glad whoever he was couldn't see me with my jaw dropped and eyes bugged, frozen, wondering how he knew my thoughts.

"What makes you think I wanna know what time it is?"

He laughed. "Because that's what everyone wants to know when they show up here."

"So, how do you know what time it is?"

"I'm on meds and they come in every couple hours, watch me take the pills and wave my little tongue around to be sure I swallowed. They were here at two and are due back about now."

He was right. Within seconds, I heard the main door open. A distant inmate called out, "The keys are walkin'." The phrase was a courtesy warning, to announce a guard was headed our way.

I tried to observe as they medicated my neighbor but couldn't see a thing.

When the guards turned to leave I asked, "Hey, what time is it?"

They didn't answer.

After the guards were gone, my neighbor blurted out, "My name's John Thomas Music. What's yours? And don't tell me you're a P.C."

"I'm John Swanger and what's a P.C."

"Protective Custody."

"Trust me, it ain't my choice to be here. Some jerk threw his shank on my bunk while I was out with my lawyer. Looks like I'm your neighbor for the next week. That is unless you're getting out soon."

I waited for a response but it didn't come. So I added "Music? You still there?"

Then, almost laughing, I heard him say, "Now just where would I go? I'll be right here til they come and take me back to Walla Walla."

"Walla Walla?" I asked.

"The State Pen. Walla Walla, a place so nice they named it twice. You headed there?"

"No, looks like I'm going to a Federal joint."

"What'd you do, rob a bank?"

"So they say. How about you? If you were already in prison, why are you here?"

"I'm on appeal, hoping for a reduced sentence. I shot a kid in the chest with a rifle. Me and three friends were stealing cars. A kid ran out and grabbed his jacket from the car. Before we knew it the kid was laying on the ground bleeding. Now I'm on death row."

I'd never met a person who'd killed anyone before. I lay there thinking about the kid just wanting his jacket and the shock of realizing how fragile life can be.

I must have been silent for quite a while because Music called out, "John, you still there?"

I shook off my thoughts and answered, "Now where would I go?" After another long silence, I added, "What's it like knowing you're going to die?"

Music took his time before answering. "It's not about knowing you're going to die. We all die. It's knowing when, that gets you."

Dinner came in a sack and I complained.

Music laughed. "Get used to it. They don't bring trays in here."

I was trying out ways to get comfortable for the night, when my new neighbor went off.

"You bastards better get me a legal pad. Hey. Hey, you sons of bitches bring me a typewriter. You inconsiderate jerks. No mercy, no compassion."

The main door opened, the guard stepped in and Music continued. "It's a Supreme Court order; all inmates are entitled to legal pads and typewriters."

I could see the guard shake his head and walk away.

Music called out, "You son of a bitch, wanna spring the trap? You wanna swing on my legs?"

The door slammed. Music was laughing.

I didn't get the joke so I asked, "Swing on your legs?"

"This is Washington State John. They still hang people here."

Suddenly my throat hurt. While I was thinking how horrible it would to die by hanging, Music asked, "Hey, John, how old are you?"

"I'm eighteen."

"Hell, you've got plenty of time to worry and whine and enough time to make something of yourself. I don't have that luxury."

"So, Music, how old are you?"

"I'm an old man John...." His voice trailed off, to a whisper, "...an old man."

I was just beginning to ponder his answer when he added, "Nineteen."

"I thought you said you were old."

"The question isn't how many years you've lived, but how many you got left."

I wondered, *how many years do I have left?* My thoughts shifted to Donna and the baby.

Music's next words startled me. "Make something of yourself," he said, "you're lucky, you still have time."

Parker had told me almost the exact same thing. Why had he encouraged me? Was there some reason I was here, next to a death row inmate?

I tried closing my eyes. Instead, I caught sight of writing high on the wall. I climbed on the bunk and read:

> *Death comes in darkness, his shadows are cold.*
> *Your life is his victim. He'll capture your soul.*
> *Great love is lost, for your life he shall take.*
> *Death comes but once. He'll make no mistake.*
> *Run away, go and hide. You're easy to find.*
> *Your life is soon taken, his last take was mine.*

May 1968

I shuddered and cupped my hand over my mouth so Music wouldn't hear me gasp. Was that poem another message for me? I took it as a warning. I began thinking, *so what if the lineup is 'tainted' or the photo show rigged. I did it and I deserve whatever comes next. Someone or something was speaking to me and telling me I needed to find a way to live right, find a way to become a better man. Perhaps God?*

I glanced again at the poem and wondered: *did the author kill himself in this little solitary box? Or was he waiting for them to do it?*

The last line kept echoing through my head. Then I whispered it, "Your life is soon taken, his last take was mine."

The week crawled by. I had nothing but my conversations with Music to move the hands of an unseen clock. I tried not to look up at the poem but I did anyway. I was determined not to let these days in the hole take my sanity. Talking with Music helped.

One night, after falling into a deep sleep, I was pulled into a nightmare complete with sound effects. *A judge's wooden gavel, striking its small pedestal, rang through my head over and over and over again. One by one, men with gray hair, in dark suits turned, sneering as each one pointed an accusing finger at me. The louder the gavel echoed the larger the men became. Then, as the gavel struck faster, calls of, "Swanger, Swanger" were interlaced with every blow.*

I jumped up to find the guard with a handlebar moustache was rapping the bars of my cell with his nightstick.

"Swanger, you plan to stay here forever? Let's go." Turning he called out, "Rack ten," and the door began to slide open. Then with a resounding bang it stopped.

I wanted to say goodbye to Music but his cell was empty. Sometime during the night he had been taken away.

On the walk back into gen pop, I was surprised to see Parker waiting at the main door. He smiled and asked, "How you doing?"

"Ok, I guess."

He handed me my bag and said, "I'll take you back to B-Block but can't guarantee the same cell."

I was hoping for cell number eleven, with the glass. That little bit of light coming through represented a point of hope. Being able to see something, anything beyond walls, was my lifeline to freedom and the outside world. Stopping at my old cell, I was disappointed to see all four bunks were taken. Reluctantly I moved back up the walkway and found an empty lower bunk in seven. I tossed my bag, my blanket, and myself on it, and sat for a long time looking at the floor.

The once polished concrete had long since given way to a filthy mix of chips and scratches. Under the opposing bunk, I spotted a roach. Pure reaction had me reaching for something to kill it with. Reconsidering, I watched as it scurried along the wall. The tiny creature moved a few inches, stopped, and advanced a little more until it reached the corner. From there he turned and took off like a shot, through a vent, to freedom. With a bit of envy and a congratulatory smile, I swiveled my body to lie down. My eyes looked straight up to the bunk above. "What? No holes to count?" Screwed into a steel frame, 10 inches from my face was a solid sheet of metal.

"Damn it!" spewed from my mouth. I curled up my left hand into a fist and smashed it hard into the bunk. Pain shot up my arm accompanied by the matchless sound of metal snapping, warping into a concave shape from my blow. I cupped my fist into my other hand and moaned. I was still angry and still staring at it when, without warning, the metal popped back into its original position. For some stupid reason that made me smile.

CHAPTER SEVEN

....

MARK IT FOR LIFE

Monday - November 15th 1971

I walked my increasingly gloomy self into the Day Room and filled my cup. Drinking coffee was the only consistent thing in my life. Sitting, preoccupied with my thoughts, I wanted the trial to be over and done with so I could move on to the next chapter. A Federal penitentiary somewhere would soon be home. Getting there would take me one step closer to freedom.

With all the waiting around, hope was growing thin. I hadn't seen Bill in weeks and had no idea where Linda was. I enjoyed seeing Donna but her visits made me sad. How could I be a dad if I was locked up? The whole family thing, the baby, me being a father, and Donna, weighed heavy on my mind.

I took my coffee and sat down at a long metal table. A guy nearby was sketching a bird on a sheet of paper using various items he pulled from a cigar box loaded with colored pencils, pens and markers. I moved over for a closer look.

"You're pretty good at that."

Without looking up, he answered, "Thanks."

I watched for a while and asked, "Where'd you get the markers and stuff?"

"I had them sent in. I was majoring in art and got busted for weed."

I asked, "What would it take to get one of them markers?"

"I don't know. Whacha got?"

I offered him a Baby Ruth and a Three Musketeers bar but he wasn't interested.

"How about a pack of real cigarettes?"

"I don't smoke."

He stood up, gathered his things then dug through the box. He pulled out a black Carters Marks-a-Lot and rolled it across the table at me.

He walked away with me calling after him, "Thanks and hey, what's your name."

"Max. My name is Max."

Back in my cell, I flopped on my bunk and took a closer look at the Marks-a-Lot marker. *Mark it for Life*, it said. Just then my focus went beyond the marker to the bunk above. A light of inspiration went off in my head.

The next few hours were spent covertly drawing permanent vent holes on the sheet metal under the bunk above me. When completed, I smiled and counted the holes, proud of my work and admiring my new implement of defiance.

I put my pillow at the foot of the bed so I could look to the spot where there should have been glass blocks above. My mind went back to the poem in the hole. I was impressed with the way its author had managed to immortalize himself with a few words written on a wall. I thought again about Parker telling me to find something I was good at. Well it certainly wasn't drawing vent holes. I looked again at my marker. It said *Mark it for Life*.

Talking out loud to myself, the words came out, "I think I will."

Climbing up and straddling both top bunks, I could reach high on the back wall. I began transcribing the words drifting into my mind from my heart and imagination.

As I sit in the darkness and look through the bars,
I gaze up to heaven and count all the stars.
I look over the sky then stare at the moon,
I think of my freedom and wonder how soon.

November 1971

Then I reached up higher, as high I could, and drew three glass blocks on the wall.

CHAPTER EIGHT

....

ANOTHER NIGHTMARE

Tuesday - November 23rd 1971

When reality and remorse collided, I was sucked into an undertow of nightmares. Most of my days were confined to thrashing around on a lumpy jailhouse bunk with my mind shackled to the past eighteen months. I was immersed in a simmering stew of fear, guilt, and shame.

Drifting in and out of sleep brought visions darting through my brain, sending rivers of distorted emotions into my dreams. *My little brother David's tormented face as that jerk running the orphanage beat him with a willow switch.* Like a horror movie with nonstop images blazing through my mind. *I lunged for the gun that Marty held to Bill's head. With my left hand curled into a fist I swung it up into his jaw. I felt skin hit bone and heard the crack. He was down and I was straddling his chest, pounding his face with both my fists, desperately trying to knock him out, to shut him up. But the harder I hit, the louder he screamed.*

"No. No." I heard myself yell and bolted forward. A sharp pain let me know my head had become intimate with the steel bunk above. I fell back onto the frayed mattress and used my sleeve to mop the bloody sweat from my face. The blow had derailed the latest in my series of nightmares. But I was still in jail, headed for prison, locked in a real life nightmare with no end in sight.

The crack on my head must have slapped some sense into me and made me aware of what day it was. A painful swelling rose up in my throat, rivaling the lump on my forehead. I stifled the urge to cry. A jail cell was not where I expected to celebrate my 19th birthday.

Afraid to fall asleep and face another nightmare, I rolled off my bunk and headed for the Day Room. I needed relief. I needed coffee, especially today.

At dinner one guy gave me a pack of Camels. Another gave me a couple candy bars. How did everyone know it was my birthday? I had told myself, no big deal. I tried not to let the gestures grab me but it was nice to be remembered...real nice.

I was finishing my meatloaf and mashed potatoes when Max, the artist, walked by. His arms were filled with paper bags...he was heading out. I was pleased to see him leave. Maybe he'd go back to school and make something of himself.

Talk at the end of my table let me know a severe thunderstorm was on the way. I thought, *so what? In here, who cares?* I wondered how many storms, or for that matter, how many birthdays would pass before I'd feel rain on my face again? I took my candy bars and cigarettes and left.

As I walked toward my cell, I could see it. There, in the middle of my bunk, sat the cigar box full of colored pencils, markers, and pens. Perched on top was a card with a hand drawn butterfly escaping to freedom between the bars of a jailhouse. Inside, a simple note.

Happy Birthday John
Max

Given my circumstances, the day had turned out better than expected. Then melancholy hit. Where was my mom? Was she thinking about me, wondering where I was? My emotions compressed into words I had to expel. The paper came from somewhere, or was it cardboard? I took a marker and wrote.

HELL

I lived for myself. I lived without a Soul.
I died in a gunfight for money I stole
As I lay on the ground shot twice in the head,
I knew it was over and soon I'd be dead
Under the streetlight I lay fatally hit.
I felt the change coming and I knew this was it
Inside my casket I lay in my grave.
Fear let me know I'd soon be a slave
Then all of a sudden the world broke through
And I fell down to someplace full of fire and I knew
I was locked here forever in the chambers of Hell
Fire rose around me, burning flesh I could smell
Ripping and tearing, flames bit at my skin
I knew I was paying for robbery, my sin
Satan stands watching the losers inside.
The fire keeps on burning; there's no place to hide
Torture keeps you moving as you do your fire dance
There's no God in Hell and there's no second chance

King County Jail, Seattle, Washington 10 pm, November 23, 1971

CHAPTER NINE

STORM

❖ ❖ ❖

Wednesday - November 24ᵗʰ 1971

Little did I know there's something about being locked in a cage, high off the ground that terrifies even grown men during a vicious storm. Sitting in the Day Room, petrified, you'd have thought we were all waiting to be executed. When lights flickered or thunder shook the building we all gasped. One kid was visibly shaken and ready to cry.

A big black guy jumped up and yelled at him, "Stop it dude. You're freaking me out."

Just then a guard came in to announce, "You guys should turn on the TV."

We tuned in Channel 4, KOMO evening news and were instantly glued to the screen. Someone named D. B. Cooper had hijacked a plane . . . from Seattle. There was no political motive, no demands for a free trip to Cuba. Cooper wanted $200,000 ransom for the return of all passengers and crew. It was a different venue but a heist none-the-less. Inmates cheered when they heard the details of Cooper's clever robbery in the sky. This breaking story kept our minds off the raging storm. The guard let our 10:00 p.m. lock down pass and said, "Since tomorrow is Thanksgiving, you can all stay out til midnight."

The concussion from lightning strikes against the building jerked me to the memory of another storm. I was seeing Mom's face, terrified, as she watched agents swarm outside her house. In my mind I could see the old broom fall from Mom's hand, bouncing off the porch into the mud.

CHAPTER TEN

REFLECTION

❖ ❖ ❖

Thursday - November 25ᵗʰ 1971, Thanksgiving Day

It was easy to be thankful for Nanny and Pa, my aunts and uncles, and for the many times they'd taken me in. Remembering the good times, I was thankful for my siblings too. I was super thankful for my mom. She'd done her best to make something out of nothing, trying to hold our family together. But it still hurt to remember being shipped off to live away from mom and being sent from one orphanage to another.

There was no way I could give thanks for my dad and three step-fathers, especially Walt, Mom's third and last husband. For a while, I thought he'd be the father I so desperately wanted and needed. Each one of those men had abused and abandoned Mom, my siblings, and me. Rejection is hard to forgive. I wasn't there yet.

It may seem strange but I was thankful for Bill and Linda. They had come into my life shortly after Walt kicked me out for the third time. It crushed me to realize he really wanted me gone for good.

I found a place to live and was hanging with adults, hustling at Times Square Pool Hall above Don's Coffee Shop at the corner of Carroll and Main. Eight ball was becoming my profession. I was developing a reputation. Along with playing high stakes pool, I was buying grams of crystal meth and cutting them into quarter papers and dime bags, more than doubling my money on each deal. Growing up poor, I liked having cash in my pocket. It never occurred to me how sad Nanny and Pa would be if they knew how their grandson was making a living.

One evening while banging a few balls around, practicing my game, a guy named Danny came in to tell me, "Hey John, there's someone downstairs you need to meet."

Danny introduced me to Bill, a distinguished looking gentleman and his girlfriend, Linda, a beautiful young woman. He was in his early forties, balding, and wore an expensive suit with a silk tie. She was a 19 year-old blond who looked like a Hollywood movie star. We sat.

Bill eyed me with a gaze that could harvest more information than any words I might muster. "Danny tells me you can acquire anything a person needs or wants."

With a touch of arrogance, I asked, "What do you need?"

"A shotgun," he replied.

"No problem." That answer rolled out before I could think about it. Bill handed me a piece of paper with his address. "Deliver it by six tomorrow evening; I'll give you $40."

I agreed. That was the beginning of an eighteen-month friendship with Bill and Linda. We became a family.

The echo of a nightstick against the bars was our call to dinner. We celebrated Thanksgiving with jailhouse turkey. Somewhere out there D. B. Cooper must have been dining in style. He received the ransom money, let the passengers go, and disappeared. We, however, were all still present and accounted for, in King County Jail.

CHAPTER ELEVEN

DOG & PONY SHOW

Monday - December 13th 1971

Showing up at court in a gray jumpsuit with K.C.J. stenciled on the left pocket and even larger letters across the back, would make anyone look guilty. I lay in my bunk thinking about the impression I was going to make dressed like a jailbird. If only I had some of the fine clothes Bill had bought for me.

They called me out of my cell before breakfast and walked me down the hall.

"No handcuffs?" I asked.

"Not yet. First we need to get you changed."

I was grateful to hear that. The thought of wearing street clothes gave me hope. We stepped into a big room. The guard said, "Drop em" and tossed me a bright orange jumpsuit with FEDERAL INMATE K.C.J. emblazoned across the pocket and the back. This was not the improvement I'd expected, so I asked, "What's with the new outfit?"

"Federal inmates are not allowed out of the building unless they're wearing orange. In fact you should have been in orange all along."

"Great." That observation came out of my mouth in a low, cynical growl.

"If your family brought civilian clothes, you'll get them at the Courthouse."

My words were almost inaudible, "Family . . . right . . . in my wildest dream."

An elevator lowered us to the basement. After signing a few papers, I was handed off to a marshal who walked me through a tunnel to the Federal building.

I was left in a holding cell for over an hour then moved to a conference room where I met with my attorney, Garry Bass.

"How you doing, John?"

"Okay. I guess."

"Linda is being charged in the National Bank of Commerce robbery and will be brought to trial with you."

"She's here?" I was surprised and excited.

"She'll be at the table next to us in the courtroom."

"Can I talk to her?"

"I don't think so. And it wouldn't be a good idea in any case."

Disappointed, I asked, "Any offers for a deal?"

Garry shook his head and continued shuffling through a stack of papers. I sat watching. Once finished, he stood and said, "I'll be right back."

Minutes later a guard escorted me to the holding cell. Around nine o'clock my handcuffs were replaced with a chain around my waist and my hands shackled to the chain. They shackled my ankles too. When I moved, the noise reminded me of when I was fourteen, working with Walt, chaining up cars to repossess them.

One marshal in civilian clothes walked me through the tunnel. Four armed guards in uniform escorted me and my clanking chains into the courtroom. A gasp welcomed me as I was ushered to my seat. The place was packed with prospective jurors and a massive table full of prosecutors. Donna was there, as she had promised. I was surprised to see her mother, Mary, and several unfamiliar spectators. I tried not to look at Linda or her attorney.

My shackles were removed and shoved around, making way too much noise. Garry rolled his eyes and whispered, "That's all for show. They want to convict you before the trial begins."

Linda looked sharp in a dark blue suit. Her hair was tied back in a conservative style. A string of pearls fell around her neck. She looked more like an attorney than a defendant. Our eyes met. She smiled quickly then looked away. We hadn't seen each other in nearly a year. That glance brought back an avalanche of memories. Linda, Bill, me . . . we'd been a team, good at what we did. But more than that, we were family.

Linda's lawyer was fat, about 60, with gray hair. He wore an expensive black suit and exuded experience and confidence. My attorney looked younger than his 30 years, tall, thin, dressed in gray tweed and appeared scattered, which did nothing to sooth my anxiety.

Donna sat as close to the front as she could, but had to shift back and forth to look around people in front of her. Seeing her offset the gawking stares and nasty whispers aimed at me.

"All rise." We stood as the clerk announced, "United States District Court for the Western District of Washington, The Honorable Judge Walter T. McGovern presiding."

When he had taken his place, the clerk added, "You may be seated."

The Judge thumbed through a pile of papers. He rattled off a few phrases, which were mostly filled with numbers and letters salted with my name and Linda's. I didn't understand any of it. As the judge gave instructions to begin the process, Linda's attorney stood and requested a motion to sever the trial.

I leaned in and asked Garry, "What did he say?"

"He wants Linda's case to be separate from yours."

The judge turned to the prosecutor who stood and asked that charges against her be dismissed. Everyone except Linda's attorney were surprised. I was shocked. Within two minutes they were out the door.

The next few hours were filled with legalese and questions. At first I couldn't figure out what was going on. Soon things started clicking. I was learning a lot.

Jury selection was pure monotony. I discovered that having a jury of your peers doesn't mean twelve bank robbers. The final selection was six women, six men, all nicely dressed and well groomed; everything from college kids to older professionals. I thought, why don't they just say twelve people? No one in that jury was qualified to be my peer.

Tuesday - December 14th 1971

Tuesday mimicked Monday. Except for the absence of Linda and her lawyer, we had the same Federal Marshals, same dog and pony show. I was still decked out in orange with rattling chains.

I turned to look for Donna and Mary. They were sitting closer to me this time. Mary gave me a quick thumbs up. Donna showed me her crossed fingers. I smiled.

The floor to ceiling door burst open as Judge McGovern entered. We all stood for his majestic emergence. This seemed to me much ado about nothing but at least the trial had begun. I sat listening as witness after witness took the stand and pointed their accusing fingers at me. Each one sank me deeper into my seat. One by one, Garry cross-examined them all with questions that changed nothing. The biggest debate was during testimony of the agent in charge at my arrest. Garry drilled him on whether my Miranda Rights had been properly administered. We did win that point, pointless as it was.

By 11:30 the prosecution rested and I took the stand. Garry asked if I was right-handed, I answered, no. He asked if I robbed the bank, again my answer was, no.

I couldn't believe it when Garry said, "No more questions Your Honor."

I was left-handed? That was my only defense? What was my lawyer doing?

Stuart Pierson, the U.S. Prosecuting Attorney approached the witness box and shoved a photograph at me. He was on my right side so I took it with my right hand.

"Do you recognize this photo?"

"No."

Before the word was completely out of my mouth Pierson said, "Of course you don't and it doesn't matter. The point is you took the photo with your right hand!"

I snapped back. "That's because you pushed it at me from my right side. I'm left-handed but it doesn't mean my right one is useless."

Pierson smiled and faced the jury, "My point exactly." He turned and headed back to his seat, and added, "No more questions Your Honor."

I began to see our side was clearly outclassed. After five minutes of closing arguments from each side my fate was in the hands of my peers. I was taken to a conference room.

Minutes later, Garry entered with Donna. "You have a few minutes then she has to go."

I placed my hand on her belly, then quickly turned away to wipe my eyes. Time passed quickly and soon she was gone.

"Ok Garry, what's next?"

"We wait. Could be later today, maybe tomorrow. We'll be called when they're ready."

"What do we do til then?"

"If you're a praying man, now would be a good time."

Garry assured me he'd be back before we re-entered the courtroom. In less than a minute the marshal showed up and took me back to the holding cell.

I sat there for what felt like forever, replaying the events of the day and of my life. I shook my head in disbelief, admitting I was no longer the teenaged bank robber who had shoved guns in people's faces. But it was my choice to commit robberies with Bill and Linda, going to such drastic lengths to earn the approval and attention of a man who was the closest to a real father I would ever have. And now I was a criminal, about to stand and face my reckoning.

Pray. Garry said pray. After all the appalling things I'd done, why would God listen to me now? I hadn't been in church for years and had no idea how to pray. I was ashamed to ask Him for help. Who was I that God would care what happened to me?

Around 3:00, I was escorted back to the courtroom. This time the gallery was vacant except for Donna. I sat, waiting for my attorney, the prosecutor, and the clerk to enter. Garry finally arrived.

"Looks like we have a verdict."

"What is it?" I asked.

"We won't know until the judge and jury are seated. Shouldn't be long now."

"What do you think?"

Garry took his time, "Don't get your hopes up. Watch the jury as they enter. If they look at you, it usually means not guilty. But if they avoid eye contact or glance at you and then look away . . . that's not good. Either way, we'll have to wait and see."

As the big door swung wide open, the clerk announced, "The United States District Court for . . ." Her words faded as I slipped into another world. I couldn't hear a thing as a muffled rumble filled my head. The bench began to appear bigger and the gravity of my situation tightened its hold, like fingers around my throat.

Then the echo of the judge's gavel pulled me back to watch as one by one the jurors marched to their seats. I searched their eyes, probing for a sliver of hope. But they took their seats without a glance my way. When the last man breached the door he looked me in the eye and smiled. Wow - he smiled! But I tensed up again when Judge McGovern looked at the jury and called out. "I understand you have a verdict?"

"Yes, we have, Your Honor," said the last man in. Once again he looked my way. "We the people of these United States of America, find the Defendant John Swanger . . . guilty . . . guilty on count one of the indictment and guilty on count two of the indictment."

I went numb. But it got worse. Why did Garry have to poll the jury? Did he ever consider how it would make me feel? I listened as one by one, the 12 stood and repeated the word: Guilty . . . 24 times. Each voice echoed through my head louder and louder as they rang out their condemnation.

When the last juror pronounced me guilty, I turned to see Donna running from the courtroom in tears. I was in shock. The realization of my fate suddenly hit me. But in a strange way, the verdict carried with it a sense of relief. It was done, over with, finished. I thought: *this is the hardest thing I've ever had to endure. Now it's over. Thank God.*

Later that night in my cell I wrote:

> *Life is so full of Yellows and Blues*
> *Sometimes you wonder which roads to choose.*
> *Think it out first, there's a lot to lose*
> *Two or three Yellows but hundreds of Blues*

Wednesday - December 15th 1971

It was sobering the next morning when, for the first time in my life, I woke up a convict. What a day for the coffeepot to die. I stood there blindly staring at the broken piece of crap as the guard called my name.

Oh yeah, I reminded myself. *Today we get to do the whole damn thing all over again. This time for robbing the First National Bank in the town of Federal Way.*

I was in a terrible mood. There we were in the same courtroom with the same judge, same prosecutor. I looked around and saw Donna. Her face so tired and sad, as if she was going to cry before we even started. I kept thinking, *why are we here? I'm already convicted. I'm already going to prison. Why do this over again?*

I didn't want to put Donna through any more pain. I didn't want to hear twelve more people denounce me. As they began selecting a new jury, I bent close and whispered in Garry's ear, "I'm done."

"What do you mean?"

"I mean I don't want to go through this again."

"Well you don't really have a choice. They're the ones calling the shots."

Suddenly I realized, small as it was, I had the power to control one little piece of my life.

"I want to change my plea."

"What?"

"I want to plead guilty."

"Why?"

"Like I said, I'm done."

Garry stared at me for what seemed like a long time, then stood and addressed Judge McGovern. I was on my feet as the judge asked, "Mr. Swanger, why do you want to change your plea?"

"Because I did it. I robbed that bank. I robbed the other one too. I don't want to waste any more of your time. I just want to get on with whatever comes next."

The judge looked stern yet thoughtful as he asked, "Has anyone promised anything in exchange for this plea?"

I looked at Garry because I didn't know what he meant. Garry shook his head and I answered, "No."

I looked at Donna. She was crying.

Within a few minutes I was back in the holding cell. I sat there and sobbed. The guard looked in on me and said, "I thought you were innocent?" I didn't say anything. I just turned my head and wiped the big, hot tears that wouldn't quit.

After about an hour of shivering on a cold steel bench, I heard the door open. In walked Marty, of all people, cheerful and totally out of character. This was the idiot we had worked with on most of our robberies. I hated him.

"Hey, John."

I was furious and shocked to see him. Why in the world would they put Marty in here, with me? I couldn't let him see my anger and confusion.

"Marty. What's up?"

"Trying to get my sentence reduced."

I straightened up, tried to be cool. "I heard the Shoreline Bank job went bad."

Marty pointed out each of his four bullet holes.

"Yeah, I took one here, one here and . . . ." I was seething.

"They got me good, John. Almost died."

My first reaction was to wish he had died. "What about Irene?" I asked.

"She's in Purdy State Pen for Women. I don't know where Linda is? Do you?"

"No, Marty, I don't. So, what about you?"

"I'm headed to Walla Walla. I'd sure like to know where Linda might be."

Why was Marty pressuring me about Linda?

"You two were tight. How'd you lose track of her, John?"

I just shrugged my shoulders. When he couldn't get me to say what he wanted, he became his old self, a jerk.

A few minutes later I was walked through the tunnel, headed back to my cell. That's when it hit me. Marty had been convicted on four counts of attempted murder in a Washington State court. He was never charged with bank robbery. So why was he in a Federal Courthouse? The puzzle pieces were coming together. Marty said he was trying to reduce his sentence. He was working with the Feds. They'd brought him in to testify against me. That changed when I plead guilty. Marty was trading Linda and me to reduce his prison time. I already knew he'd ratted out his wife, Irene. I was beyond mad.

CHAPTER TWELVE

CHRISTMAS

9:00 p.m. - Friday, December 24th 1971

Everyone in King County Jail was in a gloomy mood. Caught up in remembering years past, when Christmas Eve meant being with family, I decided to vent by writing.

> *T'was the night before Christmas,*
> *It's quiet in my cell*
> *No joy, no laughter,*
> *In these chambers of Hell*
>
> *No Holly, no stockings,*
> *No Christmas tree or snow*
> *These things are behind you,*
> *You're locked in this hole*
>
> *Escape through the air vent?*
> *Or stay here in bed?*
> *Shackles and Manacles*
> *Dance through my head*
>
> *And I heard the Guard say*
> *As he turned out the light,*
> *Spend your Christmas in jail*
> *See you tomorrow . . . Good night*

Christmas Eve 1971

Christmas came and went. I heard nothing from home. I was dead to them. This was the final blow, Christmas without family. Donna sent a nice card and letter with a few dollars to spend at the commissary.

During the holidays, a dismal atmosphere ruled. Time crept by and soon we welcomed the New Year. The only good thing that happened was watching Dallas beat Miami 24 to 3, making them the Champions of Super Bowl VI.

Go Cowboys!

CHAPTER THIRTEEN

THE RECKONING

Friday - February 4ᵗʰ 1972

This was it, the day of sentencing. My lawyer explained he would be negotiating for probation.

"It's possible they'll want to involve you in The Youth Act."

"What's that?"

"It's the Federal Youth Corrections Act 5010-B. If you get it, your sentence will be seven years. You serve two in prison, two on parole, then you're cut lose. If you make it through the final three years without getting into any trouble, the whole thing disappears. But I'm still trying to get probation. Keep your fingers crossed."

I stood before Judge McGovern, listening as he read the charges to which I had confessed my guilt. When finished, he asked, "Do you have anything to say?"

"Yes, Your Honor. I've been thinking about my crimes and there's no one to blame but myself. If I could back up two years I'd choose a better path but it's too late. I know my regret doesn't carry any weight, but I'm very sorry for what I've done. I never hurt anyone. I ask for your compassion and mercy. Please let me have a chance to rebuild a better life. Thank you."

Garry stood and addressed the judge. He asked for probation and added, "John's common law wife is here and is due to give birth to their child any day now. This is John's first offence and he has shown remorse. He was too young to know the full impact of his actions and fell under the influence of a much older man, a father figure who misguided him. We beg the court to consider John Swanger and his family."

Now it was the prosecutor's turn. Stuart Pierson stood, surveyed the scene, and addressed the Judge. "Your Honor, this man used guns in all his robberies. He showed no regard or compassion for his victims. We request the sentence of 20 years on each count."

In agony, I sat there for over five minutes, then Judge McGovern spoke.

"Mr. Swanger, stand up."

I stood on weak and shaking legs, faced the Judge and listened.

"I have seen your tears and heard you admit guilt. There is no way of knowing if you are showing remorse for your actions or regret in the face of sentencing. "You ask for mercy, have you shown mercy? You ask for compassion, have you shown compassion? I am sorry your wife has to be here under these circumstances, especially in her condition. But you created this situation. I pity you and your family. Therefore, I ask you, Mr. Swanger, will your child benefit more from your presence or your absence?"

His eyes never left mine as he continued; "I am compelled to sentence you to 10 years on each of the two counts of the indictment, said sentences to run concurrently and to be served in a Federal Correctional Institution."

Donna screamed, "Oh God. No."

Everyone turned to watch as the distraught pregnant girl ran from the courtroom. Her mother followed. The gallery buzzed with reactions and comments.

Judge McGovern slammed down his gavel and shouted, "Order!"

Prosecutor Pierson stood. "Your Honor, we also have the matter of the second indictment."

The judge looked again at the stack of papers before him and then added, "Ten years on that count also. Concurrent."

Convinced I'd be locked up for 30 years, I was more than relieved when the Judge was distracted and Garry had time to explain.

"Concurrent means you serve all three sentences at the same time. The most you'll serve is six years and eight months. You won't be eligible for parole until you've served one third of your sentence."

Garry stood and was invited to speak. "Your Honor, we request credit for time served."

McGovern agreed.

Back in my cell, I was numb. The cell, my life, everything was closing in on me. I grabbed my grungy plastic cup and headed to the Day Room. The coffee pot was missing. In its place was an urn full of hot water and a jar of Tasters Choice Instant. I watched the crystals disappear and took a sip. Oddly enough it tasted better than the mud being passed off as coffee. Another inmate arrived and snatched the jar.

"This is only a temporary fix so don't get used to it. There's a new pot on the way."

I'd never seen the guy before. He seemed friendly enough, about 50, gray at the temples and a slob. He shoveled two teaspoons of sugar into his cup and left a trail of granules sprinkled all over the counter.

Disgusting.

Wanting to forget the past few hours, I glanced up at the TV. Photos of Mars were being sent from Mariner 9. I thought to myself, *I'd love to do that. What an amazing trip*. My mind wandered back to earth and the reality of my pending journey . . . to somewhere.

The only thing certain about my future? I'd soon be on my way to prison.

CHAPTER FOURTEEN

....

REALITY

It was nearly midnight when banging on the bars of my cell scared me awake. I shot straight up to see a guard standing outside my cell. He was smiling.

Groggy and confused I managed to recognize the man and asked, "What's up, Parker?"

He said, "Well Dad," then read from a 3X5 card, "Jon Allen Swanger was born 8:06 p.m. this evening at Valley General Hospital. He weighed 7 pounds 6 ounces. Mother and child are both fine."

By the time he was finished, I was at the bars facing him. He offered me his hand and said, "Congratulations."

He gave me the card and walked away.

"Wow. I'm a daddy."

I was glad Parker had been the one to tell me about the baby. I was elated with his message and of course, I had to write.

February 4th 1972,
Ten years in the Pen I'm sentenced to do.
February 4th 1972,
My first child is born, his life is new.

My mind was bursting. *I'm a dad. But what good is it. With me locked away, it's like him not having a dad at all. Who am I trying to fool? Do I want to be a father so Jon will have a better life? Or do I want to make myself feel good? And, the little guy was born at the hospital where I'd stolen the get-away car used in the National*

Bank of Commerce job. Mere hours before his birth, I'd been sentenced to do time for robbing that very bank.

Strange.

The days passed slowly, filled with anxiety and the boredom of waiting. I wanted to get on with the routine of prison and visits from Donna and the baby. But I still had no idea where I was headed. It could be serving time clear across the country for all I knew.

Garry had been absent since my sentencing. I couldn't figure out why. Then unexpectedly he showed up with news I didn't want to hear.

"A couple of F.B.I. agents have asked to see you."

"I don't want to see them."

Garry insisted. "Well you might give it some thought. They want you and Bill to clarify a few details. You're not being asked to implicate anyone."

"What's in it for us?"

"Immunity from further prosecution. This could be huge."

I thought about it for a minute then answered. "When I was brought in, Bill was already here. We bunked together for a couple of days then were separated. I haven't seen him since. I want back in with Bill. There's no more discussion til we can make this decision together."

Later that evening I was Bill's cellmate. He was shocked to see me.

"What the hey?"

I smiled and said, "We need to talk about a request from the F.B.I."

After I explained, Bill gave me an approving look. "I'm impressed, John."

After we decided to take the meeting, Bill said, "There's a pressing issue we need to address." Bill gave me one of his stern looks. "I hear you got my daughter pregnant?"

Fear gripped me. Soon, Bill's angry face melted into a smile. "Just joking. Donna told me everything. That's a very unselfish thing you did for my girl. You're a good man, John." Then he added, "Congratulations Daddy,"

I smacked him on the shoulder, "Congratulations Papa."

Later that night, I realized my biggest fear was of the unknown. Worry about my new responsibilities wouldn't let me sleep. Then, I heard pleasant words of encouragement. Parker's voice echoed, *'You're a good man, John . . . it's not too late . . . do something with your life . . . find a way to become an honorable man.'*

CHAPTER FIFTEEN

OFF THE RECORD

❖ ❖ ❖

Tuesday March 28th 1972

Two F.B.I. agents sat across the table and handed each of us a stack of papers.

"Look them over, confirm which robberies no longer need to be investigated and check them off the list."

Bill said, "We're not signing anything. Check marks are all you get."

The agents nodded their approval.

Bill and I looked at each other then began reading and checking. After a while it was almost comical. Everything was ours. We both just shook our heads in disbelief knowing the reason this list even exists is because Marty was trying to save his own skin. Bill, being Bill occasionally pointed to a random item, drawing my attention to it, saying things like, "I didn't think Marty even knew about this one." Bill watched for reactions from the agents.

We spent the day reading through the list, remembering our adventures. The magnitude of what we'd done began to sink in. When tallied, the reality of how many robberies we'd pulled was shocking. The agents were in awe. Our total was one hundred and fifty six robberies spread out over Texas, Oklahoma, Kansas, New Mexico, Arizona, California, Idaho, Utah, Oregon and Washington State.

Bill and I ate lunch while the agents looked over our lists. Then one agent turned and asked, "Any more?"

Bill answered "Heck yeah, I'll take another sandwich."

We laughed. An agent was still laughing when he gave us each another sack lunch and asked, "Any more robberies?"

I answered, "I don't know."

Bill shrugged his shoulders. "I'm sure you remember your first arrest and the really big ones. But I'll bet neither of you can list them all. After a while they blend together. Right?"

The agents looked at each other, then to us. Bill continued, "There might be more. In fact I'm sure of it. Check back with us later; you might get a couple but not many. Marty did a pretty thorough job."

One agent pulled two folders from his briefcase. In the next hour, we discussed profiles, case studies and the history of robbery in the United States. We talked about the notorious Bonny and Clyde, Dillinger, Butch Cassidy, Pretty Boy Floyd, Baby Faced Nelson and on and on. By now our conversation was more casual, downright friendly.

I was fascinated when one agent stated, "If you take Hollywood out of it and discount legends, the best of them hit no more than 20 or so jobs. The average bandit pulls three to five hits and either gets caught, killed, or moves on." He looked from me to Bill and said, "I don't think you guys realize what you've done. You're probably the most successful armed robbers in American history."

That's when I asked, "Are we going to be in some kind of record book?"

Both agents smiled. Only one answered, "Remember our agreement? This discussion is to be strictly off the record. But we can change that if you want."

Bill placed his elbows on the table, leaned forward and said, "Speaking of off the record, how far off? Is this official Bureau business or just two agents who want to know?"

Grinning, the feds rose from their chairs. The meeting was over.

When Bill and I were alone, back to our cell, I said, "What just happened in there? I don't know what to think about those guys."

Bill looked thoughtful as he answered, "I'm not sure either. Maybe they'll write a book about us someday."

We laughed.

Friday - April 14th 1972

Every time Bill or I would be taken from the cellblock, I thought it might be the last time I'd ever see him. Then came the call, "Swanger, Chain's in the hole." I looked at Bill.

"You'll be okay John. Keep to yourself and stay quiet."

As they walked me away, Bill called out, "I love you, Son."

I looked back and under my breath said, "Me too."

I'd never heard those words from any other man. It was hard to keep from sobbing.

CHAPTER SIXTEEN

JOURNEY

By mid-morning I was shackled, signed out and cruising down I-5 in the back seat of a fairly new Chevy Suburban. The two marshals up front stayed busy discussing everything from fishing to poker. The driver began singing Truckin' along with The Grateful Dead on the radio. The other guy asked him to knock it off.

The rhythm of the highway, along with Neil Young and Joan Baez, began to sing me to sleep. A short time later, I woke up to see a familiar sign: *Winlock, Next Exit*. Instantly I thought of my childhood and the time we'd lived there. On the move from Winlock, we were all sardined into a packed van with more stuff in a trailer dragging behind. Walt was gripping the wheel. We were just beyond the edge of town when the county Sheriff flipped on his lights and siren to pull us over. Seems our landlord had reported the moose head was stolen from the rental house we'd just left. The sheriff told Walt, 'Give it up or go to jail.' I rubbed my eyes to scatter the memory.

My body was stiff. I tried to stretch and twisted my neck til it cracked. I was too curious to stay quiet. I ask the marshals, "Where are we headed?"

"To a hotel in Medford."

"Hotel?"

"Well, sort of. Yours won't be exactly like ours."

On food stops, I ate in the back seat, with only one hand free to eat, the other remained shackled. Bathroom breaks were always accompanied and complicated.

My first night was spent at the Medford, Oregon Jail, the second night in the jail at Salinas, California. Each day on the road brought reminders of towns where my family had lived when I was growing up. It felt like another punishment.

Sunday - April 16th 1972

The sun was beginning to creep over the horizon as we checked out of my "hotel" in Salinas. Heading down the coast, salty ocean air registered as more of a taste than a smell. It brought back recollections of the few months I'd spent at Corpus Christi and Padre Island, camping with Mom and David on the beach, gathering driftwood for fires . . . the best memories of my childhood.

For our next meal, instead of burgers in the back seat, we stopped at a Denny's. I said, "Why are you being so nice?"

"Don't take it personal, it's a regulation. We have to stop for at least one plate meal every three days on the road."

Steak and eggs apparently was not one of the plates allowed. But bacon and eggs with biscuits and gravy were. Coffee, truly good coffee and orange juice, made it the best meal I'd had in six months. I thanked them.

Back in the car, the driver announced, "Next stop on this beautiful west coast tour will be your final destination, Lompoc Federal Correctional Institution."

The other guard turned and added, "Hope you enjoy your new accommodations."

I somehow managed a grin.

It was about noon as we turned onto Klein Boulevard. When we came to a stop, I was escorted, shackles and all, to a larger than life gate. One of my guards pushed a button and spoke into a small box. We waited. Lights atop the gate began flashing. The deafening sound of a buzzer dwarfed the noise from the 20-foot high gate as it began to move. Everything shifted into slow motion. Each sound became acute. Movement of the huge mass of steel was mesmerizing. The mechanics of its opening paled in comparison to the crashing blow of its closing. The sounds repeated at a second gate as we exited the sally port.

We ended up inside a room marked R & D. I was seated with several other guys. The marshals removed my shackles and handed me a large brown paper bag, stapled closed along the top. Without a word, they left.

As new arrivals, we were stripped and herded into showers. Two minutes later we were dusted for lice and sent back to the showers, this time with soap. After receiving haircuts, we were issued underwear, pants, and shirts marked R & D…which I later learned meant receiving and discharge. Of course nothing fit but we were told suitable clothing would be issued later.

One by one we were taken to another room. I opened my bag of personal belongings and watched as my street clothes were inventoried: My wallet, ID and a severely faded photo of my aunt Toni. I realized then what the Feds were after, when I'd been interviewed, right after my capture. They kept grilling me about my Mafia connections. "Who is Toni Caunti?"

When the contents of my wallet were examined; they had misread the name on my Aunt Toni's damaged photo. It was written: Toni (AUNT).

Everything in my bag was listed and placed into a box labeled: SWANGER 10904-116. Back in my group we carried our bedding and personal stuff, down a long corridor past large doors labeled C-UNIT, D-UNIT and so on. A few inmates were dropped off at each block until finally we arrived at K-UNIT, my new home.

The O.D., officer of the Day or "Bull", gave me one look and said, "This ain't county jail son. You're free to move around. Within a few days you'll be issued permanent clothes and assigned to a workstation. You're responsible to keep up with your own belongings. Do you understand?"

I nodded and was given a few sheets of paper, which reminded me of school with the familiar purple ink of mimeograph machines. The pages were stapled in the corner and smelled of ammonia.

The O.D. said, "Swanger, your house number is C-7, second tier on the left."

My "house" measured 6X10 feet with pastel blue walls. One side held a bunk and mattress, with a toilet, sink, mirror, and a two-door metal cabinet on the opposite side. I threw my things on the bunk and stepped out to look over the railing. Below me was a long line of square tables in a large open area. Inmates were coming and going. Others were playing cards and chess. Back in my cell, I looked out the window. The view was of another Unit. When I shifted my gaze upward, there were white clouds moving against a blue sky.

I sat down and began reading through the stack of papers the Bull had given me. 10904-116, Unit-K, Tier-C, Cell-7 was written across the top of everything. I found some useful information and a map of the prison with my location marked. There was a schedule of "count times" with instructions to be on my bunk 5 minutes before and remain there until the "all clear" was sounded.

An appointment time was noted for Monday at the laundry to pick up my clothing issue: five pants, five shirts, one belt, all marked with 10904-116. Another paper told me where to appear for hygiene essentials and tobacco. I had no clue about hygiene stuff but I wanted the cigarettes.

The Bull handed me a bag with toothbrush, toothpaste, soap, shaving cream, razor and comb . . . no sign of smokes.

"What about cigarettes?" I asked.

"Regular or Menthol?"

"Regular."

I got two packs of Bugler Tobacco, rolling papers, a writing tablet, pens and envelopes.

"What do I use for stamps?"

He said, "You don't need them here."

As I walked away he added, "Hey, go read the last page."

In my house I flipped through and found: 'Things you should know to help assimilation go smoother.' I read on.

One: Try not to stand out. There is a pecking order here and you don't want to challenge it.

Two: Find someone you can trust and learn to watch each other's back.

Three: Don't buy, sell or trade anything with anyone. It could and usually will lead to trouble.

Four: Selling items is against the rules of the institution.

Five: Find a hobby or read. It will help time go by faster.

Six: Avoid Gifts.

I had never rolled cigarettes but figured, how hard could it be?

I was suddenly feeling scared and helpless. And what do they mean avoid gifts? I quietly said, "Oh God. If you're real, please help me get through this."

I decided to add a few rules of my own:

One: Talk half as much as you listen.

Two: Watch people; learn from their actions . . . thanks Pa.

Three: Trust your gut.

Four: Do what it takes to survive.

Tuesday, September 28, 1971

Two sought in $12,731 robbery

Detectives and Federal Bureau of Investigation agents today were seeking two armed men who robbed the University Federal Savings & Loan Association Main Office of $12,731 yesterday.

The robbers fled in a car they had taken at pistol point from Alan R. Olsen, Everett, shortly before the robbery.

Olsen told police he was accosted as he parked his car in a lot beside 11th Avenue Northeast near Northeast 45th Street at 9:45 a.m. He said he was driven around and then to the bank at 1120 N. E. 45th St. He was forced to accompany the robbers into the bank.

Police said the robbers looted tellers' cages, took money from the vault and ordered cashiers out of their cages. Olsen and bank customers were forced to stand

Man sought after $1,843 bank holdup

A hidden camera photographed the robber of the Second and Stone Branch of the Seattle-First National Bank yesterday.

Bill Headrick

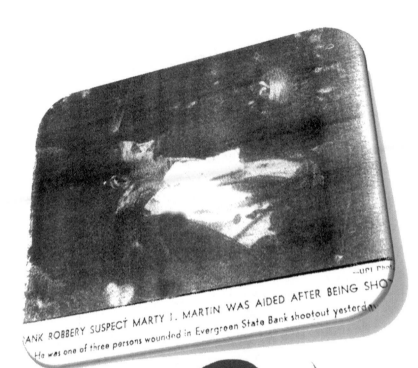

BANK ROBBERY SUSPECT MARTY J. MARTIN WAS AIDED AFTER BEING SHOT
He was one of three persons wounded in Evergreen State Bank shootout yesterday

Marty
Leon
Martin

Irene Martin

Woman sentenced for aiding husband in bank robbery

Mrs. Irene Emma Martin, 27, was sentenced today to a maximum of 20 years in prison for aiding and abetting her husband in an armed robbery of a North End bank June 25.

Mrs. Martin's attorney, Jerry R. Reiss, and the prosecutor's office had recommended a deferred sentence on the ground she has four children to support. But Superior Court Judge William J. Wilkins noted she "went along with her husband right to the end and then left the scene afterward."

The judge recommended a minimum term of five years. If the State Board of Prison Terms and Paroles agrees, she could be free on good behavior and three years and four months.

Mrs. Martin, a citizen of West Germany, pleaded guilty of aiding her husband, Marty Leon Martin, 30, in the robbery of the Evergreen State Bank, 20332 Ballinger Road N. E,

George Ritter, 39, a county police officer, and Dick Ferguson, 23, a bystander, were seriously wounded in an ensuing gun battle. Ritter has retired from the force as a result of his injuries.

Martin was shot by police and arrested near the bank. Mrs. Martin was arrested a short time later and charged with helping plan the robbery, driving of Martin to the bank and attempting to aid his escape.

Martin was sentenced last month to life in imprisonment. The Martins were married while Martin was with the Army in Germany in 1961. Their four children are in the care of welfare officials in Texas.

The woman's attorney said Mrs. Martin was following her husband's instructions, hoping to get enough money to reclaim their children from Texas.

Mrs. Irene Emma Martin left the courtroom in handcuffs after she was sentenced today.

Ladeana Ruth Pringle
(Linda Jackson)

Ladeana Ruth Pringle, left, 19, of federal court in Oklahoma City yesterday ing extradition on a charge she ro' Branch of the National Bank of Cor $3,000 April 9. She was accompan Fleener, a deputy United States

2 held in bank holdup

The Federal Bureau of Investigation today was continuing investigations of two bank robberies, involving more than $10,000, in which a man, 19, and a man, 44, were arrested in Oklahoma. its said Ladeana Ruth and Billy James were arrested Sun same address in

med in secret ed by a federal iss Pringle e April 9 Branch Con. was d a

This photo of the girl in the April 9 robbery was made by a hidden camera.

took $8,000 from the vault of the Federal Way Branch of Pacific National Bank and undisclosed amount from ellers September 7. Both rs were armed with s.

Pringle yesterday radition.

Charges against woman dropped

Bank - robbery charges against LaDeanna Pringle, 19, were dismissed in United States District Court today and the young woman was ordered released.

Miss Pringle had been scheduled to go to trial today before United States District Judge Walter McGovern on a charge of participating in the April 9 robbery of $2,991 from the Kent branch of the National Bank of Commerce. Stuart Pierson, an assistant United States attorney,

would not explain to reporters the reasons for the dismissal.

However, Gary Bass, attorney for John E. Swanger, charged in the same robbery, told newsmen the government did not have sufficient evidence to convict Miss Pringle.

Swanger's trial then began before a jury of nine men and three women.

Bass said he has not decided if he will call Miss Pringle as a witness for the defense.

CHAPTER SEVENTEEN

MAYHEM AND MURDER

Noises ramped up in my unit. I watched as a herd of inmates filled their compartments. The loud speaker blared, "On your bunks for the Count. En Sus Camas Por La Cuenta."

My cell door, which had been opened all afternoon, closed. I turned to survey my surroundings. Like it or not, this is home. I had to make the best of it.

10904-116

Today they took away my name and placed it in a box,
Along with everything I own, secure with chains and locks
Yes they took away my name and put a number in its place
Lord, thank you for this mirror so I don't forget my face

April 16th 1972, 9:00 pm
Lompoc California

The next day, walking down the corridor, I sensed something was out of kilter. The hallway was empty. Even the Bulls were gone. My instincts said, time to be cautious and stay alert. I walked, checking my back so I wouldn't fall prey to one of the crazies I'd come to accept as my new neighbors. My pace quickening, my strides lengthening, I told myself, *something bad is definitely in the air*. K-Unit was still 200 yards off. When I reached the windows to my left, I stopped for a quick look and froze. Several hundred blacks were stretched in a line across one end of the yard. About 100 feet away, facing them, was a similar line of Mexicans. It looked like a scene from a Civil War movie.

In the midst lay several dozen ignorant whites sunbathing, unaware of their pending doom. As if on cue, both lines blasted forward, crashing against each other in the middle, on top of the whites. I stood terrified, watching as knives, dumbbells, baseball bats, anything available, was being used to spill blood on the prison yard. Gunfire erupted from three of the four guard towers. The scene was terrifying, with wounded everywhere. Able inmates ran in all directions trying to escape the chaos. A few even hit the fences in an attempt to save their lives.

Alarms sounded, intercoms blared. "The Prison is in Lockdown. Return to your cells." I ran, hoping to reach my cell before the corridor became clogged. The smell of teargas seeped into my nostrils. I grabbed the door of my unit and swung it open hard and raced up the stairs to the second tier of C-7. Oddly, the cell doors were in a freewheeling mode. Once inside, I pushed my door closed until it latched.

From my window I could see inmates being held at bay with megaphones shrieking and high-powered rifle bullets streaking through the air. A Mexican man lay face down in the grass, shoes rested by his left hand. His right clutched a rosary. A growing spot of blood darkened the back of his khaki shirt.

The noise in my unit grew as cell doors were clanging shut. Minutes later there was nothing. We were enveloped in silence. I scanned the tiers across from me. My eyes landed on an unoccupied cell. It was empty, but not vacant. Someone on the yard, maybe the Mexican man I'd just seen, was perhaps the occupant of D-9. I went back to my window. Not one person was left in the yard. The Mexican man was gone too. His shoes and the rosary remained as proof he'd ever been there.

The stench of teargas grew stronger. I wet a washcloth in the sink, crushed it over my nose and flopped down on my bunk. Lying there starring at the cruddy pale blue ceiling, the awful question was back again: *How did I get myself into this mess?*

Never one to blame others for my problems or justify my actions by shifting responsibility, there was only one explanation for this mess. It was my fault. My choices had landed me in prison with at least three years and four months until I could appear before a Parole Board. My mind was running full speed. Should I become cynical about years of poverty and living without Mom, my brothers and sisters, or a real dad? And who the hell did Walt think he was, throwing me out? Sure we were dysfunctional, but who knew the difference. I thought every family lived in turmoil. The Swanger clan was normal to me. I didn't need my mom's 4th husband to kick me out and fracture our family. We'd been doing just fine without him. In spite of Walt, I'd proved myself and managed to find my own way.

My thoughts shifted to the past eighteen months. Linda had been like a sister to me and Bill gave me the fatherly attention and love I craved. We weren't ruthless criminals. In fact Bill was not your average thief. After a hit, we'd often fill coffee cans with cash and give them out to homeless people. Bill loved singing, mostly gospel songs. It seemed very strange at first, robbers singing hymns? I was surprised at how many lyrics I remembered from when I was a kid, going to church with Nanny. Bill, Linda and I actually sounded pretty good.

After a while Bill's compassion no longer surprised me. Early one morning he read a newspaper article about a congregation struggling to buy the building they were renting. Minutes later, we jammed $50,000 into a large brown grocery bag and were on our way to the church. After leaving the bag on the doorstep, we parked down the street and watched the pastor's reaction when he found the money. What a rush.

It was never about being Robin Hood…you know, robbing from the rich and giving to the poor. It was strictly selfish; all about how it made me feel to help that pastor and give coffee cans of coins to people living on the street.

Bill was the best man I'd ever known and the closest I ever came to having a dad. My clenched fist beat the stiff prison pillow until it was semi comfortable. Still preoccupied with all my questions, there was only one answer. I was at another crossroad. This was either the end of my life, or the beginning. I hadn't yet decided which.

I fell asleep to the memory of Bill singing, "*What a friend we have in Jesus, all our sins and grief's to bear. . . .*"

CHAPTER EIGHTEEN

LOCKDOWN

Consequences of the riot put us in lockdown for three weeks. Everyone was stuck in their own 6X10 foot box. Three sides were constructed of 8 inch thick concrete block walls. The front wall of each cell was made of 3 inch thick steel and faced a lengthy corridor. The only way in or out was through a steel sliding door in the front wall of each cell. Opening, closing, locking and unlocking cell doors, was controlled by guards. For the last 21 days, they'd had a vacation from pushing buttons to move our doors.

Our cells would have been totally claustrophobic except for the 12X18 inch window in the door. Each window was divided into four panes by one metal bar installed horizontally and one vertically. Panels were 6X9 inches. Three of the four panes were see through glass for observation. The forth panel was open to allow conversation while the door was closed and the passing of small objects in and out, such as food or the mail.

Being brand new in prison, there had been no time to acquire books or anything to read. I did have the pen and paper, but boredom dominated my time until night when I was plagued by reoccurring nightmares and too much time to ponder the reasons I was here.

Nick Nash was the prisoner one cell over. He was a twenty year old military guy from the south. We had many long discussions. Later, we became work out partners, lifting weights.

When lock down was complete and we had the ability to move around again, there were still people on my check list, officials I had to see who were handling my case.

I also planned to sort out the leadership in my unit to see who was in control and how they ran things. Getting the scoop on life in my new surroundings was a priority.

CHAPTER NINETEEN

R. R. KELLY

"Holy shit, you robbed how many places?"

Those were the first words from my liaison officer, R. R. Kelly.

"One hundred fifty-six, sir."

He looked at me in disbelief, shaking his head. "And you're how old?"

"I turned nineteen four months ago."

He shook his head again and asked, "So how do you intend to spend your time with us here at Lompoc?"

"I plan to go to school. Perhaps get a degree, sir. I plan to be a model prisoner."

"Let me tell you something."

He got up and shut the door, sat back down and looked at me shaking his head. He pulled a sheet of paper and pen from his desk, drew a graph, and said. "Look, you come in here all fired up, trying to be Mr. Perfect, you start way up here and end up hitting the Parole Board in the same place. Not very impressive. In fact, you may even get tired of playin' the role and start losing ground. You've accomplished nothing. Twelve honest men said you are a zero and you come in here claiming to be a ten? Kind of like calling them liars, isn't it?"

"I see what you mean, sir. That makes a lot of sense."

"Smart kid. Now, let me tell you what really works. You need to stop acting like a model citizen and let them see you as the zero they think you are. Here's what you do Swanger, go cause some trouble."

I sat there speechless.

"Did you hear me?"

"Yes. Yes, sir."

He went on. "Nothing huge, just enough to let people know they pegged you right. So, now you start here." He pointed to the bottom of his graph. "Then you begin the trip to becoming a model prisoner, your progress is obvious. The system pats itself on the back and everybody's happy."

"Man, that's so cool. But why are you telling me all this?"

He pushed his face forward, drilled me with a hard, concrete stare, and said, "Because I think you're salvageable."

"Thank you. Thank you, sir."

Kelly raised his hand as if to stop me and said, "You ever tell anyone we had this conversation, I'll deny it. It won't be easy. You may have to catch a stint or two in the hole, but I think you're smart enough to make it work. Okay, Swanger here's how things operate around here. You and I will meet on a regular basis. It's mandatory. If you're having problems, needed a transfer to another unit, you come see me. You want an education, take classes, you come see me. Mainly I'm supposed to help map out a program for your time in prison. Most important of all, I'm here to develop your parole program."

That was the word I wanted to hear. "I like that, sir. Thank you."

"Okay. Now, are you good at anything? What kinds of jobs have you held?"

"I've worked at a grocery store and managed a gas station."

"That's a good start."

"But mostly I've sold drugs, hustled pool, and robbed super markets and banks."

Kelly just smiled and shook his head. He went on to tell me about some of the work stations I might be assigned to fill.

"Corridor Orderly, Kitchen duty and things like that; you do those when you're scheduled, but it beats sitting in your cell. Makes the time go by faster. There's no pay. Where you get money is in the Prison Industries. Everyone wants a job there. You probably will too."

That got my interest. "What kinds of jobs for pay . . . and how much?"

Kelly's face turned almost pleasant as he answered. "We have a Cable Factory, where electronic cable is made. The Furniture Factory restores desks and chairs from government offices. The Print Shop produces tons of government documents. The Sign Factory makes license plates, and all kinds of highway signs."

Kelly leaned back in his chair, placed both palms behind his neck and said, "Eventually you can take your pick, but you gotta wait in line. Everyone wants those."

"Wow. There's a lot going on around here."

Kelly nodded.

"And how much do those jobs pay?"

"Well, they all start at 21¢ an hour. But with good behavior and performance they improve. The longer you are there the more they pay, 31¢, 41¢, and top out at 51¢. It goes on your commissary."

I thought to myself, *Oh well, no cash, just trade for commissary.* I decided, even if 51¢ is a joke, it's better than nothing.

Kelly went on to say, "Eventually, you may even qualify for B-Unit."

"What's that?"

"It's an honor unit where we put the men who excel. They have a key to their house; except for count times, they come and go as they please. If you're in B-Unit, you pretty much do what you want inside these prison walls because you've proved worthy of our trust."

Kelly tilted his head slightly and gave me a quizzical look. "You wanna make that a goal, Swanger?"

With my own head tilt and quizzical look, I said, "Sure."

Kelly cracked his knuckles, stood up from his chair and said, "Okay, we're done."

He moved toward the door. I followed til he stopped abruptly. With a stern look, he spoke in low tones. "Remember, keep your mouth shut."

"Yes sir."

He opened the door and shook his head. "You kiddin' me? One hundred fifty six?"

"Well actually sir. That's not exactly true. They missed one. My first."

"Holy crap! One hundred fifty seven?"

CHAPTER TWENTY

DR. BLISS

In my short time at Lompoc, I'd seen riot and murder and knew first-hand how dangerous prison really was. It made me think of Bill's last piece of advice, *Stay quiet and keep to yourself*. Kelly had just told me the exact opposite . . . he said make trouble. I had to think that one over, make a plan. There could be no mistakes.

I lay in my bunk rehashing events, still looking for answers. . . . Stuff was buzzing through my head like items on the evening news. Bass told the judge I'd fallen under the influence of a father figure who misguided me. He was wrong. But the judge's observations were right. Out loud, to the entire court, Judge McGovern had said, while looking straight at me, 'You created this situation. I pity you.'

I didn't want pity from him or anyone else. But my situation was piti-ful. Why had I been so willing to become a thief? I needed to find help in order to turn around.

I stood by her door observing the big brass name plate, "DR. BAR-BARA BLISS." *Are you kidding me? A psychiatrist named Bliss?*

Hilarious.

She stood in front of a book case, obviously looking for something. She heard me enter and turned.

"May I help you?"

"I hope so."

She asked my name.

"Swanger, John," I answered.

She scanned her schedule then looked at me. "When was your appointment?"

"I don't have one."

"Then why are you here?"

"I robbed banks and that's not normal. I want to fix my life."

"That's a tall order but refreshing. I'm not used to men in your position willing to confess their faults as well as their needs. You're in the right place."

"Well thank you, ma'am. I'm not assigned to a work station yet, so I'm free anytime."

While she scanned her book, I did a quick appraisal of Dr. Bliss. She was short, full figured, with touches of gray hair showing. I'd heard she was 53. Her blue eyes sparkled with kindness. The woman was instantly likable.

"I have an opening from two to three this afternoon. Will that work?"

"I'll be here."

"That gives me time to pull your jacket. You know . . . your file?"

I thanked her and left.

The noon meal was less than an hour away. Killing time in the Day Room would give me a chance to read headlines in the L.A. Times. Hiding behind the paper allowed me to observe prison life. But nothing much was happening, so I read up on politics. Nixon dominated the news.

Lunch was okay . . . beans and franks, vanilla ice cream for dessert. No chocolate sauce, no nuts or sprinkles, just naked vanilla ice cream. At least there was a dessert. I couldn't complain.

Time crawled by as I waited for 2:00. I was restless. Finally I was sitting in front of Dr. Bliss.

"John Swanger." She read from the brown folder open on the desk. Looking up, she continued. "The people I see here are generally ordered to come. It's not often someone requests counseling." Doctor Bliss put her hand on my file. "This tells me about a thief, who was sent to prison, stripped of his identity and given a number. But, I want to know about the man named John Swanger." She waited just long enough to smile, then said, "Tell me your story."

That took me by surprise. Not so much because of her words but the way she said them, no psychobabble, no guessing what she meant.

"Starting where?" I asked.

"At the beginning."

"How long do we have?"

"One hour twice a week til your story brings us to the present. I want to hear about your life and all the stuff that goes with it."

She never took her eyes off me. I shifted in my chair. Dr. Bliss stood, and pulled her chair around her desk until we were face to face.

"This will be more comfortable," she said.

I agreed and asked, "Now?"

"Whenever you're ready."

"If you want my whole story, you're right; may as well start at the beginning."

We both laughed.

"I was born, the 23rd of November, 1952, in Nashville. I don't remember much about Tennessee or what went on there because in 1955 our family moved to Dallas. I was three. Jack, my real father, moved with us but didn't stay long.

"Mom told us stories, probably a blend of fabrication and exaggeration, as to why their marriage crumbled. After years of broken promises and a shattered heart, her description of my Dad was short and to the point. 'He was a no good, worthless, abusive, drunken, lazy drifter who couldn't hold a job.'

"Mom said he beat us with lamp cords, shoes, sticks, and whatever he could grab. My older sister, Evelyn, said he beat me the most. I was so young and his treatment so traumatic, maybe that's why I don't remember. Eventually violence, the lack of money and the burden of supporting four kids gave way to strong resentments. Mom hung in there as long as she could. Dad skipped town shortly after the divorce and was nowhere to be found . . . so they say.

"From my little kid perspective daily turmoil had been the norm. After Dad left, nothing was ever the same again. Mom, my siblings and I, took our grief and pain in different directions, everything from denial to destruction.

"All these years later, I still remember sitting with my face pressed against the living room window, my breath clouding up the cold glass. I spent a lot of time watching, waiting, and hoping to see Dad coming back. I still tear up when I think of those days, as a little boy, wondering, 'Why did my Daddy go away?' He may have been an abusive bum but I loved him. And I missed him."

I tried not to get misty eyed but finally had to use my sleeve to mop up the uncontrollable tears that wouldn't stop rolling down my cheeks. Dr. Bliss remained silent. I wondered what was behind her eyes. What was she thinking? I didn't have long to wait.

"John, I'm so sorry you had to go through all that."

I wiped a final tear. "It was tough. But I'm just getting started. Wait til you hear the rest of my story."

Her kind eyes spoke loudly, encouraging me. "I'm ready," she said. "Incidentally, you have quite a way with words, John."

"Thank you, ma'am." I was anxious to go on. "Should I continue?"

"Only if you're okay with dredging up more painful memories. When you least expect it, long forgotten hurts tend to show up."

"I'll be fine. I gotta do this."

"Now why don't you tell me about your mother?"

"Mom? Well. . . ."

"You did have a mother . . . right?

"At times I didn't feel like it. I loved her more than anyone but felt no love back. I'd say, 'I love you Mom.' she'd say, 'me too.' But I always said it first. It never came from her."

At that point, the memories surfacing were unexpectedly raw, a bit much to handle.

Dr. Bliss seemed to know just the right thing to say. "John, tough memories like yours take time to heal. Hang on. You can do this. Talking it out is a great first step and I'm here to help."

Her words were exactly what I needed. But it was still embarrassing. "Big boys don't cry. I've heard that all my life. Crying is for wimps."

Dr. Bliss kept her eyes on me. Her voice stayed mellow, her eyes full of compassion. "It's no slam on your manhood to have feelings. Children growing up in abusive and broken families, often sustain damage beyond their ability to understand . . . and carry it with them for a lifetime. Some poor souls use drugs, alcohol, sex, murder, even suicide to cover their pain."

I shifted in my seat and said, "I pretty much tried everything but murder and suicide."

She gave me a knowing look. "Drugs, sex, and so forth, are bad choices, creating problems of our own making."

I hung my head. "I agree. I've decided, my worst enemy is me. I'm really tired of running from myself."

"You are one very sharp young man, wise beyond your years. Wisdom is a great resource. Learn to use it."

"I've made too many mistakes to consider myself wise. I have no idea what it means."

"John, you came in here saying you want to fix your life. Making that happen will take work, but one day, you'll figure it out. My job is to prepare you for a better future. You'll get there by understanding your past. As we spend time working through your story, you'll gain insight. I promise."

Her words sounded great, but the doubter in me was thinking, *fat chance*. Even so, I went on. "Dr. Bliss, what you just described is exactly what I crave. Because when I try to sort things out myself, I end up more confused than when I started. So, if you're serious about helping, I guess you're stuck with me."

Without hesitation she said, "You're on."

I'd never met anyone like this lady. After a long pause I decided to level with her. "I've crammed a lot into my 19 years. Life has taught me to be suspicious of everyone. My instincts say you're different."

"Thanks John. My instincts say you're pretty special yourself. Along with that, I believe each person is unique . . . no two of us are alike. Now, tell me more about your mother."

I squirmed, cleared my throat and jumped right in. "Well…even though she married three more times, after my dad, Mom was single most of my younger years. Times were always tough but marriage never solved any problems. In most cases things got worse. Mom was constantly struggling to make ends meet and trying to create the illusion of a normal family. Playing with us and having fun was rare. Mostly she stayed preoccupied, searching for Mr. Right.

"Mom was a beautiful woman. Even after five kids she had a great figure and looked like a fashion model. She could always attract men, whether she wanted to or not. Most were losers who had no clue about love and loyalty.

"Lonnie was Mom's second husband, stepfather number one. We never knew much about him other than he was the father of our baby sister, Tammy . . . or at least that's what we were told.

"Over the years we wondered why Lonnie was short, fat and balding, with sandy colored hair, while Tammy grew to be tall and thin, with thick black hair, and bore a striking resemblance to Carl, one of Mom's friends. She claimed it was just a coincidence. Carl was a nice Cajun man, who had the rear end of the alphabet all squeezed into his last name. He visited quite often.

"I was nine when Bill Roland, stepfather number two, came along. He was tall and thin with dark curly hair. Mom told us Bill's mother owned the Hagar Slacks Company. I think somebody was pulling the polyester over someone's eyes. We were still poor.

"When the Beatles invaded America, David and I wanted to look like Ringo Starr. Mom's reply to a Beatle haircut was a resounding no. Bill added his louder, more definite no.

He enjoyed beating us for the slightest infractions, real or contrived. One day he took off his belt and told me to whip David. He said, 'John, if you don't do a good job I'll beat you like you should have beat him.' I didn't . . . he did. Bill was truly evil. The next day I told him, 'You can either beat us or sleep, but you can't do both.' He wasn't with us much longer.

"Mom was single again and money was scarce, so David and I were sent to live with Uncle John a few times, three times with Uncle Bobby, a couple of times with Aunt Toni and I've lost count of how often we stayed with Nanny and Pa.

"While living with Mom, I remember guys coming over to spend the night. As a little kid, I wasn't sure what happened but I could always tell when she had been crying. Young as I was, I swore I'd never treat a woman like that."

When I stopped to catch my breath, Dr. Bliss asked, "You said your mom had five children...so you have four siblings?"

"Donnie is the oldest. Evelyn is next. I'm right in the middle. David is number four and then baby Tammy."

"Got it," she said."

We settled in our chairs and I continued. "One day this guy showed up at the restaurant where Mom worked. He spent a lot of time flirting with her. She could handle his type. A brush off usually worked. But this guy wouldn't back off. He showed up night after night, promising to take care of Mom and us kids if she would just marry him. She turned him down."

My pause was intentional.

Dr. Bliss gave me a quizzical look. "I don't get it. So your mom deciding not to marry someone?'

"He wasn't just someone. His name was Richard Speck."

Dr. Bliss sat up straighter. "The man who killed all those nurses?"

I leaned forward. "Yeah, that's the guy. But we didn't know who he was at the time."

Looking thoughtful, as if she was processing, she said, "Wasn't Speck caught about five years ago?"

"Yes, I was 14."

"So, Speck could have killed your mother?"

"Oh, yeah. The few times I saw him, he looked really strange to me."

"How did you feel about a man who would do such vile things to all those young women?"

"I was scared. When the papers came out with pictures of all the nurses, one was really pretty, with dark hair. She looked so much like my Mom." Once again the tears threatened to flow but I continued with determination in my voice. "I'm sure I would have killed Speck if he ever laid a hand on her."

"How did she handle the situation?"

"She told us kids to forget it, move on and be glad nothing happened. But I know she must have been shook up knowing that, instead of them, it could have been her."

"That's amazing, John. What about now, are you over it?"

"I think so...well maybe not. I've always felt protective toward my sisters. But the thought of my mom possibly being murdered still does something to me. When I see women being mistreated, it's like I go on auto pilot, I have to stop it."

"Like a knight in shining armor, John?"

"No, like a guy who can't stand by and let a woman be harmed . . . physically, mentally, or emotionally."

"That's a very positive statement and a good place to end our session."

We agreed on a time to meet again. I thanked her and left. This had been a totally unexpected encounter.

CHAPTER TWENTY-ONE

···

LERMA

Many of my fellow prisoners wanted a cell in the top tier, or the Ghetto Penthouse, as it was called. It was a good place to hide out. The bottom tier was popular for easy access. The middle tier was, well . . . the middle. For some unknown reason the powers that be liked to shuffle us around like a game of musical cells? Maybe it was a control thing. Nick Nash had been moved to F-20 and I was still on C.

Late one evening I headed up stairs to see Nick. Turning the corner where Tier-E connects to F, there sat a Mexican, all alone on the floor. He held a letter in his hand. He was crying.

"Are you okay?" I asked.

He quickly buried his head in his sleeve, to wipe away tears. Looking up, he shook his head to let me know he didn't understand English. I sat down next to him. Without either of us speaking the other's language, I deciphered that the letter brought sad news of his brother's death from an overdose of heroin . . . what the Mexicans call 'cheva' or 'muerta.' Apparently, this poor guy next to me had shared his loss with prison friends. Some had responded, "Wow, what a way to go." Not the comment I'd want to hear, especially if it had been my brother.

Before we parted company, I learned his name was Jesus Lerma Fuentes. I called him Lerma. Over the next weeks, months and years I taught him English, he taught me Spanish.

I remembered item number two on the mimeographed list of things I'm supposed to know. 'Find someone you can trust and watch each other's back.' Lerma was a good guy and became my trusted friend. We watched each other's backs.

CHAPTER TWENTY-TWO

······································

MAC'N MEL

Because of my accent, I was instantly tagged "Tex." I considered it a good thing when the name Tex began attracting attention. It went against Item Number One on the mimeo sheet. 'Try not to stand out. There is a pecking order here and you don't want to challenge it.' I didn't want to challenge the pecking order, but I had my reasons for welcoming visibility.

In the short time I'd been at Lompoc, my observations had become my education. Living with 130 people in my cell block meant a lot of personalities to deal with, or not.

Mac'n Mel was a big black guy; well known as the top Pressure Artists (or Gallo) in K block. His real name was Melvin. The Mac'n part was synonymous with yacking. He considered himself a smooth talker. Several other Gallos operated in our area as well. Because of their size and tactics, these men would prey on newcomers, the young, the fearful, and guys who were too weak and scared to fight back. We had a few gays within our population. But there were a whole bunch of scared kids who had no idea how to protect themselves. Targeted simply because they were small or too young to shave.

One evening, I came back to my house and found a box of commissary in the middle of my bunk. I had learned the usual and accepted way to handle this overture, was to place the box in the corridor and ignore it. The Gallo would see it as rejection and carry it to some other bunk, as bait for another potential victim. But I had another agenda. I left the box right where it was and went down the tier to see Lerma. I told him what was going on and asked, "Hey, you got a shank?"

"No, but I have a blunt."

A blunt is a piece of pipe filled with lead on one end and wrapped with electrical tape on the other. I took it and arrived back to my house just before the 8:00 rack in, when all cell doors would close. I sat on my bunk checking out the contents of the box. In no time, I was sipping Pepsi from a can, eating Doritos, and munching on Hostess Oh's in between. The box was loaded with more food items, plus a full carton of Camels.

I saw him out of the corner of my eye. Mac'n Mel was standing by my window. His face pressed against the open pane. He seemed surprised that his commissary box was still sitting on my bunk. He grinned, looking real proud of himself, thinking he'd fished me in.

"Hey man, I see you like the stuff I got for you."

I looked up. "How'd you know I smoke Camels?"

"I been watchin' you. I think you're a good guy. But we gotta figure out some way you can pay me back."

I said, "Oh, Yeah, I like that."

I'd been keeping track of the time until the cell doors would be opening. I'd only have three minutes before they'd lock again. I moved toward Mel, as the announcements began, "Racking A. Racking B." Just as the words "Racking C" came echoing through the building. I yanked Lerma's blunt from under my armpit and bam, I wacked my visitor in the face. He went down and he was out.

In seconds, when my door opened, I grabbed Mac, drug him to his cell, and left. At 10:00 p.m. I went back to his cell. Mac was sitting on the floor, groaning. He held a bloody washrag next to the huge knot on the side of his bruised face. His eyes registered panic when he saw me. I knelt down to his level so I could leer at him eye to eye as I spoke.

"Here's the deal. Every week you bring me a box of commissary. Understand?" He nodded. I left him on the floor, moaning.

The next morning, I checked on him again. Mac looked worse. By now, his black face was blue and purple, with a tinge of green. Again, I got in his face.

"Forget about the commissary. But if I ever hear of you pressuring anyone, I will kill you. You are no longer a Gallo. Got it?"

He knew I meant it.

I had managed to fulfill item number five on the mimeo sheet: avoid gifts. More importantly, this little incident took Mac'n Mel out of the game and earned me a reputation. Word spread fast, Tex was not to be messed with.

CHAPTER TWENTY-THREE

LETTERS & LEON

Letters from Donna with pictures of her and Jon were a welcome distraction. The kid was gaining weight and growing like a weed. Donna's figure was slim again. She looked terrific and more mature. Every so often she'd sent a few dollars for commissary. I answered every one of her letters and wrote poems. I told her about Dr. Bliss and tried not to dwell on my negative life.

As months went by, the mail dwindled. There was nothing coming in from anyone except Nanny. Nothing from Mom or my siblings.

Then came the day I picked up a letter which, of course, began Dear John. Only this one truly was a Dear John letter. Donna had met someone. My heart was broken. But then again, I was in no position to be a father. I spent the next two days in my cell. I cried . . . a lot.

Several new, younger prisoners began showing up and asking me for help to keep from being raped. I tried to show them the ropes and told them, "You have to stand up and fight back, show them you can't be messed with. It's either that, or check into the hole for protection."

One day Leon, a young kid came looking for me and said, "Twelve black guys said they're going to rape me. I am supposed to meet them at the end of the second tier at noon. What do I do?"

I told him, "You can fight, give into them or go to the hole. Or I'll back you. I'd rather not back you because then they'll just think you're my punk."

There was just enough time for me to see Lerma and ask him for a shank. He ran to get one and just as the 12 blacks were about to take the kid, Lerma showed up with about 80 Mexicans.

Outnumbered, the Gallo and his entourage left. I announced, "This one ain't yours."

CHAPTER TWENTY-FOUR

BLISS, TAKE 2

"Glad to see you, John."

"Good to see you too, Doc. Excuse me, I mean Dr. Bliss."

"How about you just call me Barb?"

I was surprised. "Really?"

"Yes. I think we're on the way to being friends and friends call each other by their first names. Right?"

"If you say so. I'd like that."

"Good. Let's just start where we left off."

Barb took her seat. "Okay, John. Where to next?"

"Well, when circumstances improved and tips were good, Mom would find a place and gather us back to live with her. She drove an old Junker, a Ford Falcon with the shifter on the column. When the shift lever broke off, it took both her hands to go through the gears. She didn't seem to mind. We were all learning to make do and be grateful.

"Sometimes Mom would park behind a Safeway Store where David and I would dig through the dumpster looking for discarded food. I vividly remember Mom using a razorblade to cut bruises from peaches and hand the good parts to us kids. My sister Evelyn was humiliated. David and I couldn't understand why she was so upset. After all, the food was free and it was an adventure.

"With her small income as a waitress, Mom never had enough money to support all five kids. I didn't realize how tough it was on her to send David and me across town to live with her folks at the south end of Dallas. I loved David. We were close in every way, including age. Being older, I felt responsible for my kid brother. No matter what, we had each other. Sticking together was our way of coping.

"Life with our grandparents was less hectic, more secure. We still had times of being homesick, but Nanny's homemade banana pudding eased the pain. Best of all, we had our own room. The curtains were ugly but we each had a cozy bed. With Mom, sometimes we slept on the floor.

"Most grandmas bake cookies. Nanny made pies. Apple was my favorite. Her fried chicken was the best ever, cooked with lard in a cast iron skillet. With Nanny and Pa, we never went to bed hungry.

"One day Pa announced we were going on vacation. He spoke of the fun we'd have visiting relatives. I couldn't wait to get going. Being only six, I had no idea how long it would take to drive from Dallas to Nashville or what we'd see or do along the way.

"Our journey began late one Tuesday night. David and I fell asleep the minute we landed inside the car. An hour down the road we were jerked wide-awake by horrible noises. It sounded like a washing machine shaking out of balance. Nanny's hands flew up to cover her ears. She was yelling, 'My word.' At the same time, David and I were screaming, 'what's the matter Pa?'

"'Seems the drive shaft's goin' out on this ol' Willys Jeep. . . could break lose any minute now and come through the floorboards.'

"Since we'd been sleeping on the floor, David and I scrambled onto the seat and stared over the edge. We didn't want to miss it if something came through the floor. Pa turned the Jeep around and took us home. We were glad yet disappointed.

"One year later, Pa's dad, my great-grand father, died. I knew him as Papa. Again we headed for Tennessee. This time a heavy blanket of sadness covered us all. The long trip gave me plenty of time to imagine what I'd see at a funeral.

His obituary said Papa died of natural causes at age 94. But rumor had it that he'd lived mostly on Jack Daniels and Red-Hot candies the last few years of his life.

"Papa hand carved slingshots and whistles. He sent them to us kids wrapped in brown paper, bound with a white string. We were thrilled to receive those special gifts, all the way from Tennessee to Texas. It made me realize how much he loved us. Though I don't remember meeting him, I cried along with everyone else at Papa's passing.

"At the family viewing, the clan was seething when they saw Papa in his casket. The undertaker had cut his hair, shaved his long beard and put him in a suit. Orders had been to clean him up, dress him in a new union suit and bib overalls and let him be. I'd seen pictures of Papa in that outfit, with his beard to his belly and white hair down his back. It was the way everyone remembered him and that's exactly how the kinfolk wanted him buried. Right then his casket was closed so no one else would see our loved one in such a dreadfully unnatural condition.

"I didn't understand most of what went on during the funeral. Afterwards, Uncle John crammed seven other relatives and me into his Ford Fairlane for our trip to the cemetery. On the way, we stopped for burgers. When we arrived at the graveside, Papa was already in the ground. It took Nanny two years before she'd let us off the hook for that one."

Barb was smiling. "You have quite an interesting family."

"Even if we hadn't been around each other much, loving came naturally. Just from hearing adults talk, I had a good idea who was who. But, I have to tell you, looking at Papa seemed strange. David and I were both confused about how we should feel. When we saw him in the coffin, Papa looked like he was taking a nap, but Nanny told us Papa wasn't in there. She said, 'He's gone home to be with Jesus.' It was difficult to visualize our great-grandpapa in two places at once. But if Nanny said it was so, we knew it must be true."

Barb asked, "John, how do you feel about your Papa's death now?"

"Actually, looking back, it seems amusing, especially about Papa showing up in the wrong clothes. Everyone was pissed. Excuse me. . . . Upset."

Barb maintained her smile and asked me to go on with my story.

"From the cemetery, we went to someone's house. There were cars parked everywhere. The place was filled, inside and out, with people eating and talking. Tables were loaded with food. Ladies rushed around replacing empty casseroles with full ones and adding more desserts. Everyone who came brought food. It was great.

"Kids were running around everywhere. I was related to most of them. Some I'd met in Texas, but most lived in Tennessee. The fact that we were kin was important and jump-started us into friendships right off the bat. We played games all day and hide and seek in the dark. Then it was time to go back home to Texas."

"Was your mother there?" Barb asked.

"No. She didn't have the money and my older siblings were in school.

"Tell me about her parents."

"Mom's parents were wonderful, but that didn't keep her from having a tough life. Her sister, Aunt Toni was really nice and her four brothers all served in the military, had decent jobs and were great guys."

"John, apart from being an excellent storyteller, you have remarkable insight into your own situation. Did you know that about yourself?"

"No."

"Why not?"

"I may have insight, but what can I do with it? Sometimes it's like I can't see through to the other side of things. It's like I'm trying to look through a mirror."

"That's good, John. Very good." Barb looked at her watch. "We still have 20 minutes. Tell me more?"

"The trip back home to Texas was long and sad. Papa's funeral really affected Nanny. She began going to Church and insisted Pa and David and I go with her. One Sunday night she wouldn't let up til we were in the car headed for the coliseum to hear Billy Graham. The crusade lasted 15 days and we were there every night.

"I had no idea what that preacher was talking about but he made Nanny cry. Four nights later she went down for the alter call and was baptized. The next few nights she'd look at Pa and start crying. Finally he went forward and Nanny couldn't stop smiling. The next evening she was at it again. This time her target was David and me. We went forward, clueless. We thought *if it stops Nanny from crying, why not?* So at the age of seven, I was baptized by Billy Graham.

"I've since come to believe even though that whole experience meant little to me, it was important to God. He has honored it even though I haven't."

"That's a very profound observation, John. What about now? Where is God in your life?"

"All I know for sure is, I've experienced a lot of near misses. I'm still alive and you're helping me find a better life. It can't all be good luck. I'm thinking there has to be a God."

Barb said, "I think you're right." She settled back into her chair and asked me to go on.

"Nanny was the glue that kept our family together. I always looked to her for assurance that everything would eventually be okay. She wasn't very tall and she was sweet in spirit. When she came home from the beauty parlor with blue hair, I thought she looked pretty and I told her so. It always made her smile.

"Nanny always told David and me how much she loved us. When I was scared she reassured me. If I was sick, her hugs were better than chicken soup. And when I needed to talk, she was more than just an available ear. With her compassionate heart, I felt more love from Nanny than from anyone. She's a wonderful grandma and I'm sure her prayers are what keeps me alive. Of all of our relatives, I enjoyed living with Nanny and Pa the most . . . because I knew they really loved me. They stayed put, they weren't always moving."

I leaned back and took a breath. Barb kept her eyes on me. She always did. It made me feel as if my life interested her and that I was important. Being with Dr. Bliss was a peaceful detour from my chaotic existence.

"John, are your grandparents still alive?"

"Yes, ma'am."

"You call your grandfather Pa. I'd like to know more about him."

"Pa is amazing. He taught me how to fish. He showed me that putting soapy water on the ground brought night crawlers to the surface. We used them for bait. We dangled our fishin' lines off the bridge down by Love Field where we mostly caught catfish and perch. With just a cane pole and a string hanging off the end, Pa could out fish a whole tackle box full of gadgets.

"One sunny afternoon Pa was out back melting lead to use for sinkers when we go fishing. I ran to see what he was doing. Not knowing the three-pound hunk was fresh out of the mold, I picked it up. As the scorching hot ball flew out of my hands Pa tried not to laugh.

"Didn't take you long to look at that did it?"

The doctor said I had second-degree burns on my fingers and thumb. I remember thinking I would no longer have fingerprints."

Barb said nothing, just smiled.

I smiled also and said, "Wrong."

She laughed and added "Go on?"

"My second trip to the emergency room came after playing Tarzan in the back yard. As I swung through the air, my older brother Donnie began whipping the portion of rope that hung below me. I was thrown upward, landing on the phone lines running to our house. I ricocheted into the air again. When I finally fell to the ground, I landed on my right arm. The cast remained in place for several months."

Barb's expression was priceless as she listened. She finally had to laugh and say, "You paint quite a picture. I could see you bouncing off the phone lines. Sad you broke your arm but it was really funny…like a circus act the way you described it."

"Circus, that's a good word. Parts of my life were indeed like a circus. You'll see what I mean when we get there."

"Let's go on with your Pa, shall we?"

I crossed my legs and settled in my chair.

"Pa still works for the City of Dallas in the sign department. He spends most of his life painting stripes on streets. People might think his simple job means he's simple too. Actually he's one of the smartest men I know. To this day, I take to heart the advice he showered on me, wisdom that could have only come from the hills of Tennessee. Things like, 'Potential, means you ain't worth a hoot . . . yet.' But the greatest thing he taught me was, 'People say you should learn from your mistakes. I tell you, if you're smart, you'll go to work for an idiot and learn from his.' Over the years, I've been blessed with a lot of idiots in my life and filled that roll myself numerous times.

"Pa liked Moon Pies, Peanut Patties and R.C. Cola. He hated white bread. His favorite songs were *My Blue Heaven* and *Goodnight Irene*. I loved to hear him sing along with the radio, tapping time on the steering wheel of his red Ford pickup. He was so proud of that truck. It was always clean and neat, inside and out. He kept it washed and shined until it sparkled.

"Every week Pa would give me a couple of quarters, just because he loved me I guess. Though he never said it in words, he showed it in many ways. The biggest treat was when Pa took me to the Waffle House. I'd sit for hours listening to him reminisce about his childhood, telling me stories of his life as a boy growing up in Tennessee.

"I love my Pa."

CHAPTER TWENTY-FIVE

KELLY AGAIN

"Okay, down to business. So how the hell did you let yourself get messed up with this Bill guy anyway?"

What a way to start our session. I didn't dare react. Instead I looked straight at Officer Kelly, smiled, and answered. "I was hustling pool at a place near downtown Dallas called Times Square. Danny, a guy at the pool hall where I hung out, introduced me to Bill and his girlfriend, Linda. Bill was looking for a shotgun. I told him I could get it for him."

Kelly rolled his eyes and crossed his arms. I paused.

"Don't mind me," he said. "Go on."

"Bill hadn't mentioned details: make, model or anything. I thought, *who cares*. It could be another payday. The thought did occur to me, he might be a cop just looking to clear a few guns off the street. I told myself, nah, even if I don't know Bill yet, I trust Danny.

"The only shotgun I could get my hands on was in my grandpa's closet, an old double barrel 12 gauge his father had given him. After an hour bus ride, I was in my grandparent's house. They were both at work so I had time to wrap the gun in blankets and get back on the bus. I scared myself to death imagining what might happen if anyone discovered what was in the bundle. I got off at Carroll Street and walked the final few blocks without being detected.

"Bill answered the door and invited me to take a seat on the couch while he went to the kitchen. He reappeared with two beers, handed me one, along with two $20 bills. Before I could pocket them, he surprised me by saying, 'If you're interested, I have a better offer.'

"'I'm listening.' was all I could think to say. Then Bill said, 'Trust me 'til tomorrow and I'll pay you $100 instead.'

"I gave him the 20's and left. By the time I arrived home I was having doubts. Their apartment was virtually vacant, no personal effects, no clothes lying around and the kitchen was bare. I hated getting ripped off but figured, *what the heck, it didn't cost me anything. No big deal.*

"Later that day, I lost all my cash at the tables and someone ripped off my last two grams of crystal. The previous 24 hours had been a bust. I was pissed. With no money, no meth, and no way back onto the tables, I had to keep my appointment with Bill and Linda the next day.

"As I walked down the hall, they came around the corner from the opposite direction, overloaded with bags. We met at their door. With a welcoming smile, Linda said, 'Hi, John, come on in.'

"Both were in a good mood, laughing and joking. Again Bill handed me a beer. This time he invited me to dinner. 'We're having steak and baked potatoes.' I was hungry and accepted.

"Bill motioned for me to sit, turned on the TV and left the room. Just as I was getting comfortable, he returned and held a large grocery bag in front of me.

"'Take a look at this,' he said.

"Inside was Pa's shotgun, shortened to about 16 inches, the barrels were sawed off to the stock and all serial numbers were gone. The butt had been fashioned into a pistol grip and wrapped with friction tape.

"As I admired the piece, I said, 'Whoever did this is quite the craftsman.'

"Bill handed me a Benjamin and asked, 'How do you like your steak?'

"I put the money in my pocket and shrugged. 'I don't know, never had one.'

"Bill smiled, 'Medium rare it is.'"

Kelly unfolded his arms and pushed back in his chair. "Were you aware that no matter how great the craftsmanship, your grandpa's shot gun was highly illegal and a favorite weapon of gangsters in organized crime?"

"I really didn't think about it at the time."

Kelly crossed his arms again. He was getting fidgety, so I continued my story, "During dinner that night, Bill offered me another job. My rent was due and all I had was the C-note he'd just given me. I told Bill, I was very interested. That's when he said, 'How would you like to be a babysitter for a week? I'll pay you 500 when I get back.'"

Kelly sat up straight and interjected, "Babysitter?"

"Yeah. Bill said guys from a whorehouse in La Grange were trying to kidnap Linda."

Kelly said, "Wow, those La Grange guys are infamous."

"I know. Girls are forced to work until they're useless, then they'd mysteriously turn up dead."

"Okay John, get on with it."

"Bill handed me a chrome plated Smith & Wesson .38 Special with a shoulder holster. He said, 'Don't let Linda out of your sight. You'll stay here while I'm gone. Your job is to protect her, no matter what.' Then he said, 'Be back by10:00 tomorrow morning. Okay?'

"I said, 'Count on it. I'll be here.' I took the .38 with me."

Kelly raised his hand like a traffic cop, "Okay time's up, I want to hear more about that next week, so be ready." He looked down and flipped through a few papers on his desk. "Oh yeah, here we are. Your workstation assignment will be in the kitchen." He looked at me and said, "I'm sure you're thrilled."

"I actually have kitchen experience." My answer was not meant to be a smart remark but Kelly took it that way.

"Okay, wise guy."

"Seriously, I worked in a restaurant, same one as my Mom."

Kelly whipped out a piece of paper. "Here's your schedule. Be on time and don't make waves."

Even though we were alone, Kelly spoke cautiously, almost in a whisper, "There's a new guy . . . checked in this morning. He's scared to death of being approached by some Gallo. I told him to find you."

I followed Kelly out the door. At the main hallway, he turned right. I turned left.

CHAPTER TWENTY-SIX

BARB

Back in my cell, I was still remembering Linda and our babysitting adventure. I lay down on my bunk and allowed myself to admit I was really tired. Since the day I set foot in Lompoc, I'd been on my guard and dealing with one stressful situation after another. Along with the occasional fish that came around looking for protection, now Kelly started sending them to me. Like it or not it seemed my reputation was spreading.

Exhaustion had finally caught up with me. I was asleep darn near the minute I hit the mattress. My usual nightmares had all but disappeared but I hadn't figured out how to shut off my mind. Every night, pictures from my life still rolled like movies into my dreams. Tonight, I knew Linda's story would be the main feature.

I was glad when morning came. A restless night had left me groggy. Seeing Barb was on the day's schedule. She'd said my past was pulling me down. She was right; it was a burden I couldn't carry any longer.

In her office, I began by unloading what was bothering me. "Barb, before we get into anything I want to say something."

"Yes?"

"I just want to tell you . . . I just want you to know that I stole my grandfather's shotgun."

Barb just looked at me kind of puzzled like.

I went on, "Of all the things I have done, that is the only thing I am really, honestly sorry for. It's the one thing I really feel, you know, remorse for. Stealing Pa's shotgun."

"Because?"

"Well you might think it's because it was the beginning of my life of crime. But no. It's because . . . it's because it was my grandfather's. And he knew I took it. He never said anything about it. He never confronted me. He just . . . let it go." I began to cry.

Barb handed me a box of Kleenex then just sat without saying anything for a bit. She asked, "Do you want to go on with that?"

I wiped my eyes and answered, "No."

"Very well then. Where should we go?"

I took a few breaths and cleared my thoughts, "Linda and I bonded because we understood each other. She had lived a tough life also and like me she felt alone. For eighteen months she was like a sister. But yesterday, in Kelly's office, she surfaced and I need to get it off my chest."

Barb said, "Go for it."

"When I met Linda, she was nineteen. Her 42 year old boyfriend was named Bill. He hired me to be a babysitter, as he called it, for a week, to protect Linda while he was away. Her life had been threatened."

Barb raised her eyebrows. "I can hardly wait to see how this turns out."

"No kidding, Barb. This is exactly how it happened. When I arrived at their apartment the next morning, Linda was alone. We were both hungry and went looking for breakfast. It felt strange to be with someone else's girlfriend and packin' heat. I tried to act cool but Linda knew better. She asked me if I'd ever worked as a bodyguard before.

"I told her, 'Actually, no.'

"She said, 'Relax. You're doing fine. And, don't worry; the situation isn't as bad as Bill makes it sound. He's overly protective of me.'

"During our meal Linda began telling me the sad story of her childhood. It made me feel accepted, like she trusted me.

"Her parents are very controlling. They live in a posh, upper class neighborhood near Albuquerque. Linda was adopted. Maybe having a kid was not what they expected. No matter the reason, their rejection was more than she could stand. At 15 she took off and hitchhiked around the country for a while. That little detail gave us a connection. I'd done that too, a couple of times.

"I told her I thought hitching alone, for a girl, was dangerous. She said most people felt sorry for her. In Hollywood she landed a job as a production assistant for a company making B-movies. She became a makeup artist and landed a few roles acting in low budget Biker Flicks. She was making it on her own. When she saved enough money to visit her parents, they wouldn't even let her in the house. They were afraid of being blacklisted if their fancy friends found out about Linda's movie career. She was heartbroken and went back to California in time to find her boyfriend packing for a move to Dallas. She moved with him but two weeks later he dumped her.

"Linda and I were still finishing breakfast when our waitress interrupted with refills. That gave me a minute to realize Linda's hard-luck life was getting to me. She was so nice and way too young for so much rejection.

"She said there were no other choices, so she hired on as a topless dancer. She told me those places were horrible, but that's where she met Bill. Linda's eyes got real soft and her face changed into a wonderful smile when she mentioned Bill. She told me, 'One look at him, I was mush. He came to my rescue during a police raid. Bill and I have been together almost a year.' To see her smile at the mention of Bill, yet tear up when she spoke of her parents was heartbreaking. It was obvious her memories were still painful and she needed to vent. I'm glad she saw me as someone safe, a place where she could keep her secrets. While she was a girl I could have fallen for, my growing respect and admiration for Bill kept my hormones in check. When it came to women, I'd been seriously influenced by memories of the mental and emotional abuse Mom received from the men in her life. Because of Mom, my two sisters and Nanny, I had great respect for women. I wanted Linda as a friend, nothing else.

"Linda predicted I'd really like Bill once I got to know him. She told me he was very intelligent and had a lot of friends in key places, people who could pull strings.

"We spent most of the day talking and drinking coffee, with me listening to Linda's monologue of misery. Back at the apartment, we snacked on chips and dips for dinner and watched TV. Our time together had, so far, been uneventful, no threats, no danger.

"Later that evening she asked, 'What about you John? Do you have a family?' Linda had caught me off guard. 'Come on, John, It's your turn.'

"I told her she reminded me of my older sister, Evelyn. I told her about Mom sending me away to live with relatives and how that made me feel unwanted and abandoned. Linda's sad eyes told me she could relate. She said, 'At least you had relatives. I have no brothers, sisters, aunts, uncles, no family that I know of.'

"I felt terrible and that's when I told her to consider me her brother. It took a long moment before she spoke again. 'I think I'd like that.' She smiled and said, 'Okay, Brother John, what is it about me that reminds you of your real sister?'

"I started my story again. Evelyn was unhappy with our very dysfunctional family and decided to take off to California. Well, late one afternoon David, Tammy and I were watching cartoons when there was a knock on the door of our apartment. David and I tore across the room to see who it was. It was Evelyn. She pressed a finger across her lips and whispered. "I'm running away and want you and David to come. If we can get out of Texas, maybe we can have a better life."

Barb interrupted. "Wait just a minute. How old were you kids?"

"I was 13, David was 11 and Tammy was, maybe four…but we didn't take her"

"And Evelyn. How old was she?"

I had to think before answering. "She was 15."

Barb shook her head. "You were all so young. I can't imagine such a thing."

"Well, that's what happened. Evelyn helped us pack. We dropped Tammy off at Nanny's and headed into the unknown.

"My sister knew a young couple, Sonny and Ellen, who decided to try their luck in

California and invited my sister to go along. A man named Roger Carter was going too. Sonny and Ellen led the way in their car. Roger followed with Evelyn, David and me in his car. Before leaving town we made a quick stop at the Fina Service Station where Roger had been working. He shattered the rear window and in no time he was back with the cash box.

"California here we come."

I leaned back and stretched. Barb leaned forward. "No time for that. What happened?"

"I don't know. I fell asleep."

Barb tilted her head and said, "Really?"

"Really, I fell asleep. David did too. When Evelyn woke us up, we were in Sweetwater, Texas, at a cheap, rundown motel. They only had two rooms. Sonny and Ellen took one, the rest of us piled into the other. Evelyn told us to brush our teeth and left to go see Ellen in the other room.

"Once the door was shut, Roger told David and me to go to sleep . . . fast. He said, 'I got plans and you boys ain't part of 'um.'

"Evelyn returned and told Roger to take the bed. She'd sleep on the floor with David and me. When she didn't go for his "plan", the fight started. Roger flipped out a switchblade but he dropped it. When he bent down to pick it up, I hit him on the head with a lamp and David grabbed the knife. We left Roger groaning on the floor and ran outside."

Barb's eyes were riveted to mine as I continued.

"A police car was driving by and Evelyn frantically flagged him down. They went in and arrested Roger. We were all taken to the Sweetwater Jail. When Evelyn told the cop about the robbery, Roger was booked. The jailer opened a cell for us to sleep in and then called authorities in Dallas. We never mentioned Sonny and Ellen.

"David and I spent part of that night looking at wanted posters and display cases full of contraband guns, knives and brass knuckles. Two pizzas later we were sound asleep in the cell.

"Our uncles Bobby and Claude showed up early the next morning to claim us. Claude was angry and really gave it to Evelyn. He said, 'How could you put your little brothers through this? They must have been terrified.'"

Barb took a breath and asked, "Were you terrified?"

"No. Well, maybe when Roger pulled the knife. But I thought it was pretty cool that Evelyn let us go with her, then she took all the heat in the end."

Barb shook her head. "John, so far your life reads like a book." She pulled up the sleeves on her sweater as if preparing for work. "You kids were really lucky."

"When I think about how we could have died that night, it's clear to me, luck had nothing to do with the way it turned out. It had to be God protecting us." I hesitated. "Do you think that's possible?"

"Your life is so bizarre; my guess is you were quite right about your encounter with Billy Graham. Only God could keep up with your misadventures."

I had to smile. "I'm not quite sure God is real. Maybe someday I'll know."

Barb smiled. "I hope you do." She sighed and began to talk of her own past. "I don't recall much about my early years. The people who adopted me were kind and loving, just the opposite of Linda's. From first grade to a doctorate, my parents saw to it that I was educated in the best schools. I was very fortunate. I don't believe it was an accident. God gave me what I needed to be here for you. Now keep going."

"Okay. The next morning, Linda asked me to buy her a pack of Salem's. Bill had told me not to let her out of my sight but it was only a 10 minute run to the store. I returned to find Linda huddled on the couch, crying. I flew across the room and dropped to my knees beside her. Between sobs, she confessed Bill was in jail for a week and needed to pay a fine in order to get released. I felt so sorry for her and asked how I could help. Linda wiped her tears and told me about a woman who drove a Plymouth beater and took the same route every night to make a bank deposit. Some people Bill knew were going to relieve the lady of the deposit. That money was supposed to pay Bill's fine. Linda was crying again as she said, 'They backed out.'

"That's when I told Linda, 'I'll do it. I can jump in the car when she pulls up to a stop. I'll draw my gun and tell her to drive on. When she stops at the next corner I grab the bag, jump out and take off down the alley. There's got to be an alley somewhere on her route.' Linda listened, shocked and speechless but I kept going. 'You wait in the alley. I'll jump in the back seat of your car and lie down, out of sight, while you drive us back to your apartment.'"

Barb shook her head as she said, "Unbelievable." She took a deep breath and asked, "Well . . . did you do it?"

I just smiled. We ended the session.

CHAPTER TWENTY-SEVEN

SLINGING SLOP & THE HOLE

What can you say about kitchen duty? Everyone hated working there and wanted out as soon as possible. I was lucky enough to be transferred out after three days.

For my next assignment, I became a Corridor Orderly. The title sounded important. Actually, it was no big deal. "The Walk" identified a long corridor that connected the units. Every four hours, a team of four orderlies would sweep and mop the walk from one end to the other. I could have lasted in that job had it not been for David Becker. He owed me 20 bucks from playing Spades, but kept putting me off. Every time I'd see him, it would be one excuse after another.

One day, I was on corridor duty. I was just turning around to re-dip my mop and there he was. "Hey Becker, what's up with my 20?"

"You know Tex, I ain't gonna' pay you. I'm thinking I don't really have to."

I kicked his ass. That incident added to my reputation and got me at least $20 worth of satisfaction. It also landed me 30 days in the hole for assault.

Solitary confinement in prison is different from what I'd experienced in jail. The medical doctor came in to make sure I was okay physically and Dr. Bliss showed up to assess my mental health.

"Are you okay?" she asked. Her tone showed genuine interest. I was so glad to see her. But it was not a visit that allowed conversation. It was strictly to make sure I wasn't suicidal. She had boxes to check on a mandatory list.

R. R. Kelly's responsibilities included keeping track of me to assure my welfare.

"Thirty days is a long time. You gonna to be okay?"

"Sure, I really appreciate your support."

"Hang tough, Swanger. I'll be back."

Kelly came several times to check on me during my time there.

Just as I was thinking I would go nuts if I had to spend one more day in solitary, they let me out. I grabbed my bag of toiletries and hit the door. There I found Becker waiting. He walked up and handed me two crisp sawbucks and said, "Sorry Tex. I was wrong."

Freedom rocks!

Two weeks later, I was in a bad mood, It wasn't a good day. As I passed a guard he made a comment that hit me wrong. I went off on him, suggesting he do something anatomically impossible. I was in trouble again. Back to the hole. Seven days this time.

Insubordination.

CHAPTER TWENTY-EIGHT

ABANDONMENT

The guard called "Swanger", and opened the door to my dungeon. Sprung again. Coincidentally, I was scheduled to see Dr. Bliss. She had come often to make sure I was coping with confinement. The lady had become like a mom, sister, and friend all wrapped into one person. I could hardly wait to resume our conversations and showed up to her office 15 minutes early.

Barb greeted me warmly. "I'm so glad you're out of solitary . . . again."

"It's good to be out. Thanks for the visits. I know it's your job but it helped."

"Aside from doing my job, I personally wanted to make sure you were okay. It must be tough to spend time alone with just your thoughts."

"Having you and Mr. Kelly around made it easier. I can't begin to tell you how much. Thank you."

"You're welcome. Now let's get back to where we left off last time you were here."

"Yes ma'am, I'm ready."

"Some of what you've gone through, John, is just the way life is. And don't think that because you have questions, there will always be answers. As we talk, you'll gain insights that will help deal with your losses and regrets. But some things are not fixable. You'll have to dismiss them and not allow them to drag you down. How does that sound?"

"Sounds like Nanny. She says, 'That which don't kill you will make you stronger.'"

Barb agreed, "Words to remember from a wise lady." She knew I'd be thinking about my Nanny and needed time to shift gears. Then she said, "John, I'm curious, what do you think about during the time between our sessions?"

"Well . . . there are moments when I just want to forget the whole thing. Talking with you about my feelings makes me think of my past and what I should have done differently. I dream about it a lot. For a while I had terrible nightmares but that's changing. It makes me wonder what I'm doing here dredging up more rotten feelings. That's when I think of quitting. And then I realize my whole life has had me on the run."

Barb gave me a quizzical look. "So, do you want to continue or not?"

"I need your help."

"Good. Let's talk more about the early years. You up for that?"

"I guess so." I took a moment to think. "In 1959 our entire family, six of us, piled in with Nanny and Pa. We had nowhere else to live. That year I began my formal education at Lida Hooe Elementary in the South Oak Cliff section of Dallas. Public school in Texas begins in the first grade. I was in trouble from the start. Because David was always tagging along with me, it seemed natural to take him to school. Around lunchtime someone finally noticed he was too young to be there.

"A few days later my teacher, Mrs. Riddle, sent me to the principal for what she called swearing. I was just talking like we always did at home. After three swats, I was sent back to class. Mrs. Riddle asked me what happened. I told her. 'He whopped my ass.'

"She sent me back for seconds."

Barb's spontaneous giggle made me laugh too.

"Within two months of starting school, Mom's brother, John, was transferred to Jackson, Mississippi and he took me with him. Two weeks later he was transferred to Mobile, Alabama. By the next month we were back in Dallas. Thinking her brother Bobby was more settled, Mom sent me to San Antonio to live with him and his family. You guessed it. I no sooner arrived than Uncle Bobby was transferred to Houston. My stuff was on the truck too. Eventually I was right back where I'd started, with Nanny and Pa, at Lida Hooe Elementary. After attending five schools, I finished the first grade.

"In those early years, school was a place of ridicule. The boys from middle-class families always seemed to have money. During recess they'd pile loose change on the blacktop against a brick wall behind the gym and spit on the money until it was completely covered. Then they would back away laughing as all us poor kids scrambled to grab as many coins as we could.

"Not being a tough guy, there were times when I was beat up or spit on. I was always afraid to fight back. Once, while running from three guys who wanted to whip me, I ended up cornered on somebody's front porch. One of the boys pissed on me while the other two laughed. A man came out of the house and chased them off. He was very kind and drove me home. Along the way told me, 'Kid, you don't have to take that kind of abuse. You should defend yourself.'

"I felt so small."

I was too embarrassed to look at Barb. That part of my life was humiliating.

"It's okay John, take your time."

"If my life was stressful, I can only imagine how much worse it was for Mom. She was under the gun to provide for five kids and there was always some unsavory guy giving her grief. Mom desperately dreamed of living happily ever after but reality kept getting in the way. Her life was full of strife and turmoil, no wonder she ended up with ulcers and in need of surgery.

"One afternoon, while Mom was in the hospital, Donnie was horsing around with the kids across the street. When things started to get out of hand Donnie came home. Soon the boys were in our front yard. One guy was yelling that Donnie had stolen his wallet. They were just looking to start something.

"When a rock came flying through our living room window, Donnie called the police. By the time cops arrived, Evelyn had taken Tammy and left. David and I were hiding out of sight but we could hear Donnie talking to the police.

"They asked, 'Where's your Mom?'

"He told them she was in the hospital.

"The cops said it wasn't safe to stay in the house with a broken window and asked if there was some place else he could stay. He told them about Nanny. They said he should go there. The policeman seemed satisfied, wrote his report and left. So did Donnie. Maybe he thought David and I had gone with Evelyn. We were still hiding.

"Later that evening, a patrolman came by to make sure no one was looting. He found David and me and took us to the detention facility called 1000 Knight Street. We had no idea why we were there, until we over-heard someone say we were being neglected. They cut all our hair off and took our cigarettes and Zippos.

"Vegetarians ran the place and that's all they served at mealtime. It was gross. But we didn't have to put up with it for long because we ran away the next afternoon. Just before we snuck off, David and I watched a little kid take a beating for peeing outside. I remember thinking, *if they catch us, they'll beat us too.*

"Playing the brave older brother was tough. I was scared. When the right moment came, we ran as fast as we could. Not knowing which direction to go and running scared, we ended up right back where we'd started. We just stopped, turned around and took off again. We managed to find a bus stop. With no money, we snuck through the back door of the bus while people were exiting the front. Eventually we found our way home and hid under the bed. A few hours later, we heard Nanny's voice. Someone from Knight Street must have called her when we turned up missing.

"Nanny to the rescue.

"When Mom finally got out of the hospital, we went back home with her, but not for long. One day Mom took David and me aside and told us we were going to a nice camp, with a lot of kids, horseback riding and games. Nanny bought us new underwear, T-shirts and socks. We were excited and wrote our names on each piece with a marker as we packed for the trip. I was thinking, *Wow, nothing this nice has ever happened to us.* I knew Mom didn't have the money for such things. Eager to go, we thanked her anyway.

"It wasn't until our first morning there when we realized that summer camp was nothing but a lie. We were actually residents of Boles Home, an East Texas orphanage. I'm convinced Mom always wanted to keep us with her or at least with family. But when we were dumped off at an orphanage my outlook changed. I felt deceived and betrayed."

Barb could see emotions stirring in me and waited. Finally she asked, "Tell me what you are feeling right now."

"Remembering my chaotic childhood is always tough. I can convey what happened, what it looked like, and some of what was said. But there are no words to express the depths of my feelings . . . the gut wrenching emotions attached to feeling abandoned, unwanted and poor.

"I tell you, that first morning at the orphanage came with a shock. Even before sunrise, we found ourselves riding in a trash truck heading out to dump garbage and slop the pigs. When the truck stopped, Cornelius, a big Indian kid, and two other boys lifted the hood. With a bent metal clothes hanger, they jumped across the battery to heat the wire until it was red hot. They used it light their cigarettes. One of the other boys decided that if we didn't smoke, we might tell on them. He said either we smoke with them or face a beating. This wasn't our first cigarette, but it was the first time to be forced to smoke. We were not tough kids. We smoked.

"Cornelius became our friend. He taught us things, like, 'Sometimes you just got to go along to get along.' And 'You got to learn to make do with whatever comes your way.' A few days later, Cornelius ran away without saying goodbye.

"David and I were always in trouble. Mr. and Mrs. Gaines, the couple that oversaw our dorm, told us how we needed to give our lives to Jesus. Then Mr. Gaines would turn around and sadistically beat us for various indiscretions. I can't tell you how many times we were "disciplined," but I thought giving my life to The Lord might deliver me from the evil that surrounded me. I developed a love for Christ and a hatred for Christians. I remember praying, 'Lord Jesus, please protect me from your followers.'

"David was caught one day taking cigarettes from Mr. and Mrs. Gaines' bedroom. We'd been whipped several times before, but this was different. David had inadvertently exposed their hypocrisy. Our leaders had been smoking and drinking for years without detection. Now their sins were made public. In front of all the kids, David was whipped on his bare back with a hand full of willow switches. My feelings of helplessness were devastating. I'm torn up every time I think of how I let him down. His welts remained for weeks. But the wounds on my heart are still with me. I paused, waiting for Barb to say something. She didn't so I did.

"David and I formulated an escape plan. Cornelius had made it and we could too. In reality, dozens of kids had tried to run and were brought back. It was no secret how badly those boys were treated. But our fear of staying outweighed our fear of leaving. Then, just before making our move, Mrs. Gaines said, 'You boys have some visitors coming from Dallas.' She never said who they were.

"We sat on the porch staring down the long driveway til long past sundown. They say a watched pot never boils, but I was determined to boil this one. Finally, distant headlights turn in. It was Uncle John, his wife Ann, and Mom was with them. They were moving to Corpus Christi.

"We begged, 'Mom, please take us with you.'"

She said, "Johnny, there's no room in the car and we don't know where we'll live once we get down there."

"I burst into tears and pulled up David's shirt to expose the welts and bruises on his back. I told mom 'If you don't take us, we're gonna run away.' I couldn't stop sobbing and neither could David. Ann began crying and turned to Uncle John with an insistent look.

He said, 'Girls, make room. We're not leavin' these boys in this awful place.'

"As we drove away, it dawned on me, the lie Mom had told about a summer camp paled in comparison to the lie on the sign at the entrance of Boles Home. It said, a Christian home.

"We lived a short time in Corpus then we packed up and moved to Padre Island. Padre was the highlight of my young life. We were only there a few months, but it was a time of peace and rest and fun. We spent hours playing at the beach. On weekends, David and I cut lawns for spending money. We had a taste of life in a somewhat normal family."

I leaned back in my chair. "That's as good as it ever got. By fall we were back in Dallas."

I looked at Barb, expecting something.

"John, was your time in Padre enough to offset what happened at the orphanage?"

"No. My feelings are still as raw now as when I was 10 years old, stuck in that awful place with a younger brother who looked up to me. I felt lost and discouraged. There was no way I could have helped myself. Worse yet, I had no way to protect David. Nanny wasn't around to rescue us that time. Thank God Uncle John was."

Barb's genuine concern soothed me. "John, you have so many layers of pain and damage in your young life. Thank you for sharing your story with me." Those caring eyes of hers were hard to ignore. "My next hour is open if you want to keep going."

"Thanks. I'd like that."

Barb got up and poured me a glass of water. "If you're going to talk for another hour, you may need this."

I thanked her, took a sip and began again.

"We hadn't been back in Dallas long, maybe five months, when after Christmas Mom took David and me on another ride. I can't remember what led up to our placement at the orphanage in Stephenville. I only recall being there. Jimmy Green and his wife Carolyn were our dorm overseers. Most of the time we got along with everyone and I must say Stephenville was not at all like Boles Home.

"I learned about 4-H from a kid who was tired of caring for his pig." I tried to imitate the kid's voice, "'Ya see, John, the feed store in town sold me and some other kid's these piglets for 15 bucks apiece. They carry the bill for the feed and everything til the 4-H fair and auction. Truth be known, I hate this kinda' stuff. So if you want him, you can have my pig.'

"I accepted."

Barb smiled and said, "Great story. Better accent."

"Oscar may have started out a $15 piglet, but he'd become a 260 pound hog. I thought that kid wasn't very smart because it was only three weeks until the fair. Faithfully, I fed, watered and bathed that fat red slab of bacon every day. I could hardly believe it when Oscar took second place in his class. Top bid at the auction was 75¢ a pound. After paying off the feed store, I had nearly $200, which bought pop and candy on many weekend trips to the movie house.

"Midnight was a Black Angus raised by a girl at the orphanage named Gail. Her steer won first place and she was given a huge blue ribbon. The generous individual, who bought Gail's steer, donated him back to the home. Midnight was delivered frozen and wrapped in white paper packages. Gail cried every time beef was served and wouldn't eat any of it. We taunted her by singing *The Midnight Special*. It was funny then but I felt bad about it later.

"After spending some of my hog loot on cigarettes, Mr. Green caught me smoking. For the second time in my life I was forced to smoke. This time I was made to sit in the living room, on a chair, in front of all kids, with a milk bucket on my head while lighting up the whole pack. There's no way I enjoyed the experience but I can't say it taught me anything either.

"One morning at breakfast, David, Gail, and I were talking. She had just turned 18, which meant it was time for her to leave. Saying our good-byes made me sad. I knew I'd miss her. At the same time I was happy for her. She was finally free to go.

"There were a lot of good kids at Stephenville but to save myself the pain of parting, I tried not to get close to anyone. Gail was the exception. Most of us at Stephenville were in the same rut, living each day hoping something would change. But nothing ever did.

"Kids would come and go. Friendships were short lived or not at all. And, just like the day we arrived, I have no memory of leaving Stephenville."

Our session ended and somewhere along the walk, I began to realize how much I appreciated Barb. She was, bit by bit, helping me come to the realization that I actually could be a better man. In some ways healing is like a drug. I couldn't wait to get back to more of it.

CHAPTER TWENTY-NINE

BRINKERHOFF & HERNANDEZ

Summer had given way to fall. The eucalyptus trees around the prison formed a windbreak. They were beautiful as leaves began to change color and hide within the fog of Southern California. I learned that fog was called parole dust because if someone managed to escape over the fence and into its protection, it was like a do-it-yourself parole. An escape beyond the eucalyptus was called a Bush Parole.

Traffic within the cellblocks increased as winter pressed in and outdoor activities dwindled. That gave us more time to play cards. David Brinkerhoff was a short skinny white punk. I often thought he was straight but assumed the role as a way to cope. Actually he looked more scared than gay. He was a hell of a spades player though so, gay or straight, he was my spades partner. We sometimes played for green but mostly commissary.

Watkins and Boston were a team we often fleeced for a few trips to the Canteen. Although they were black, there was never any sign of racial tensions between the four of us. We enjoyed each other's company.

One Saturday afternoon we were engaged in a match for the typical $5 commissary per game. I glanced up and noticed Hernandez at the next table. We exchanged nods. Just as my eyes landed back on my cards, I heard cheering and shouting. "Go, go, go!" A large black man stood behind Hernandez, clutching him by the collar with his right hand and repeatedly stabbing him in the chest with his left. Hernandez struggled to his feet, trying to fight him off and get free. He couldn't. The assault danced between our tables and brushed my shoulder as the two worked their way around us, then against B-Tier, where Hernandez fell to the floor. The attacker reached down and stabbed his victim several more times before walking away.

As I looked around, there were nearly 200 blacks flooding into the tiers of K-Unit. All had come to witness the stabbing. I was shaking. Brinkerhoff started to leave his chair. I grabbed him and pulled him back into his seat. "Spades led." I said. Watkins and Boston were perhaps the only blacks within the prison who were clueless as to what was going down. The four of us just kept looking down, tossing random cards at a pile in the center of our table. I looked up to see Brinkerhoff crying. I put a finger to my lips and softly said, "Shhh, it'll be okay." The assailant slowly walked toward the exit. Twice he looked back at Hernandez. I watched as he handed the shank to someone on D-Tier. That person handed it to another, who in turn handed it to someone on F-Tier where it disappeared.

Even with blood splattered all over our table, we tried to continue our game, as if nothing had happened. The right side of my face was covered with blood as were my shirt and trousers. I held the cards with shaking hands as a drop of red landed on the seven of spades.

The loud speaker echoed, "The Prison is in Lock Down, The Prison is in Lock Down. Report to your Cells." All cell doors opened at the same time. The vacuum of blacks had cleared enough so I could see the guard locked in his office. Fear painted his face.

I ran into my cell and pulled the door closed until the clank assured me I was safe. After quickly cutting the numbers from my shirt and trousers, I flushed them down the toilet and stripped. With my bloody clothing tied into knots, to help gain distance, I threw them out the window, sending them as far to the right as possible so they didn't fall straight below. I washed the blood from my neck and face and made sure none remained on the sink. Pulling fresh clothing from the locker, I dressed, and flopped down on my bunk pretending to read.

People were yelling back and forth between cells. Some were laughing, others were loudly chanting their approval. The sight of someone being murdered was beyond disturbing. It was sickening. Hernandez never had a chance.

I felt ill.

The Goon Squad stormed our unit and began grabbing everyone to read their shirt numbers. Those from K-Unit were shoved into their cells. Everyone else was removed to the walk. Finally the roar quieted into the occasional shriek or obscenity.

From the cell next to mine came a sharp yell. "Dago, what the hell just happened?"

An answer came from somewhere, "I don't know bro. I don't know."

I wasn't in the mood for music, but anything would be better than the yelling and jeering going on around me. Through the headphones, Buffalo Springfield rang out, as if mocking my present situation.

> Battle lines being drawn
> Nobody's right if everybody's wrong
> Young people speakin' their minds
> Getting' so much resistance far behind
> It's time we stop
> Hey what's that sound
> Everybody look what's goin' down

"Strip and stand by your doors," resounded through the building. One by one, each cell opened and men were ordered onto the tier. Cells were searched and each naked body inspected for wounds. By nightfall things had settled down. Dinner was served in boxes. Meatloaf, gravy, mashed potatoes, salad and tea.

Unsweetened.

CHAPTER THIRTY

MOVES, MANDATES & THE DRAGON

For the next few weeks there was little to do. I hadn't been reassigned to a workstation so Barb decided we should meet three times a week. That was fine with me.

"Just begin where you left off, John."

"Mmm. Let me see. Mom and Evelyn waitressed at Pal's Waffle Shop. After school David and I worked there bussing tables. We had second jobs as newspaper boys. Donnie had moved to Alaska with Uncle Bobbie. They were on a great adventure while the rest of us were stuck in the same boring routine. But Donnie didn't stay long. When he returned he joined us at the Waffle Shop as our dishwasher.

"Even with all of us working, there was never enough to cover the rent. Mom tried hard to make things better for us, but raising five kids on tips didn't cut it. She would convince an apartment manager to let us move in without rent on the promise of a double payment by the end of the month. Then around the 30th, we'd pack up in the middle of the night and head to another apartment where the cycle began again.

"At times the new place would be so small we'd have to store things either in Pa's garage or in a self-storage unit. It was the same routine month after month. Donnie called it P.M.S. . . . Packing, Moving, and Storage.

"There were some good times during those lean years. Excitement ruled when Mom came home with pizza. But that didn't compare to the rare evenings when she'd take us out to eat at the pizza place across the street from the Waffle Shop. Every time I sit down in a pizza joint, I'm reminded of those times. Actually just the smell of pizza triggers memories: Six of us sitting in a booth sharing a pizza. Sometimes it was only a small, only one slice each but it wasn't about satisfying our hunger. Eating out meant we were together. I loved those times.

"By age 13, I'd lived in Tennessee, Alabama and Mississippi. In Texas alone, I'd lived in Dallas, Grand Prairie, Garland, Mesquite, Houston, Galveston, San Antonio, Corpus Christi, Padre Island, Stephenville and Quinlan. I thought I'd tasted everything Texas had to dish out.

"Nope, not even close."

Barb interjected "Wow, travelin' man."

"Yeah, while living with Mom seemed to be one escapade after another, we encountered a most frustrating situation during the infamous forced bussing era. On enrollment day we walked to J. L. Long Jr. High, just two blocks from our house. We were told we'd be attending a school across town because of federal mandates. Spence Jr. High was predominately black. I remember thinking: *David and I are predominately white*.

"We rode to and from school on a city bus which set us up to be regularly accosted by several darker skinned students who demanded our money, cigarettes, lighters, and bus passes.

"A guy named Eugene decided he liked David and me. Even though we were white, he defended us. He was a nice kid and we stuck close to him. But one day Eugene didn't show up. So once again we were jumped. David and I decided to take matters into our own hands.

"There was a burned down house near the school we were attending. On the curb we found the address. The next day, we went to the school office and told the lady our family was moving to California and we need to take our records with us. Back across town, we presented the folders to the lady in the office at J. L. Long. We watched in silence as she looked up the address.

"She smiled and said, 'Ok, let's get you boys to class.' No one ever figured out we'd switched schools.

"There was a lot of talk circulating on the subject of bussing and integration. I have come to believe no one, not whites, blacks, teachers, or even school boards wanted bussing. We came to the conclusion that people in Washington, D.C. were forcing their ideas on us. It seemed to me we were living in a world which spoke out against racism on one hand and promoted it on the other. Bussing brought about nothing but violence and animosity in Dallas."

Barb and I looked at each other in silence for a long moment before she gave her feedback. "Why am I still surprised that, even as young as you were, you came up with such common sense solutions? I'm learning to expect the unusual from you. It's the essence of who you are and your logic seems to push you toward your own moral standards."

"I'm not sure what that means."

"It means you have a strong sense of right and wrong. It's nothing you learn or sign up for. With you it's pure instinct, every bit as intense as your need to be loved and accepted by a compassionate mom and caring dad."

"I think I get it now. You're good Dr. Barb . . . real good."

"Glad you think so John."

I looked up at the ceiling, then down at my feet. I left my chair and walked around, then back at my chair, I whirled around and sat, leaning forward, looking straight into Barb's intense blue eyes.

"I deserve to be here in prison. I did wrong so this is right. But I feel like a caged animal."

Barb was ready with an encouraging answer "You'll make it and I'll be here to help you." Then she urged me to go on.

"Nothing about our family was normal. Nothing was ever permanent. We were always on the run from something. My teen years went from pain and rejection to a life of crime. Even since being here, with all the limitations of prison, I haven't been content to sit back and let time pass. Acting like my life was put on hold the moment I was arrested isn't working. I don't want to walk out of here the same person who walked in. And that, Barb, just isn't acceptable. I need to find a way to fix what's wrong and I know that rehabilitation will be in spite of the system and not because of it. No one's gonna fix me. I have to do it myself. And I thank you for being willing to help"

Before saying anything Barb stood, took a few steps and leaned back on her desk. "There you go again, John. Seeing through problems is your gift. In a previous session you mentioned feeling as if you're looking into a mirror. I believe you need both a mirror and the clear glass to find your way. Am I right?"

"I need a compass too…a father who is consistent and caring, to teach me about life and how to be a man. I've been stumbling all over looking for the right path, but I can't seem to find it on my own. I'm lost, Barb. Just lost."

"Chances are, you'll have to find your compass another way. Let's drop the past. How do you see the future?"

"I have no idea. Making it through each day so I can get the hell out of here is a priority. My life is so small, compressed and boring."

"Obviously your life has been simplified, but your past is still complicated. What we do in these sessions is supposed to help clear the muddy waters of your life. Is it working?"

"I think so. Without you I'd be a nut case. So where do we go from here?"

Barb checked her watch, "We're still on the clock. How about another story?"

My glass was nearly empty. Another swig and it was. I wiped my mouth on my sleeve and kept going. "Okay, next chapter. We were all together, living with Mom. I can still hear her voice, all the way to my room. 'Johnny, come out here.' Responding to her call, I had to step over a chair blocking the hallway. That seemed strange. In the living room, there was a large man wearing high top Converse tennis shoes, sitting on the couch next to Mom. Donnie and Evelyn were sitting there too, so I sat. I couldn't stop staring at his shoes. I don't think I had ever seen an adult wearing black high tops. When she called David, he shoved aside the chair and joined us. Last, she called Tammy, who was mad about something and refused to leave her room.

"Mom introduced us to James E. Razor or Walter Dean Morrison, depending on which ID he was using. We called him Walt. He became Mom's forth husband, stepfather number three.

"Walt was larger than life, six feet plus and well over 300 pounds. Once he began talking, he didn't hesitate sharing his impression of us kids, especially me. 'John, I believe you're the one headed for trouble. The way you handled that obstacle in the hall indicates your approach to life. You walked on like it wasn't even there. With that attitude you'll be the one to end up in prison. Stick with me and I'll show you the ropes.'

"At the time I had no idea how tainted his advice really was. This guy sounded like he might be interested in me and my future. Maybe he was trying to impress Mom, but I let myself believe he cared.

"Walt was a jack-of-all-trades and it turned out he was more than qualified to 'teach me the ropes'. He'd done two years in Huntsville for auto theft and a Federal stint for interstate transportation of a stolen vehicle. Automobile repossession was a trade made to order for Walt and at the age of 13, it became mine too. Walt's C.B. handle was The Texas Dragon.

"One day I asked, 'Hey, Walt, why the Texas Dragon?' his answer 'Cause that's what I do, I'm always draggin' cars around.'

"Within a few months my skills were impressive. I could hotwire just about any car on the road and pick locks like a pro. I could point out every year, make and model of Chevy just by looking at the taillights.

"We began with me at the wheel, steering as Walt pushed from behind using an old Dodge pickup with a tire lashed to the grill to soften the blows. One tap on his horn meant I was to turn right, two meant turn left. In no time I was backing cars down side streets at breakneck speeds, usually at 3:00 in the morning, while angry debtors threw rocks and insults at us in an effort to regain their heaps.

"I loved it.

"Walt had a talent for talking his way out of most bad situations. He used a combination of intimidation, finesse and logic. It was a gift.

"Once I was under a car, placing a tow hook on the axel when the owner came running out of his house. He was armed and fired into the air. Then he drew a bead on us and said, 'Get away from my car or I'll kill you both.'

"Walt threw down the other tow hook and marched across the lawn, gesturing and yelling, 'You better lose that shotgun before I stick it up your ass.'

"Sorry, that was crude."

Barb nodded her head and thanked me.

"The man opened the door, stashed the weapon, and watched as we rolled out of his driveway, his Buick in tow.

"After my nerves settled I asked, 'Hey Walt, you got some kind of death wish or something? Man, walking up to that guy with a shotgun aimed right at you?'

"I was dumbfounded yet impressed with his reply. He said, 'That man showed his hand when he fired into the sky. If he really wanted to kill us, he'd have done it when he first came out. That ole' boy was bluffing.'

"Okay, so Walt had used mostly intimidation and not so much finesse. He certainly got the right result and my attention.

"As repo men, Walt and I worked long hours and were good at our jobs. It was actually enjoyable and certainly more exciting than going to school. I never was what you'd call a regular attendee. I thought going to work two or three days at a time was cool. It certainly was a great way to make living.

"Occasionally we had to take a car by force. When things turned ugly and it came to a fight, we always won. We recovered cars, busses, trucks, wedding rings, television sets, farm equipment, house trailers, one airplane and 15 Charolais steers."

Barb raised her hand. "Wait. One airplane and 15 head of cattle?"

"All in a day's work. Most memorable was the day we were commissioned to pick up a brand new Cadillac in a rather questionable area of Dallas. Three heavily armed men were standing guard over it. We entered a high-rise and climbed three flights of stairs to the car owner's apartment. Numerous well-equipped militant types answered Walt's knock. They immediately yanked us inside and shut the door. We had stumbled into the Dallas headquarters of The Black Panther Party. It crossed my mind: *these could be our last few moments on earth.* Watching Walt stand there all cool and calm, I figured I'd best try to do the same, but I was freakin' out. We withstood accusation and interrogation.

"Finally someone asked, 'What the hell are you doing here?'

"Walt showed the leader our bank orders. Someone called in an associate. They exchanged a few whispers. When the keys came flying across the room, Walt caught them and we were shoved out the door. By the time we reached the curb, all personal effects had been stripped from the vehicle. The three sentries were gone.

"I can still smell the leather . . . Sweet. Once I was over being impressed, I asked Walt, 'Were you afraid of those guys?' He just looked at me and grinned.

Again Barb broke in, "First Richard Speck, now The Black Panthers? Where are we going next?"

"Well, Walt had grown up in the country and always talked of raising chickens. He said it would be a great experience for us kids. Our next home was a small farm near the town of Weatherford Texas. But this move was different. Donnie wasn't coming with us. He was on his way to Viet Nam. Evelyn was unhappy about living in the boonies. She wasn't happy with Walt either. Actually she wasn't happy with life in general. I think she was still miffed about our failed escape to California. David and I still wondered what would have happened to us if we had made it. I admired Evelyn. She'd never approved of Mom's way of life or her choices. She never liked Walt either. She certainly didn't see him as Mr. Right.

"One day we came home to find Evelyn unconscious. She had downed a whole bottle of pills. Mom and Walt rushed her to the hospital. David, Tammy, and I were told to stay put. We spent hours worrying and wondering if our sister was going to die. She survived but didn't come home. She moved in with friends. Her failed attempt was never discussed.

"Sometimes wounds need to be cleaned out. Other times its best to just let it be. We raised 50 chickens that spring. Then for reasons unknown to me, we packed up and moved on."

CHAPTER THIRTY-ONE

GYPSIES

I was on a roll and Barb was a great listener. Before she let me go on, a question came up for which I had no answer.

"John, what happened to all the chickens?"

"I don't know. That was Walt's big idea. Meanwhile, us kids were stuck doing all the work. Actually, that's when he decided to quit repossessing cars. We ended up in the small town of Matlock, Washington.

"Once a week, David and I would go on a torturous four-mile walk to buy Mom a carton of Raleigh cigarettes at the combination grocery store, post office. On the return trip, we'd duck into the bushes, open each pack from the bottom and carefully remove two cigarettes from the center. We'd reseal each pack with glue and return them to the carton, seal it up and head home with 20 cigarettes of our own.

"We were getting away with something until the day Mom opened a fresh pack, shook out a cigarette and wham, the pack collapsed. She ripped into them all, one by one and counted. Finding only 18 where there should have been 20. Mom was so mad she wrote to the cigarette company. She even called their main office to complain and told everyone about the incident, mimicking the big shot who finally took her call. 'Only 18? Ma'am, that's not possible.'

"To appease her, Mr. Who-ever-he-was sent Mom two free cartons and several hundred Raleigh coupons. After a few months, she finally let it go. Thank God.

"Walt found a job hauling logs for Weyerhaeuser. Within just a few weeks he rolled a loaded truck off a cliff, barely escaping with his life. Then he either quit or was fired. I'm not sure which.

"We left Matlock and settled in Winlock, a slightly larger Washington town further south. Though Walt was still driving a logging truck, this time there were no mountain roads, so he lasted a bit longer. But Walt, being Walt, grew restless. We packed up and took off again. Within the next few months we lived in several Oregon and Northern California towns. We were moving around like a pack of Gypsies. Loading up and hitting the road was no longer a burden, but a well-practiced skill.

"We seldom settled long enough to go to school. Though we may not have known what was happening in the rest of the world, we knew what was going on in Saigon. We listened for news concerning Viet Nam. Donnie was still there fighting.

"Moving was an adventure for David and me. Relocation involved bologna, American cheese and Miracle Whip on white bread. We ate in the car as we rolled down the road. To this day, I still love those terrible sandwiches.

"We slept in shifts and showers were a blast.

"Literally.

"We dressed down to cut off blue jeans. Then we'd all head to the quarter carwash, which served as bathhouse and Laundromat. What fun. All that, Rolling Stones and the Beatles . . . nice.

"In Redding, California, Walt landed another job behind the wheel of a logging truck. This time the mountain had two spiral roads, one for empty trucks ascending, the other for loaded trucks descending. It was much safer for everyone.

"Walt often took David and me with him. We waited for him down the road from the loading dock. On occasion we even switched places and I'd drive.

"Mr. Franklin, owner of the gyppo outfit Walt worked for, was no bigger than a minute but had a mouth as big as Texas. He was missing his right arm, which made it awkward for him to reach over the steering wheel to shift gears. Still, he insisted on driving a little red Corvair with a standard transmission. That's why, at times, he'd be seen driving rather erratically.

"Unfortunately Mr. Franklin found David and me riding in the truck with Walt a couple of times. He'd get all red faced and say, 'I catch them boys in my truck again and you can kiss your job good-bye.'

"Apparently he was suspicious because one afternoon, as we were coming down the mountain, Franklin came up the road and met us head on. I was driving. I locked up the brakes and just barely stopped in time to avoid crushing the little red car with Franklin in it. As other loaded trucks stacked up behind us, we jumped out to watch Franklin struggling to get out of his car. He slammed the door behind him and yelled at Walt.

'I told you not to let them boys in my rigs. And now you got 'um drivin'? You take that truck to the barn this minute and don't come back. You're fired.'

"David and I weren't surprised when Walt hauled off and threw the keys into the canyon. 'If I'm fired, you take the @%&!n truck to the barn.'

"Mr. Franklin's face turned the same shade as his car. We walked home laughing. Then we packed . . . again. I never figured out why we ended up in Reno except that Walt wanted to put miles between us and Franklin.

"Life in Nevada was one long nightmare of wondering where we'd find our next meal. One thing was certain: Walt could never pass up a blackjack table. The sound of him skidding into the driveway and slamming the car door was a dead giveaway that he'd lost everything again. The only thing worse than being addicted to gambling, is being a really bad gambler and addicted.

"Mom seldom argued with Walt. Instead, she'd cry, act sad or look disgusted. But, there came the day when Mom had no more tears. Her only emotion was anger. Boy oh boy, was she upset. Walt had taken our last three dollars to buy milk and bread. He never made it past the slot machines in the entry of our local grocery store. We were absolutely penniless. Well, not quite. He seemed repentant when he arrived back home, that is until he noticed David sitting at the table spinning a quarter. Walt grabbed the coin and took off out the door.

"Mom made a beeline for the bedroom and began packing. She'd had enough. I think she could have lived with Walt or lived in Reno, but not both.

"We were broke, two months behind on the rent and the landlord wanted us out. I wasn't sure if Mom was packing to leave Walt or just packing. Either way she was slamming things into suitcases and boxes just as fast as she could.

"We didn't hear the car door close or the house door open. The first we saw of Walt was the big grin on his face as he threw a wad of money on the floor. Somehow he'd parlayed David's quarter into well over $1,000.

"I remember a short discussion about paying the rent or moving on. We moved on . . . back to Dallas.

"Walt and I were once again repossessing cars. This time with a nice tow truck. Two months later we moved to Fort Worth were we became well established in the repo business. Walt put a sign in the back window of our tow truck, which read:

~ *Want to get back on your feet? Miss a payment.* ~

"One evening Walt's boss called. I heard the guy's booming voice through the phone. 'Three hippies are coming in from California with a repo and are looking to crash for the night. I told them they could stay at your place.'

"Within an hour the trio arrived. Walt told them our back yard was available but there was no room inside. They seemed fine with that arrangement. Mom gave them something to eat. They were grateful.

"I'd never really seen hippies before. They were interesting, to say the least. I went out to see. Eventually Walt joined us and said, 'Hey, John, you wanna go with 'um?'

"That took me by surprise. He said, 'When I was your age, you could give me $10, drop me off anywhere in the country and within two days I'd have a job and a place to live.' Walt reached into his wallet, flung his hand in my face and said, 'Here's a sawbuck. Go with 'um.'

"Walt's sudden eviction notice was crushing. Memories of my earlier childhood with all the pain of abandonment came back. I had let myself believe Walt was my friend. But he'd just kicked me out. I felt more unwanted than ever. As wild and crazy as the past few years had been, we'd stuck together as family and survived. Hurt and confused, at age 15, I left with the hippies.

"At Denton, 35 miles north of Dallas, we bought a few burgers, some pot, and ended up in an apartment with a group of really weird college kids. I thought, *Way cool.*

"I spent only one night with those strangely dressed, super educated people and learned a lot. They taught me about quarter papers, lids, matchboxes, and dime bags, Jerry Garcia, Martin Luther King, and incense. I saw my first collage, and found Nirvana somewhere between the brownies and the patchouli. They taught me that bombs were bad, and sex was good. I was set for life."

Barb giggled but motioned for me to go on.

"The next afternoon I woke up all alone. Living on my own had been great but it was time to head back. Walt was less than pleased with my accomplishments. In fact he read me the riot act. He said, 'If you can't make it more than one day on your own, you'll never be able to cope with the real world.'

"Just how far did you expect me to go on 10 bucks?"

"He came back at me with, 'Look, you big mouthed idiot, I've had it with that smart ass attitude of yours.'

"A few days later they packed up and headed to Oregon. I stayed behind."

Barb's eyes seemed a bit misty. She rose from her chair and extended her hand. "Thank you John, I'll see you day after tomorrow."

I valued the warmth of her hand and that of her kind spirit.

Back in my cell, I was alone . . . just me, my memories, and a truckload of emotion. Falling onto my rack, I decided Barb was right. I'd been hauling around a lot of baggage and I had to let it all go. This was a different kind of battle. It was a fight for my sanity.

Mom & Nanny

Robert Hall Clothes
Nanny's Job

John
&
Pa

Tammy, John & David

John
and
David

Toni and John

David, Mom, John
and Tammy
Headed to
Matlock
Washington

Tammy

CHAPTER THIRTY-TWO

HARD LESSONS

One day I was leaning against a wall along the walk watching other cons pass by, I felt like I had no idea who I was. It put me in a serious inventory mode. I was looking for answers. I came to the grim conclusion that no one liked me. In fact, I realized no one ever did.

My analysis revealed I'd spent my whole life trying to win approval by impressing people. I was so totally convinced that I was unlikable, my need to become a different John had ruled my life. It was all done in hopes that someone; anyone would notice me. But if they did like me, it wasn't really me; it was the plastic image I'd created. In the end, there was no John Swanger. He had always been a façade, a fake. No wonder people didn't like me.

Call it desperation or revelation, it was at that point I made the best decision of my life. If you don't like me, there are billions of other people in the world and someone else will. I would no longer spend time living up to other people's expectations . . . or what I thought their expectations might be. Trying to act like a person I am not, is a cruel circle that leads nowhere. How could I expect others to like me if I had no regard for myself? I finally decided to be myself. Like it or not, I am who I am. I was pleased with my discovery and labeled it my healthy don't-give-a-shit-attitude. Oddly enough, it was then, after leaving the plastic John behind, people began to like me.

Time passed slowly til my next appointment with Dr. Bliss. It was still difficult to grasp the idea that she'd given me permission to call her Barb. Because of my upbringing, it just seemed disrespectful for me to call her by her first name. Wasn't sure I'd ever get used to it. I approached her open door, entered and after greeting each other, we sat down. Barb wasted no time in starting our session. "You know the routine. Where we going next?"

"Well, Bobby is Mom's baby brother, my youngest uncle. He married Ceil and adopted her son David, who we call Big David, my younger brother became Little David. Later while stationed in Alaska they adopted baby Jo Ann. Uncle Bobby had always been my favorite. He had a heart like Nanny and I moved in with his family in Garland, Texas. Big David and I were the same age. We were really tight and enjoyed being together.

"When the time came to enroll at school, Big David and I were issued the usual papers for Uncle Bobby to sign. The next day we told the lady in the admin office that we'd lost the papers. She gave us replacements. We filled out the second set ourselves so we could forge Bobby's name. This way, if we skipped school we could write our own notes with matching signatures. It was a great plan and worked well until we skipped three weeks in a row. Big Dave and I managed to live through getting busted, but just barely.

"Moving seemed to be what our family did best and that included Uncle Bobby. At our new school in the town of Mesquite, rumor had it that Randall Oatfield was the toughest kid on campus. It was common knowledge that if Randall couldn't take you, his older brothers could and would. Big David and I came up with a great idea. We made friends with Randall. He liked coming over to drink Dr. Pepper and hang out. We usually ended up slap boxing in the front yard, all in fun of course. Randall would pull his shirt off real slow to be sure we all saw his flexed muscles.

"My friend Samantha was afraid of Randall. He followed her home several times and made threats, saying one day he'd have his way with her. She felt safe with me and I listened with compassion as she shared her fears. Her trust should have done wonders for my confidence. But I was the kid who still ran from fights.

"One afternoon as Big David, Randall, and I sat watching TV, Samantha called. I didn't want anyone to hear me so I used the phone in the den. She told me Randall had broken her bedroom window the night before. That's when I lost it, not just because of Randall but suddenly I was remembering all the bullies I'd known throughout my life. Back in the living room, I began slap boxing Randall. He reacted in his usual challenging way. 'So, you want to go outside?'

"I agreed and out we went. After two or three playful taps, Randall stopped to pull off his shirt. As it went over his face I let him have it with both fists and feet. He yanked his shirt back down and said, 'Hey, you're for real, aren't you?'

"I didn't answer but kept swinging. We went at it for what seemed like hours. Exhausted, I fell on the ground and Randall fell on top of me. He said, 'I'm not letting you up until you say you're sorry.'

"I think he out-weighed me by a good 50 pounds, but I wouldn't give in and he wouldn't get up. Finally the man next door came over and pulled Randall off of me.

"We went back inside. I opened two Dr. Peppers, gave one to Randall and took a big swig from the other. I stood in front of Randall, glared at him square in the eye and said something I could have never said before that day. 'I'm going into the bathroom to wash my face. When I come out we'll finish our drinks and then finish the fight.'

"When I came out, Randall was gone. That was the last time I ever lost a fight. To realize I could defend myself and do it rather well was a great feeling. I'm not sure how good a thing that really was, but the pendulum had swung.

"A few weeks later Big David and I began experimenting with glue and paint as recreational drugs. I had told him about pot but we couldn't afford such luxuries.

"We were so high one night we forgot baby Jo Ann was in the house. We were supposed to be babysitting. After roaming the neighborhood for several hours, we arrived back home to pandemonium. We told the cops that two men came in with guns and made us inhale paint and that we were confused.

"It was pitiful but it was the only story we could think of. No one believed us. Through weeks of arguments and tears, Big David and I stuck to our story. Tension seemed somewhat relieved once the house was back in order. In our stupor, we'd spray painted several walls . . . dark green.

"Over a quiet breakfast one morning, Uncle Bobby got our attention, 'Boys, Ceil and I believe you.'

"Big David and I were stunned.

"Uncle Bobby went on to say, 'Now let's consider this matter a closed subject.'

"Wow. They were finally convinced. But within seconds, Big David crumbled with guilt and confessed. I was totally dumbfounded. Just as we'd gained victory, wham, the screaming, crying and lecturing started all over again. I was declared a bad influence and put on the next bus to California.

"Mom and Walt were living in Placerville, a little town between Reno and Sacramento.

The locals called it Old Hangtown. Friends of Walt's ran the local truck stop and restaurant. They were calling it quits and wanted out. Walt wanted in.

"Uncle Bobby must have let Mom know I was on the way because when the bus stopped to let me off, Walt was standing right in front of the door when it opened. I had barely cleared the last step when, without a word, he thrust another sawbuck at me and walked away.

"I was so angry I headed straight to the highway and caught a ride to Reno. This time I was determined to make it on my own or die trying. That's when it dawned on me. I didn't say goodbye to Mom.

"Through the Reno newspaper, I found a nice old lady with a room for rent. She took pity on me when I told her I was new in town, had no money, but was earnestly looking for a job. By noon I was the dishwasher at the Mapes Hotel. They even gave me a draw at the end of the day. So between the day's take and tips, I was able to pay my landlady.

"Two weeks later I hired on full-time as a stocker at the grocery store. My wages went up two bucks an hour. I was so proud of myself I called Nanny to tell her. She was pleased for me but grief stricken for my brother Donnie, who was finally home from Viet Nam.

"'He's in rough shape Johnny and needs family, but nobody's around. Please come home? For Donnie's sake?'

"Nanny's words haunted me as I thumbed my way back to Dallas.

"I took the bedroom at the rear of Nanny's house and started decorating with flat black and bright yellow paint. Black lights and a strobe finished the decor. It was the era of war and Rock'n Roll. I didn't know the world was upside down. It was easier to just go with the flow. I learned to appreciate Led Zeppelin and cheap wine. Dazed and confused and often depressed, I was lost somewhere between the immaturity of being a teen and the need to take care of Donnie.

"Viet Nam had taken my brother's heart and soul. Once strong and confident, he now seemed fragile and lost. I felt like Donnie's parent and protector. We spent a lot of time together accomplishing absolutely nothing. It was great. Donnie introduced me to Salty Dogs, a crude mix of gin, salt and grapefruit juice. We discovered that we could vastly improve the drink by simply leaving out the grapefruit juice and salt. I'm still astonished that I was never caught playing bartender in the back seat of Billy Shire's silver SS-396.

"I had acquired a taste for alcohol. As the result of an excessive celebration of my new found fondness of liquor, I attended a kegger at Lake Ray Hubbard. I vaguely remember lying down to rest somewhere along the white stripe in the middle of Belt Line Road. I woke up in an isolation cell at the Dallas County Jail. No one could tell me why I was there. That really scared me. What had I done?

"My cell was a cold, 4X5 foot box with no light. Twice a day a little door in the wall opened and a small tray of food was shoved in. The toilet was a hole in the floor. I was in the dark, literally and figuratively. No one would talk to me. Five days later I was released without explanation or notice. I read my release order: Drunk and Disorderly, Resisting Arrest.

"Barb, at the time it meant nothing to me. But now, looking back, I'm so thankful I didn't hurt anyone."

"John, that in itself is progress. Go on."

"Okay, back to sanity with my grandparents. Pa got me a job at the City of Dallas Water Department. I signed on with a survey crew locating water mains and sewer lines. In the first week a co-worker tried to break loose a manhole cover and accidentally hit my hand with a hammer. While mending with a mutilated hand, I was temporarily assigned to the drafting department. I became very good at tracing water mains onto city maps and my lettering skills were so good, the department head asked if I wanted a permanent position.

"'John, go get your G.E.D., pass the Civil Service Draftsman III exam and you're hired.'

"I had lied about my age on the job application, saying I was 18 when actually I had just turned 16. *Would they let me take the G.E.D. without a birth certificate?* There was nothing to lose so I decided to give it a shot. I passed all the exams, became a draftsman and was really enjoying my new position until Big David called.

"'Hey John, I'm moving to New York. Wanna go?'

"'When?'" I asked.

"'How long will it take you to pack?'

"The next day, I approached my boss. 'If I quit my job do I get paid right away?'

"He gave me a questioning look, 'Not unless you're fired. If you quit, you'll have to wait until payday.' I showed him my driver's license and pointed out the birth date.

"Big David and I began hitchhiking early the next morning. Rides were coming steadily and by evening of day two we were on the outskirts of Baton Rouge. The next ride was with a somewhat inebriated man who drove way too fast and talked non-stop. 'No matter whacha do, boys, don't ever get stuck in Gonzales, Louisiana. They really hate you long haired hippie types.'

"Around 6:30 the man said, 'I'll buy us all some supper.' He pulled into a gas station next to a restaurant. 'You boys grab a table. I'll fill up 'n be right in.'

"We did as he asked, sat down and waited. When we finally looked out the window, the man's car was nowhere in sight. We found our backpacks stacked by the gas pumps along with a hand written note that said, *Welcome to Gonzales.*

"I'll bet he's still telling anyone who'll listen about the stupid trick he played on us. Gonzales, as it turned out, wasn't nearly as bad as he'd said.

"At New Orleans we bedded down under a bridge for the night. We never should have done it. While sleeping, we were brutally attacked by an angry gang of ruthless mosquitoes. I woke up anemic. Leaving Louisiana in the broad daylight was another mistake. We spent the day roasting in the sun and never did catch a ride. Instead, we walked all the way to Mississippi, about 15 miles, facing backwards the whole time, thumbs out. Nothing was going as planned. We'd hoped to make the trip without spending any money, saving what we had to set up in New York. Just when things looked hopeless, a very nice guy picked us up and treated us to a meal. That was a welcome change.

"Hitching along the gulf coast was great. Days were mild and nights were cool. Near Pensacola, we crashed at a rest stop. Morning came with a jolt of reality. My head was whirling. I struggled to wake up. There was blood on my shirt, boot marks on various other parts of my body and a lump on the back of my head. When I spotted Big David I realized something more than mosquitoes had jumped us this time. He looked terrible. Whoever they were had taken our backpacks, our money and our dream. We gave up on New York and headed back to Dallas.

"Our first ride took us all the way to College Station, a small Texas town. The young lady who picked us up was easy on the eyes. We truly enjoyed her company. She was headed to Texas A&M and worried about falling behind schedule. Problem solved. We all shared the driving. Lots of conversation, coffee and a few restrooms later, we arrived at her destination. As we said good-bye, it was obvious our paths were heading in vastly different directions. She was on a full ride scholarship with a future ahead of her. We however, didn't know what was next.

"We walked away hoping to catch a ride going north. I was lost in thought, til David slapped my arm. 'She was one nice chick, the highlight of our trip.'

"I told him, 'Yeah, nice of her to give us a few bucks too. We must have looked pretty down and out, especially you David.'

"He looked at me with a scowl and said, 'Yeah, but now what?'

"I told him we were almost in Bryan City.

"He said, 'Come on, John, there ain't nothing in that town but railroad tracks and a tiny little café.'"

I answered, "Yeah but, it's a good place to rest and take advantage of refills." So, after an hour of coffee and small talk, we'd had enough. Ten seconds out the door, one of Bryan City's finest looked at us and decided an investigation was definitely in order.

"He assessed our crimes as, no visible means of support, no luggage, no local address. That made us vagrants. I thought to myself, *Great. More trouble. Just what we didn't need.*

"The officer said if we have the funds, we were welcome to catch a Greyhound back to Dallas. Otherwise we'd be spending the night downtown.

"Downtown turned out to be just across the street. A quick u-turn and we were there. They only had one cell and it was overly occupied. So we were locked inside someone's office. I called out several times during the night for an escort to the restroom but my cries were in vain. By morning we were released to continue on our way. We walked fast, praying we'd hit the county line before anyone noticed the nearly full Mason jar I had hidden in the bottom drawer of the desk."

Barb stifled a giggle and I joined in. Looking back it was amusing.

"Don't stop now, John. Go on."

"Back home, I was the subject of Walt's ridicule, again. I can still hear his crotchety voice saying, 'What the hell is wrong with you? Making it on your own is a piece of cake, that is, unless you're a looser.' Then he really let me have it for leaving Placerville without seeing Mom. I was sorry for not taking the time but I was so angry with Walt for pushing me out again, I didn't even think about Mom until it was too late. Walt railed on while I fought back tears and rage. By then he was yelling. 'When are you gonna quit screwin' around and start makin' something of your life?'

"He stopped to catch his breath and I gave it right back to him. 'Hey, you and Mom had to come back to Dallas too. No matter where you go, you can't keep a job. You're the one who's a @%&!'n failure.'

"That was a mistake. Walt jumped up and ran towards me with fists raised, yelling something about me not being man enough to whip his ass. Even though I wanted to, I thought I should decline. Mom defused the situation. But Walt couldn't let it go. He went on, 'and you're wrong taking Nanny for granted and moving in with her. You're a burden to that old lady and you're not staying' with her anymore.'

"Mom agreed with him, but when Nanny heard about it, she had her say. 'You can't control me. This is my decision, not yours.'

"Nanny defended my right to board with her. When we were alone, that was when Nanny said to me 'Whatever don't kill you, will make you stronger.'"

Barb smiled, "Like I said last week, your grandmother is a wise lady. Did things settle down then?"

"Walt invited Donnie and me to dinner, then drilled my brother about the time he'd spent in Alaska. We heard all about the great taste of caribou sausage, elk hunting, and the awesome fly fishing. Finally Walt tipped his hand. 'Ever wanted to go back?' he asked.

"Donnie was surprised. He said, 'If I had money to make the move and get set up. You bet.' But I was stunned when Walt matter-of-factly said, 'Take Johnny with you and I'll finance the trip.' Bam, just like that. Then, to seal the deal, Walt slaps $500 on the table in front of Donnie. But a sawbuck remained in his hand. Walt popped it a few times then asked, 'Do you boys know why they call this a sawbuck?' My anger was mounting as Walt explained, 'In the olden days, $10 bills had the Roman numeral X on it. It looked like a sawhorse, known back then as a sawbuck, or a buck. The name stuck.' Slowly and deliberately Walt laid the 10 spot on the table and with a pointed finger slid it to the edge of my plate. He was smiling.

"That did it. I guess the third time was the charm. So at barely 17, I felt as if I no longer had a family. Walt didn't just want me out of the house; he wanted me gone for good. I couldn't understand why he'd changed from the cool guy in Converse tennis shoes, wanting to take me under his wing, to the self-appointed dictator who had written me off. Saying goodbye to Mom and the agony of that day is still painful."

CHAPTER THIRTY-THREE

HOO RAH

Visiting Barb three times a week was great. Her encouragement kept me going and the stories rolling. Her patience was amazing. I was getting a lot of crap off my chest and her ability to see through my difficulties and give wise council made me feel as if she really cared.

"John, I can hardly wait to find out, did you make it to Alaska?"

"I guess we were born with adventure in our blood. Just the three of us heading to. . . . Did I mention Charlie?" Barb gave me a quizzical look. "Charlie was Donnie's pet monkey. Just a little guy but he was cute. We were disorganized but determined. Well, it didn't take long before we realized Donnie's '57 Chevy would never make the 50 hour trip. It was geared for the quarter mile and drag racing on the streets. Near Bozeman's Pass in Montana the car broke down. Somehow we ended up on the university campus, selling everything we had: cameras, Donnie's guitar and finally Charlie. We soon ran out of money. Homeless, the local mission took us in. We were so hungry that listening to sermons was a small price to pay for a semi-full stomach.

"Several days had passed before we hitched back to check on the Chevy. As we stood there, stranded, a Marine recruiter offered us a ride. Having the two of us as a captive audience, he began to talk about the great careers available in the Corp. When Donnie mentioned he'd just returned from two tours in Nam, we were invited to the guy's house on base.

"After dinner, Donnie said, 'John, if you sign up, I'll re-enlist. How about it?'

"The thought of Donnie returning to Viet Nam was scary. I figured if I went along, I could help him deal with it. We agreed. The recruiter was thrilled. Our host was quick to say, 'Gentlemen, it will take a few days to get the paperwork in order and another week for parental authorization, since you're under age John.'

"We spent the next couple of weeks being shuffled from Great Falls to Helena, Butte and Billings. Preparing me for my physical, the recruiter said, 'Keep your arches off the floor. If they see you have flat feet, they'll reject you.'

"I made it through physical and psychological testing and finally the swearing in ceremony. At the last minute, Donnie decided not to re-up. He sold the Chevy, bought a motorcycle and took off back to Dallas.

"Crap. My whole intent was to be there for Donnie. Now I was the one needing help. Before I could figure out what to do next, I was airborne, on my way to San Diego. It was my first trip in a plane.

"I'd never gotten myself into a situation I couldn't get out of. This was my biggest challenge ever. Plus, Donnie had lied to me. Now he was free and heading home. And I? Well, I was a Marine.

"Hoo-Rah."

Barb was on the edge of her seat. With wide eyes and a half grin she asked, "Are you kidding me?"

"Seriously. I have pictures."

"I'm sure you do. So how was boot camp?"

"Boot camp was, well, boot camp. Our platoon began with 70 plus recruits. After five weeks of exercises, drills and inspections, we were down to 23 men. The next morning at roll call our Drill Instructor said, '22 of you will be heading to Nam right after graduation.' Remembering what that war had done to Donnie, I realized anything was better than shipping out. I decided to become number 23, the one not going to Nam. That afternoon while marching, I twisted my ankle, which immediately began to swell. For the rest of our day I kicked the other ankle until both matched. They were terribly swollen, not a pretty sight.

At roll call I showed up bare footed. I remember thinking, *be careful John, you don't want to make your D.I. mad.*

"The usual call was made, 'All sick, lame and lazy, deaf, dumb and crazy, fall out.' The Sergeant noticed me and snapped, 'Private, where are your boots?'

"I can't get them on, Sir.

"He wanted to know, 'Why didn't you make sick call, Private?'

"I pushed out my chest and told him, 'I wanted to be a Marine, Sir.'

"He gave me a pass to sickbay. The doctor examined me and sent me to a specialist. I stood along a wall waiting my turn. The guy in front of me asked, 'You wantin' out?'

"I told him, 'You bet.'

"He said they were weeding guys out, but to be careful not to make them mad. He told me to listen at the door and follow his lead. Three doctors voiced their opinions. They asked if he wanted out. He said, 'Well, not really.' They told him, 'Soak your feet in this, wear these pads in your boots and take these pills. Then report back here Monday.' He was pissed as he stormed out. I entered to the sound of the doctors whispering among themselves. Finally they looked at me and said, 'Private, you have flat feet.'

"'Yes sir. Crooked ankles and a bum knee too.'

"'Do you want out of the Corps?' they asked.

"'Yes Sir.' They handed me a paper, which said: Immediate transfer to Casual Company pending discharge.

"Barb, in my mind I shouted, *Hoo Rah!* I was thrilled. My plan worked. Even if I had to stay in San Diego another month, going to Viet Nam was not in my future. I returned to the quonset and handed the paper to my drill instructor.

"He started yelling, 'I thought you wanted to be a Marine!'

"I tried not to grin, when I told him I'd changed my mind. That's when he ran into my barracks, turned over a couple of beds and dumped out a locker or two. He told me to clean up the mess, pack my gear and report to his office.

"I couldn't help it, the words just poured out. I told him, 'If you look, the paper says immediate transfer. So I'm no longer under your command, clean it up yourself.'

"He stomped out in a rage, I packed. Later, in his hut, he handed me an envelope and told me to take it to the Commander of Casual Company. On the way over I opened the envelope to find I had been recommended for an Honorable Discharge rather than a Medical and suggested I receive the rank of P.F.C. They gave me the Honorable but not the P.F.C.

"One week later, I became a civilian. Just seven and a half weeks before, I was cold, broke, hungry, and 1500 miles from home. Now I was warm, fed, and on a plane headed to Texas with $200 in my pocket. How much better could it get?

"Mom and Walt had moved back to Oregon. I was glad to hear it. I really didn't want to see them. But it was good to see Nanny and Pa.

"I found myself a small apartment and hired on with three of my uncles. They had become partners in a service station. I opened at 6:00 in the morning and more often than not closed up late at night. Working 80 plus hours each week became the norm. It felt like I was working non-stop. Completely exhausted, I told my uncles, 'I've worked every day and night for a solid a month. Can I at least have this Sunday off?'

"They huddled and discussed my request, then told me, 'We can't do that.'

"Disappointed, I couldn't believe they had nothing else to say. Maybe they didn't mean it but I took it as an insult. I felt like a mere employee, not their nephew. I was angry, tired, and disappointed. I quit."

As if she needed time to collect her thoughts, Barb was silent. Then she said, "John, I'm amazed at the way you tell your story. You've got a talent and I want you to use it."

Listening to her compliments felt great because I knew she meant it. Then it hit me, use it? So I asked, "Use it how?"

"Mr. Kelly and I have been comparing notes. We both want to know about your time with Bill and Linda. I'll be gone for the next three weeks and during that time, we'd like you to write a journal of those 18 months of your life with them."

"Wow, Barb. What makes you think I can write?"

"From the way you talk. There's no doubt in my mind. Pretend you're talking to me but put it down on paper instead. Simple."

"Easy for you to say."

"John, I know you can do it. Oh, and Kelly has a gift for you to help with your writing."

As we parted company, I stopped and turned to look at her. "I'll miss you. Three weeks is a long time."

"I'll be in Michigan at a conference on rehabilitation and then some much needed vacation. I'll miss you too, John. I can hardly wait to read your manuscript. I'll see you Tuesday the fourth. The day after Labor Day."

Walking to my cell, my mind was running double time. *Manuscript. That sounds so . . . I couldn't even put a name to it. Damn, that lady is smart. Now she's got me writing?*

CHAPTER THIRTY-FOUR

....

KELLY AGAIN

"Nice to see you out of the hole, Swanger."

"Nice to be seen, Mr. Kelly."

"From what I saw during our visits, solitary didn't mess you up too much, did it?"

"I'm good. But I'd rather not go back there any time soon."

Kelly gave me one of his quirky sideways looks and said, "That's up to you," He shifted his swivel chair and continued, "Okay John, you left me hanging with the old lady and the bank deposit. I told you to be ready to give me the rest of the story next time you were here."

"I remember."

"So are you ready."

"Yes sir. Here goes. Linda had been a makeup artist. She performed magic with her kit and a coat. I didn't recognize myself. The coat made me look bigger. A fake moustache, wig, and glasses with tinted lenses made me look like I was 25 years old.

"Linda drove. I tried acting nonchalant, but it didn't work. I was nervous. We went over the plan a few more times then suddenly we were at the corner. Within seconds after I was dropped off, the old Plymouth pulled to a stop almost in front of me. It was all happening too fast. I hesitated. A voice inside my head yelled, *go dummy go!*

"I stepped off the curb and grabbed the door handle. Immediately, I felt a huge adrenaline rush, blood pulsing in my neck, my heart beating loudly. Everything shifted into slow motion as I slid in right next to the lady and stuck the gun into her side. Reacting with shock, the poor woman tried to put distance between us.

"'Drive.' The word flew out of my mouth.

"She tightened her grip on the wheel and drove. Without turning, she said, 'I don't want to see your face. I don't want to know who you are.'

"Our eyes met for an instant as we both looked into the rear view mirror. I saw fear in her eyes and I hoped she wouldn't see the fear in mine.

"I disguised my voice, trying to sound older to match my new persona. 'I'll get out at the next corner.'

"I reached for the bank bag and could see her hands were trembling. I told her, 'Drive to the bank, same as always. I have a car following you. Vary from your route and they'll start shooting. At the bank, go inside and notify the police. Don't risk your life. Do as I say. Understand?'

"She nodded. I grabbed the bag and opened the door at the next stop sign. I quickly wiped the door handles with my coat sleeve and stepped to the curb. The old Plymouth drove off. Linda was waiting in the alley with the engine running.

"'Mission accomplished,' I said as I jumped in. Lying flat on the back seat staring at the headliner, I couldn't stop thinking, *I've just experienced a rush that dwarfed repossessing cars.* The euphoria I felt while holding a gun on the lady was like no drug I could imagine. I felt powerful. I felt important.

"By the time we pulled into Linda's parking space, my wig, moustache, glasses and coat were stuffed into a large grocery sack along with the bank bag and pistol. Linda stepped out, looked around and said, 'It's clear.'

"It took a while to calm down. I washed the remnants of glue from my upper lip and combed my hair. Linda emptied the money bag onto the table and made two piles of roughly $800 each. I'd never seen so much money in one place before.

"I said, 'Redo the split.' The look on Linda's face was a mixture of fear and confusion as if she thought I was somehow not pleased with my share. I pushed the piles back together and took 500 off the top. 'That's to get Bill out. Now we split the rest.'

"She burst into tears.

"I wasn't sure what to do so I patted Linda on the shoulder and said, 'Come on Sis. Let's get some dinner.'"

Kelly kept his eyes on me as he uncrossed his arms. "Was that your first time out?"

I was distracted, watching the front legs on Kelly's chair come off the floor as he tilted backwards. I thought, *what if he pushes too far and falls.* It didn't seem to worry him; he just kept on pushing and talking.

"Swanger, I said was that your first time out?"

"Ah, yeah. First one."

"Okay, let's get serious about work assignments. You only lasted three days on kitchen duty and 30 days as a corridor orderly, so I've been thinking. You need a more creative, hands on job. The sign shop is a better fit. They will have an opening in a little over a month and I have managed to secure the spot for you."

"Wow, too cool! Thanks."

"Okay. Now, change of subject. Yesterday I had a conversation about you with Doc B. You know she'll be gone for a while?"

"Yes sir."

"And you're aware of the journal project, about your time with Bill and Linda?"

"Yes, sir."

"Doc and I hope your story will give us a better foundation for developing the next step of your rehabilitation."

I wanted Kelly's take, so I asked the same question I'd asked Barb. "What makes you think I can write?"

"You tell a damn fine story when you're talking to me. Bliss says the same thing. Write it down."

"Doc said you have a gift for me?"

"Oh yeah, thanks for the reminder. Doc put you in for an MSA and I got it approved today. Twenty bucks."

"What's an MSA and why?"

"Meritorious Service Award. We are placing $20 on your books so you can get commissary. You know, pick up a few things."

"Why?"

"Doc figured it might keep you out of trouble and off the card tables so you could focus on the manuscript."

"Wow, thanks a bunch. Are you going on vacation too?"

"No. But this approach, writing down your history, will free up time for us to discuss your program. We haven't done much on that yet."

"I'll need paper."

Kelly rummaged in his desk and pulled out three nice blue notebooks and three pens. "How's this for starters."

Without even trying, I smiled. "Thanks, this is great."

"Remember, we don't need another War and Peace or Gone with the Wind, but we do want details."

CHAPTER THIRTY-FIVE

LOOK WHO'S WRITING

Looking at page one of the notebook, made me wonder, *what's my first word*? I thought about it for a while. I already know this stuff. How hard could it be?

Once I began writing, it seemed to pour out. As memories kicked in, so did my emotions, from joy to sorrow and everything in between. Except for the tears, I actually enjoyed writing. It came rather easily. The most difficult of all were the times I spent agonizing over my feelings of rejection, poverty and a dysfunctional family. They weren't excuses for my actions, but the past did influence my criminal behaviors. Ultimately, the final decisions were mine alone. With that settled, I was ready.

Finding John Swanger was centered on the first page of my notebook. The more I looked at it the more I disliked it. But I couldn't think of anything else. I told myself it was only a working title. After that was settled, I just started writing.

CHAPTER THIRTY-SIX

THE FAMILY

1st Journal Entry: Monday, August 13th, 1973 - 3:23 pm

Meeting Bill and Linda just happened. From then on it was a roller coaster ride. I'd proved myself reliable and that got Bill's attention. As a hired bodyguard for his girlfriend, Linda, he was impressed with me. When I committed a robbery to pay the fine needed to spring him from a stretch in jail, he was even more impressed.

It was noon on a Wednesday. We were at the Dallas County Jail waiting for Bill. Finally around 3:00 p.m. he appeared, unshaven with his clothes all wrinkled. He looked terrible. Linda tried to hug him.

"Later, honey. I smell like a goat. Taking a shower in jail is something to avoid."

As we hurried to the car, I could tell Bill was uncomfortable with the entire situation. Linda was excited to see him and eager to tell him how I'd come to his rescue.

It was embarrassing. I kept quiet. Bill didn't seem interested. He was just glad to be out of jail and back with Linda and desperately wanting a shower.

As we entered the apartment, Bill talked all the way to his bedroom door. "Do you two have any idea how good it is to be home? John, just relax. When I'm presentable, we'll talk."

I read a magazine article and watched TV. Finally, Bill and Linda came in and sat down across from me.

"Linda tells me you weren't happy with an even split on the take."

That seemed like a strange way to start a conversation. "I was okay with the split, after we took out the 500. Springing you was the reason for pulling the job in the first place."

Bill looked and me and asked, "What are you going to do with your take?"

"Well, I need to pay my rent and. . . ."

Before I could finish, Bill interrupted. "Why don't you grab your things and throw in with us? We have an extra bedroom. It could save you a few bucks." Bill gave me his serious look, staring intently, connecting man to man. "I like the way you operate, John. I think we could work well together."

No rent and the thought of Linda's cooking sounded really good to me. Bill smiled as he tossed me the keys to his Caddy. I smiled back and left. Within the hour, I had my stuff and was headed for my new digs. Bill greeted me at the door.

"That didn't take long."

"I don't have much."

"Get dressed up, we're going out.

I showered and 20 minutes later made my appearance. Bill and Linda looked at me then at each other.

"Hey, I did my best with what I had."

Bill left the room and returned moments later with a tie that blended perfectly with my blue shirt. I cringed as he tightened the noose around my neck.

"We'll go shopping tomorrow."

Sarcastically, I muttered, "I can hardly wait."

We ended up that night at a swank restaurant somewhere in north Dallas. When the waiter placed the napkin in my lap, I was startled and looked at Bill. "Man, I wasn't expecting that."

Bill didn't laugh or poke fun. For all his seriousness, he had a gentle way of dealing with my lack of social experience. We talked over dinner about my past, growing up poor, feeling rejected and kicked out of my family. It just spilled out all 17 years' worth.

Bill looked at me thoughtfully and said, "Repossessing cars with your step-dad. That'll come in handy."

He asked questions and listened intently to my answers. More than that, he seemed genuinely interested in my abilities, strengths, and opinions. That was a first. Best of all, Bill made me feel important.

"Sounds like you've learned to survive everything life has thrown at you so far."

That comment took me by surprise. "You're the only one who's ever noticed."

Bill looked at Linda, then me. "Guess you'd probably like to hear my story."

That really got my attention. "I sure would."

Apart from what Linda had told me, I knew nothing about the man seated in front of me. He began, "I've been busted a couple of times for fraud and a few elaborate confidence schemes."

He went on for nearly an hour talking about his years in the military and his travels. By the time dessert was served, it was clear. I was in the presence of a genius. Though he operated on the wrong side of the law, he had an ethic and morality all his own and a way of carrying himself that was deliberate and sure. Bill was unlike anyone I'd ever known.

"John, I promise you this. Trust me and I'll teach you how to live. Show me I can trust you and I'll see that you get everything you've ever wanted. Stick with me and you'll see the world. But turn on me and I'll turn on you."

Before I could even begin to process what I'd just heard, Bill reached for his wine glass, and said, "John, Don't ever cross me."

Bill offered a genuine smile as he and Linda reached across the table. Then as our glasses touched, accompanied by the chimes of delicate crystal, we became Family.

The tip Bill left was more than the entire tab at the pizza place Mom used to take us.

That night, lying on a comfortable bed between soft sheets in my new room, I reflected on the day. What a contrast to my old life. I was in fast company. How fast? I had no clue. But one thing was obvious, I was at a major crossroad. - J.E.S.

I wasn't ready to stop but the doors were racked for chow. Since I was hungry, my journal established a resting place within my locker. I found myself exchanging shoulder punches with Nick as we made our way to the stack of trays at the head of the line.

Meatloaf and corn.

After dinner, Nick diverted me to the pinnacle table. The more I won, the less I thought of my journal. Some people get loud as they lose, but these two were over the top. The 10 green I won eased my guilt, but did nothing for my massive headache. I probably would have been better off writing.

Lights out.

CHAPTER THIRTY-SEVEN

CLASSROOM

I opened my eyes and checked my head. Sweet, no pain. As much as I wanted to dive back into my journal, I was starving and ran to the chow hall as soon as my cell door began to roll away. As soon as breakfast was on my tray, I piled the bacon and eggs onto my toast, into a sandwich and scooped it into a bag. I headed down the walk, back to my cell. Thank God for coffee because I had a lot to tell my journal and needed the wake up.

2nd Journal Entry: Tuesday, August 14th, 1973 - 8:30 am

I awoke the next morning to the smell of bacon. My favorite. I was motivated for several reasons to dress in a hurry and start the day.

"Good morning Sis."

"Hey, bro."

"Smells like my favorite, honey baked."

"That's all I buy. It's the best." Linda turned a few slices and said, "You know I didn't find out about bacon until I was in junior high."

"Are you kidding me?"

"John, I was raised Jewish, remember? At a sleepover, my girlfriend's mom served bacon for breakfast. I passed it up . . . afraid if my parents found out I'd eaten pork, they'd disown me.

Linda's sadness was obvious. But the sight of Bill coming down the hall swept away the painful memory.

Bill greeted me and hugged Linda. "Something smells wonderful."

Linda smiled. "If you boys do the dishes, I'll be the cook."

I was quick to agree. "Count me in."

Bill poured us both a cup of coffee and announced, "School starts today kids. We're going to learn to think outside of the box."

After breakfast, Bill and I did the dishes. Class began once the last spoon was dried and put away. Session one? Bill's view of robbery. He dissected the subject to the last meticulous detail.

"A successful robbery has three basic parts: preparation, action, and get away. We'll never approach the venue without thorough research, groundwork, and rehearsal. Success leaves nothing to chance. Never enter a situation you can't get yourself out of."

"We need to know what strengths each of us bring to the table. Write them down, even if you don't think they're important. We'll discuss them when you're finished."

I'd never inventoried my capabilities before. I wasn't looking forward to talking about myself. Bill called on me first.

"I can hotwire any car on the road, pick locks and I'm an above average driver. I can think on my feet, know how to handle a gun, and I'm not afraid of anything or anyone. I guess that's it."

Bill added one more. "John, I believe your temperament allows you to remain calm in a tough situation."

Linda agreed. This was something new for me, being built up instead of torn down. Validation by my new friends felt great.

"Okay, Linda, you're next."

"Well, I'm a makeup artist, especially good at creating disguises. I can be a convincing actress and I'm not afraid to handle a gun. I've had only myself to rely on since I was a kid and that's made me pretty good at reading people."

I was beginning to see what Bill was after. Knowing how our talents and abilities complimented each other would make us gel as a unit.

Bill was a gifted tactician with amazing organizational skills and a knack for ingenuity. His communication style and meticulous approach was something I'd never experienced before. Bill was in a league of his own. It was easy to learn under someone so willing to teach and share, not only about his profession, but life. Bill had a way of commanding my attention.

"Understanding your opponent is of primary importance. It's the only effective way to anticipate his moves and maintain ultimate control."

I hung on Bill's every word.

"What causes a flame to come out of a match is the striking, the friction. You can cause a flame to ignite only when you know how to make it happen. Likewise, you can keep the flame from erupting. It's your choice. The match doesn't have control, you do."

Bill remained quiet and let us think about that one as he concentrated on writing a list of words: diversion, confusion, fear, deception, hope, communication, distraction, anticipation, anger, drama, intimidation, and force. He held up the list and explained.

"These are tools at our disposal, to be used against the opposition. Look up each word and study it. Think about how you would employ it and how your opponent might react. If the tables were turned, what would you do? Always anticipate your opponent's moves and be ready with a counter move. Consider every possibility. Prepare so your reactions are automatic, until you respond instinctively."

I was amazed. "Bill, I've never heard anything like this. It makes sense."

"That's the whole point John. It's all about making sense; getting into your opponent's mind . . . the person we call "the Target", the person with the cash. Find a way to diminish the value of the money you want to take and focus it on something the Target values more. If your Target sees the option of losing either the money or something of greater worth, he'll always choose to protect what he values most."

Man, this was getting serious. We agreed on a set of guidelines:

1. Never hit a convenience store, service station or liquor store. They net a fraction of the cash available at grocery stores but carry the same amount of prison time.
2. Never rob an Asian establishment. They will protect their property and that of their bosses. They would rather die than lose face.
3. Never hit a privately owned store. When people work all their lives to create something, letting a robber walk away without a fight is not likely.
4. Never take money from the working class.
5. Take only insured funds.
6. Never hit the same place twice. No matter how sweet or easy the venue, we don't want over exposure.
7. No alcohol within 24 hours of an Appointment.
8. No drugs allowed, ever . . . except what the truck drivers call west coast turnarounds, uppers or pills to help us stay awake on long trips.

Bill left no detail unexamined or unexplained, including how the police look for an M.O.

Bill kept going. "Did you know most criminals eventually get caught by inadvertently leaving a trail of clues exposing how they habitually do things? That's why we will always employ a hidden and a visual M.O. We'll leave intentional clues that constantly change so no two Appointments can be tied together."

When Bill stopped, I had a question. "I'm hearing words I don't understand. What is an Appointment? And you said something that started with a v?"

"Venue?"

"That's it."

"From now on, we'll use Venue when referring to the store, the hit, the mark, the location. Appointment is what we will call the robbery. So the Appointment will occur at the Venue. Target is another term we'll be using. That would be a store manager or person in charge…the person with the money. So, The Venue is the store, the Appointment is the actual heist, and the Target is the manager." Bill looked at Linda and me. "Got it?"

We confirmed in unison. "Got it."

I was totally impressed. Appointment sounded much better than a "job" or "heist." Over the next few days I realized we were taking armed robbery to a whole new level. I also thought everything sounded so sophisticated. I decided to never use the words "Stick Up," I'd find a better way, something a bit classier.

I'd known a few guys who had used guns to rob convenience stores. They either ended up dead or in jail by the second or third time around. Bill's style was precise and calculated. I couldn't imagine investing so much time in planning for anything, let alone a robbery. This sounded infallible. Bill had my complete attention.

"Every element must be covered in order to promote maximum confusion in the mind of our opposition. Most robbers are afraid of getting tied up in traffic, so they avoid rush hour. We'll use rush hour to get lost in it. While the typical robber will throw down and draw his weapon to hold the entire group of customers at bay, we'll keep our weapons hidden to diminish the witness base. We'll throw down only when necessary.

"From now on, we will be known as "The Family". Some Appointments may require more than just the three of us. We'll carefully consider bringing in someone from the outside. They will be called Imports, hired hands. Not voting members.

"Linda will share in my take. Any Import will have his fair share but wives or girlfriends will not. And last, we will do nothing without unanimous agreement. No matter what the situation, The Family will have total control of each Appointment."

For a poor teen-aged, dropout kid like me to become part of such an elite outfit was beyond belief.

Bill warned, "To be more than just idiots with guns, we'll look at every possibility, every situation and find reasons not to employ arms. Your mind is a more powerful weapon; use it before taking action with bullets."

Bill recognized he'd put Linda and me through an intense day. Leaning back in his chair he said, "Ok. That's enough school. We're going shopping."

They weren't unkind about it, but Bill and Linda had decided I needed clothes that wouldn't ID me as a pool hustling drug dealer. I ended up with several sharp western shirts, nice jeans, and two western cut suits.

Bill paid for everything with a credit card. - J.E.S.

Nick startled me as he jammed his head into the window of my cell door. "You coming out soon? Time to go work out."

Writing about my past had me on a bit of an adrenalin rush. Reliving those times was getting to me, I needed a break from my emotions. I grabbed my gloves and headed out. "Lunch first?"

Nick laughed "Dude, you missed lunch an hour ago. Let's hit the boneyard"

CHAPTER THIRTY-EIGHT

ROAD TRIP

Work out was long and hard. Back arms, lats, curls, and then three laps around the yard to cool down. My body was sore but my mind was still racing. I asked Nick to grab me something from supper and I headed back to my house.

3ʳᵈ Journal Entry: Tuesday, August 14ᵗʰ, 1973 - 5:15 pm

When Bill suggested a drive to Austin, I was ready. That was the first of many trips and let me say, traveling with those two was pure luxury. No broken down vehicles, no thumb out to catch a ride with a possible maniac. I could hardly believe how drastically my life had changed. While Linda napped in the back seat of Bill's '68 Cadillac. I rode up front.

"Here's something you may not know, John, anybody who is any-body wears boots that make a statement. If you dress like you're some-body and act successful, people will never question your character."

Bill's statement sounded good to me.

It was late afternoon when we entered Capital Saddlery. Charlie Dunn was an old man who'd been making custom boots since Moses was a kid. He had me stand on butcher paper. It tickled when he traced around my bare feet with a soft lead pencil. Charlie held another piece of paper beside my foot to draw the profile. When he was finished measuring, he helped us pick out leathers and colors, styles and cuts.

Bill ordered one pair of boots for himself, two for me. Again, Bill paid for everything with a credit card.

Charlie was smiling as he walked us to the door. "Show up tamarra, 'round four a'clock, and yer boots'll be ready fer the first fittin'." The old man waived as we drove off in search of food and rooms for the night.

In the morning we followed an armored car making its rounds . . . with Bill explaining and teaching the whole time.

"You'll notice that Friday is typically payday for most of the general public. A lot of people head straight out to buy groceries. As a perk to their customers, stores will cash paychecks. Without that service many stores risk losing shoppers to their competitor. That's why thousands in cash will be delivered by armored car each Friday. Keep notes while we drive, make a log of times in and times out, when and where each drop is made, and note the number of bags delivered."

I recorded everything. After logging several stops, we evaluated and discussed each location and which would make the best Appointment.

Later that afternoon, at Charlie's, we tried on the lower section of our boots.

"Well? Wadaya think boys?"

I was in awe. "I've never seen anything so beautiful or felt anything so comfortable."

The old man's crinkled face produced a grateful smile. "Well son, that's just what I like to hear. Cum on back in a couple a days and you'll be walkin' outa here wearin' yer new pair a boots."

We thanked him and left to go shopping at a grocery store we'd selected earlier in the day. We cased the place while acting like ordinary customers. From a sign in the window next to the front door, Linda wrote down the manager's name, Tom Cook. Bill walked through the store noting where the office was located, the appearance and configuration of the front windows. He checked for alarms and cameras. Out back, I found the pole with phone lines servicing the store. We scanned the neighborhood for a covered parking area to make the Exchange. After cruising around the area for a while, we found everything we needed, plus a safe route to the freeway.

Back at the motel, Bill ordered pizza so we could keep on working. While details were still fresh in our minds, we ate and continued formulating a plan.

Bill explained, "Major grocery chains are prohibited by their insurance underwriters from keeping weapons on their premises."

"Come on Bill, you'd think a store manager would want a little protection."

"No, John, it's not like that. Insurance companies would rather pay 40 or 50 grand to replace stolen cash than possibly millions in death or injury claims. Clerks are instructed to cooperate with the bandits and bring the ordeal to an end as quickly as possible. If you remain calm, the Target will too."

Bill found the manager, Mr. Cook's address in the phone book and took us for an after dinner ride. We watched his kids play in the yard and waited to see if the man pulling into the driveway was indeed the right guy. He was the Target.

Later, over coffee, when the day's lessons ended, I asked Bill, "Why did you pay for my clothes and boots when I have money now?"

"Glad you asked. These credit cards are hot and can become cash at will. They remain undetectable for two, maybe three weeks. Once the cards show up on a hot list they're worthless. Some store owners will check cards for me against the list. For a small fee they'll tell me when to lay off certain card. They make a few bucks and so do we. Here's something else. You don't have nearly enough cash yet to cover one pair of Charlie Dunn boots, much less two."

Early Saturday morning we drove to the Target's house. We watched as Mr. Cook left. When his wife drove their two kids to a soccer game, we followed. At the field, we took seats on the sidelines and cheered as if we belonged there. We overheard Mrs. Cook cheering for her daughter Lisa. When she moved away to greet a friend, Linda approached the son.

"Aren't you Lisa's brother?"

"Yes."

"She's doing a great job out there."

"Yeah, pretty good for a girl."

"Do you play soccer . . . sorry, I forgot your name?"

"Ben. I love soccer. When I have my birthday next month, I'll be old enough."

"Well, happy birthday a month early, Ben. See you."

We were back in the car when I asked, "Where to now?"

"To the Target's house."

I watched Bill check out phone lines. He took the contents of their mailbox and we drove off. Back at the motel, we took all the information we had and laid it out on the dining table. The rest of the day was spent rehashing everything. By the end of that night we had a solid plan.

The next day we shopped the Salvation Army and Good Will stores for appropriate outfits, hats, scarves and gloves. We visited several beauty shops and bought wigs, false eyelashes, fake moustaches and beards. At several different hardware stores we bought bolt cutters, a hacksaw, hatchet, duct tape, rope, wire, and alligator clips. At a costume shop we bought an assortment of eyeglasses. Last on our list: band aids and surgical gloves.

Later, at the motel, I watched Linda rummage through her makeup kit. She held up two small porous balls. "Bet you don't know what these are for."

I moved closer for a better look. "I have no idea."

"Insert these into your nostrils, your nose would look wider and flared."

Linda had gold caps for teeth and all sorts of things to create amazing disguises. Among her many containers was a bottle of liquid resembling rubber cement.

"When I mix this with water and coloring, I can make authentic looking scars."

Linda handed me a few pebbles. "Here, John, put these in your shoe and I guarantee you'll walk with a limp."

"I'll take your word for it." - J.E.S.

I saw him out of the corner of my eye. Someone was peeking through the window of my door. He jumped back when he saw I noticed. I laid my journal aside moved toward him. Almost cowering was a small, dorky looking, redheaded man in his 40's, with freckles and acne. Immediately he started apologizing for looking into my house.

He wouldn't make eye contact but instead looked at the floor. In a near stutter he asked, "Why do you stay in your house all day?"

"Who wants to know?"

"I'm Dennis Newsome and I watch people in the unit. I mean I don't watch them, that's kind of creepy. I just notice what they do."

It was obvious to me that Dennis wasn't all there. I reached my hand out through the window and offered to shake his. He quickly yanked his shirt tail out of his pants and wiped his hands profusely on it. Several times. Then he glanced up at me and shook my hand.

"I was just thinking that if you don't come out much you'll miss all the going's on in the world."

I must have looked confused because he started rewording his thoughts. "I mean the news. I like to watch the news and read lots of newspapers and magazines. I take notes. There's a guy in D-18 that never comes out either. His name is Paul, Paul Stavenjord. Why you don't come out?"

"Well, to tell you the truth, I am writing in my journal. I'm writing my life story."

His eyes got big and he said, "Wow! Paul doesn't come out because he is always reading. Wow, reading and writing! I make notes about the news and give to Paul so he gets lost in the world. I mean doesn't. You should really meet him. Can I give you some news notes too? I would."

"So Dennis, your name is Newsome and you want to give me 'Some News?' That's pretty cool, some news from Newsome." It was like a light came on in his head and he realized that sharing the news wasn't just his passion, it was his destiny. "Yes Dennis, I think I would like that."

He shoved a scrap of paper into my hand and raced around to D-Tier to see his friend Paul.

News August 14ᵗʰ 1973

1. Johnny Unitas sues Baltimore Colts for ¾ of a million.
2. America stops bombing Cambodia.
3. Ferguson Jenkins of the Chicago Cubs freaks out after being pulled from the game and throws several bats from the dugout onto the field. He was restrained and led away.

I looked across the tier to see Dennis talking with his friend Paul. Obviously he was talking about me because he kept pointing toward my cell. I smiled.

CHAPTER THIRTY-NINE

GARY

Just a few days had passed, but I was already missing Dr. Bliss. My next usual Wednesday appointment was still about a month away.

4th Journal Entry: Wednesday, August 15th, 1973 - 10:35 am

Our next stop was Grapevine, to meet with a guy named Gary. On the way Bill briefed us.

"He's a longtime friend, handy with electronics, guns and explosives; he's also a pilot, a machinist, an accomplished safecracker, and the artist who modified your grandfather's shotgun."

I was impressed, if it was true. "Bill, he sounds like too much for one person."

"That's not all. Gary's greatest talent is grilling."

Our journey took us over back roads with the worst and biggest potholes ever. Three miles later we stopped at a large house by a peaceful lake in a secluded wood. As the car doors opened, we were ambushed by the smell of a well-spiced brisket roasting on the grill. Gary stood waiting. His 200 pounds was packed into a strapping five foot eight inch frame. Well-developed muscles gave him the look of immense strength. He stretched out his arms in a welcome.

"Where you guys been?"

Bill laughed, "I wanted to make sure we didn't have to wait for dinner."

I ate my fill. Roasted corn on the cob and brisket belong together. I complimented our host several times.

"Glad you like my cookin', John. The secret for corn is ta slather honey, butter 'n paprika all over them ears before I wrap 'um up in foil."

Gary's potato salad was out of this world, with relish, diced onions, celery, mustard and real mayo. I'd grown up on margarine and Miracle Whip. I'd never tasted the real thing. Conversation during dinner was enjoyable. The guy had a special way with words. He could find humor in a rock. We'd make eye contact and start laughing.

After dinner we broke out pistols for a little target practice. I was pleased with how well I did and amazed at the cluster Linda put together. Gary disappeared and came back with more weapons. I must have looked silly with my eyes bugged and mouth open when he demo'd a Thompson.

"Hey, Gary, I never realized a Tommy gun could empty its clip so fast."

He smiled, "How old are you anyway?"

"Seventeen."

"Kid, at your age, I didn't know that either."

By the time we finished coffee and dessert, I felt as if I'd known Gary for years. I liked him. Before we left, a deal was struck for a dozen pistols. As our purchase was loaded into the trunk, I overheard Bill's parting words.

"I'm pretty sure we'll need your services very soon."

Gary replied, "Ya know where ta find me."

We all shook hands and headed for the car. Suddenly Gary took off for the house, yelling, "Wait just a minute." Soon he was back with a foil-covered pan of leftover brisket. "Throw summa this in a skillet, crack a few eggs on top an' wham, you got breakfast."

On the drive to Dallas, Linda curled up in back while I sat up front with Bill.

"I like your friend Gary. He seems like a good man."

"He's that and more. But John, let this soak in and never forget it. Don't ever under estimate the value of a friend, but don't over estimate his loyalty either." - J.E.S.

The best thing about Wednesdays in the joint? T-Bone steaks. Well the third Wednesday of each month at least, and that's reason enough not to miss dinner.

CHAPTER FORTY

THE APPOINTMENT

The steak was great, but on my way back to write, I was hijacked by Brinkerhoff. He had a couple of guys lined up for a pinochle match and begged me to sit in. Five green. Nice, I couldn't resist. However one game turned into four. We won three and lost one. It was late, but with a sawbuck in hand, I headed to my house.

There, on the floor, I found a single sheet of paper:

SOME NEWS from NEWSOME
1. 3 people murdered in Athens Greece by radical group Black September.
2. USSR blows up a Nuke.

I had to smile at Dennis's move toward professionalism.

5th Journal Entry: Wednesday, August 15th, 1973 - 9:15 pm

Thursday, we drove back to Austin, checked into a hotel, ate lunch and stopped by Mr. Cook's store for a final walk through. Bill told me what to do.

"John, take a last look around. Linda and I will wait here in the car."

I walked to the customer service counter near the manager's office and picked up a bus schedule. Pretending to read it, I slowly scanned the Venue until I spotted the Target. I studied him until I was certain I'd recognize him at show time.

Next, we drove by the Target's house looking for changes or anything out of place. Satisfied that all was well, we headed to the Exchange. We verified the lot where I would "borrow" a get-away-car. Then we drove back to the Venue. The Target was just leaving his store. He was consistent.

The next morning, as I pried my eyes open, it struck me, the real thing was only few hours away. I pulled on my robe and followed the scent of coffee. The door to Bill's room was open. He was packing his suitcase.

"John, get your stuff together so we're ready to roll."

I poured myself a cup, took a few swigs and headed to the shower. My body was still damp as I pulled on one of my new tailored western suits. While grabbing a handful of change and my wallet from the dresser, I caught a glimpse of my image in the mirror. I couldn't help smiling. "Not bad, John."

I crammed everything into my vinyl case, slammed it shut and left the room.

Linda whistled a catcall. "Hey, hey, bro."

I felt my face flush, "Thanks, Sis. You're looking pretty good yourself."

Linda smiled. She was stylish in a simple but expensive blue dress with flowers all over it. Bill wore a gray flannel business suit and a dark gray Fedora. He looked sharp.

"Ok, kids, in the car. Time for dress rehearsal."

At the Venue, we strolled through the store, stopping like everyone else to look at merchandise. I observed the Target in his office for as long as I dared. As the lead, I'd do the talking and carry the goods. Linda's job was to stay nearby, pretending to be an ordinary shopper. She would pull her gun only if someone walked up behind me.

Back at the hotel, Linda transformed me into someone else. She first showed me how to effectively apply a false moustache. It looked like the real thing and made me appear older. I wore a black wig over my dark hair. Linda poked a small lock of blond behind my right ear. I thought to myself, *that'll fool 'um*. Faded blue jeans, a Cowboy hat and sunglasses completed my disguise. I was ready.

When Bill came in he looked at Linda then at me.

"John?"

I answered back, "Who's John?"

"Man you look so much older. Great job Linda."

"Thanks."

Linda tweaked my hair and handed me a mirror.

"Wow, I don't think even my Mom would recognize me."

Bill was amused. "Hopefully she won't be around to put it to the test." Bill's tone turned serious, "And, John, use your right hand if you need to pull the gun. Since you're left-handed, it will be misleading if an eye witness were to report anything."

Bill had taught us about using ordinary props as a distraction. The more things a witness had to look at, the fewer details they would remember. Linda placed a Band-Aid on my cheek and a red bandana in my back pocket. We were set and ready to go.

So as not to be seen, Linda and I used the rear door to enter the parking lot. Bill checked us out of the hotel and left by the main entrance. We met at his car.

Show time was 1:35pm. The armored car was scheduled to deliver at 1:20. At 12:55 we pulled into the alley behind the Target's house. Bill left the car to cut phone lines with his hatchet. He pulled out a plastic bag containing a wallet, which held a driver's license with a Houston address and $30 cash. Turning the bag over, Bill let the contents fall to the ground.

Next, we drove to a remote parking area by an office complex where I hotwired a fairly new red Mustang. Linda and I jumped in and drove to the Venue. We entered the store parking lot as the armored car was pulling away. It was 1:25pm.

Perfect.

At the rear of the Venue, I flashed my headlights at Bill, signaling him to cut the phone lines. One slash and he was back in the car, driving to the Exchange.

I looked at Linda. "Okay, Sis. You ready?"

She smiled, opened her door. We stepped out in unison.

As we entered the Venue, my heart pumped hard and fast, just as it did with the lady and the bank deposit. But this was different. The past few days of anticipation only added to the rush. And as before, everything shifted into slow motion.

The Target was near the rear of the store, kneeling while stocking cans on a shelf.

"Excuse me, Mr. Cook?"

He looked up. "May I help you?"

I pulled my jacket open with my left hand and covered the weapon with my right. It was just enough to reveal the pistol nestled in its holster.

Quietly, I said, "Sir, this is a robbery. Please come with me and no one will be hurt." As he stood I said, "Tom, I have men throughout the store. If you try anything, they might lose control. We wouldn't want that to happen now, would we?"

"What do you want me to do?"

"We're going to walk to your office. Just be your normal self. Act like you know me. Don't indicate anything out of the ordinary is happening."

As we moved through the store, he responded with a nod, greeting one of his clerks. I smiled and carried on what turned out to be a rather one-sided conversation. "You're doing just fine . . . keep it going. By the way, Lisa sure plays a great game of soccer. Are you going to let Ben join a team anytime soon?"

The look of terror in the man's eyes let me know I had him. A few more steps and we were in his office. "Tom, trust me; do as I say and your kids will be fine. Put those three canvas bags from the filing cabinets and the contents from those cash drawers into these grocery bags."

He rushed to do as instructed.

"Take it easy man, you're doing great." When he was finished, I continued, "Now, carry the bags and come with me to the front door."

Linda remained several feet behind us. Tom Cook never knew she was there. Once we were outside, I said, "Tom, wait five minutes, then you can call home. I took the bags, thanked him for his cooperation, and made sure he saw me get into the Mustang. Linda passed him as he reentered the store. She jumped in with me and I drove toward the freeway.

One block later we took a right turn. Linda watched to see if we were being followed. Two blocks further we turned into the parking garage. Bill had backed into a secluded space. We pulled in next to him. I wiped off the steering wheel and gearshift lever with my red bandana. Linda grabbed the bags. We both wiped door handles. After a quick look around, we stepped into the trunk and pulled the lid down. Bill drove. We removed our makeup and disguises.

A few minutes later Bill said, "It's safe."

From the trunk, I push through the back seat armrest, opening our passage into the car. Linda climbed up front. I remained in the back seat.

I lit a cigarette to help me calm down. Linda was combing her hair and applying normal makeup, as if what had just happened was no big deal.

As Bill turned onto the Interstate, he said, "Guess what kids, there's still time to visit Charlie and pick up our boots. This Caddy is headed to town."

Linda turned on the radio, "No one was hurt in the daylight robbery by a single gunman, with blond hair, of medium height, in his late twenties. Information suggests the lone bandit may have been from the Houston area."

Within a few minutes another report quoted me as saying, "This is a stickup." It really pissed me off because that's not what I said.

Bill turned off the radio and began singing *Amazing Grace*, which seemed like a strange thing to do. But then, again, we had just robbed a grocery store. How strange was that? - J.E.S.

Out of my journal-writing, into the reality of prison, I was exhausted. I thought I'd be asleep before my head even hit the pillow. Wrong. Tired as I was, thinking of the past and wondering about the future, kept me awake until 4:00 am. Just before drifting off I thought of Bill singing that hymn. It reminded me of Nanny and the times she took me to church with her.

I fell asleep wishing I was back there. . . .

CHAPTER FORTY-ONE

BOOTS & BAR-B-Q

Writing in my Journal was going good . . . better than I had anticipated. After a while, the sadness of remembering became easier to handle. In all, I was pleased with my efforts to write down things that Barb and Kelly would find significant. That was my motivation to keep writing.

6th Journal Entry: Thursday, August 16th, 1973 - 9:20 am

Charlie had all three pairs of boots finished and they looked great. To think that old guy had made them all by hand was impressive. We were surprised when he showed us belts to match each pair of boots.

"Those are on the house, boys. Thought ya'll would look sharp with belts to complete your outfits."

Bill smiled. "You've outdone yourself, Charlie."

I was grinning ear to ear, "This is incredible. Thank you so much."

"My pleasure, son."

No one had ever treated me with such kindness as Bill and Linda and their friends. We picked out buckles and in no time they were affixed. Bill helped me find a Stetson and a nice straw. He threw it all on a card.

"Thanks for the business boys, Ma'am."

We bid Charlie good-bye and left with our treasures.

Though we hadn't eaten all day, we decided to drive the 60 miles to Killeen, where Bill said he knew of a terrific restaurant. We stopped at a gas station, filled the tank and grabbed a six-pack of Pepsi. Linda dug through the glove box and found the bottle opener and we were on our way. I remember thinking; *I've just lived through the most incredible day of my life*. We sang old gospel songs as we headed North. Bill's favorite was, *Washed in the Blood of the Lamb*.

Killeen wasn't very big but it had lots of character. I was fascinated to see people still riding horses through town. Guys walking around with pistols on their hips made it feel as if we'd gone back in time to the old west.

The restaurant was very common looking and sparsely decorated. We were seated in a corner booth. No tablecloth, candles or crystal. It was just a little Bar-B-Que joint, not even close to what I'd expected.

Bill offered me a menu, waited a moment and asked, "What's on your mind."

"Well, I'm almost embarrassed to say."

"Say what?"

"Going the extra miles to get here, I thought this would be some kind of fancy place."

"John, there's fancy restaurants and then there's fancy food. But you'll never find a better plate of pulled pork this side of the Mississippi."

There were lots of side dishes, drinks and dessert on the menu. Bar-B-Que was the main dish. All kinds of Bar-B-Que.

Bill gave me a nudge. "So what'll you have, John?"

"I'm not sure."

"It's all good. But you need to break your bad habit of checking prices before ordering. From here on out you eat what you want, not what you think you can afford."

For a kid who knew all about eating cheap, ordering what I wanted was a totally new concept. Over the years I've tried to act on Bill's advice. And to this day I've yet to taste better Bar-B-Que.

There was barely any conversation as we ate. I almost said something about the day's events. One glance from Bill let me know he was reading my mind again. We'd talk later.

The last leg of our return trip was quiet. I even fell asleep for a while. We arrived home around midnight. When we were safe inside, with the door locked, Bill dumped the take on the dining room table for the tally. One canvas bag held rolls of quarters, dimes, nickels and pennies.

"Sorry Bill. Should I have left the heavy stuff behind?"

"No, always grab the change. It serves a special purpose. Tomorrow you'll see."

Our total take was around $38,000. I almost burst into tears when Bill handed me $19,000. I was in shock and didn't know what to do with it.

Literally.

Bill and I removed the bands from around the bundles of bills. We opened each roll of coins and dumped them into two coffee cans. In another can we burned all the bands and wrappers. Bill flushed the ashes down the toilet. Then he carefully cut the bank name from the canvas bags and discarded them in the same way.

Debriefing the Appointment was interesting. Bill called on me first, "John, what did you do or say that worked well?"

"I told the Target there were several men in the store to back me up. He must have forgotten since the radio reported a lone gunman. I assured him no one would be hurt if he did as he was told. He gave me no trouble."

"Good. Anything else?"

"When I mentioned his kids, I'm sure it influenced his cooperation. And Linda played her part perfectly."

Linda smiled at me, "Thanks, John. It wasn't difficult."

We consumed a whole pot of coffee while discussing possible weak points and the prospect of integrating more sophisticated techniques for our next Appointment. I had only one thing that needed an explanation.

"Bill, the wallet you dropped behind the Target's house? I don't get it."

"I found that wallet two, maybe three years ago. It was empty, except for a driver's license belonging to some guy in Houston. I kept it, thinking it might come in handy. I put cash in it to make it more convincing. The point was to indicate we were going south."

"From the news report, sounds like it worked?"

Bill smiled and pulled out a bottle of sparkling wine or maybe it was Champagne. I didn't yet know the difference. We drank a toast and turned in.

I lay in bed wondering if I could ever sleep again. Only a couple of weeks earlier I had no clue where my next meal would come from and now my biggest problem was trying to figure out how to stash more money than I'd ever seen. Adding up all the dollars I'd made in my life so far, it wouldn't come close to what I'd just made in five minutes. As hours rolled toward dawn, I was still too wired to sleep.

Faintly in the distance, I could hear Bill and Linda talking but couldn't make out their words. Perhaps they were discussing how well I'd handled myself during the Appointment. I hoped Bill was starting to believe in me and trust me.

I felt grateful for the changes in my life. But, I didn't know who to thank or why. - J.E.S.

I jumped up from my bunk to look out and see what all the noise was about. Across the tier I could see Buddha, a big Samoan dude that looked like a Sumo wrestler. He was dancing around in circles, in his underwear, with his hands in the air, and blasting, *My Sweet Lord* on his radio. I didn't think anyone minded, but the hack made him turn it down anyway.

Love George Harrison.

CHAPTER FORTY-TWO

IMPORTS

I was beginning to really like this writing stuff and the events of my former life as an outlaw was starting to heat up. I could see it all playing out like a movie in my mind. It often occurred in my dreams which helped me write down all that I was remembering.

7ᵗʰ Journal Entry: Thursday, August 16ᵗʰ, 1973 - 7:20 pm

The next morning I sat down next to Bill. He was reading The Dallas Morning News. He looked up and said, "I only read the paper for news. Comics and sports are for people who don't know how to think."

"What about the business section?" I asked.

"That's for thinkers who don't know how to live."

Linda approached the table, "You boys are on your own for breakfast. I'd like to get an early start on shopping."

Bill replied, "Sweetheart, you can have anything this side of a new sports car."

Bill had errands too, so the three of us went our separate ways. Heading for the door, Bill cautioned me, "Have fun, but don't flash around too much cash. We don't want to draw attention."

I grabbed 50 bucks and left. Breakfast at the Waffle House was first. I still ordered the special because it cost less. Some old habits are hard to break. I bought a carton of Marlboros. I'd never bought a whole carton for myself. It had always been a luxury beyond my means. There was nothing else I wanted or needed. Less than an hour later I was back at the apartment. The rest of the morning was spent hanging out, watching TV. Bill and Linda were both back by mid-afternoon.

"John, how about you and I go spotting."

"Spotting?"

"Yeah, scouting Venues for future Appointments."

Linda stayed home.

I enjoyed driving around with Bill, spending time one on one. He always had wise things to say, such as, "You know John, if you think you can, or think you can't, in either case, you're right."

We drove to several grocery stores. One in particular stood out. Bill said he was interested in the Safeway because it had a lot of posters in the windows and the safe was in the office. He didn't like stores that kept their safe right out in front. This particular establishment had no alarm system or security cameras. The manager was a skinny, educated looking kind of guy who wore a wedding band, a class ring, and glasses.

"John, I'm guessing maybe 40k. What do you think?"

It felt good to have Bill ask for my opinion.

"Honestly? I couldn't even make a good guess."

"There's another consideration. I think we need three men to pull off this one."

Bill told me about Floyd, someone he'd met during his week in jail. "The guy had a brother. Floyd and Donnie Houston are in their 20's. They've never been involved in anything like what we do. I'd like to invite them over to check them out."

The sun was setting but Bill wasn't finished yet. "John, what do you say we make a couple of detours?"

"To where?"

Bill just smiled and drove downtown. We entered an alley and stopped. He motioned for me to get out of the car. I watched as he opened the trunk and removed one of the two coffee cans full of coins. Beside a dumpster, an old shirt lay draped across a duffle bag. Bill walked to it, placed the can under the pile and returned to the car. He was smiling.

Near the other end of the alley we found a similar site. Bill nodded and I placed the remaining can under an old sleeping bag. Somehow the act of giving away some of what we'd stolen made me feel strangely proud. To my surprise, our next stop was a pool hall I never knew existed. We met a guy who handed us a couple of jars of meth tabs, two kinds: baby crisscrosses and black beauties.

Later that afternoon, when we entered our apartment, Linda, who was now a brunette, met us at the door. She had even died her eyebrows. Bill was impressed.

I excused myself to take a walk, something I realized that I should do regularly. There was an old movie house close by. It was a good place to spend a few hours.

A double feature was playing: Bonnie & Clyde and M.A.S.H. On the walk home, I tried to figure out what was behind Bonnie & Clyde's death wish. They were still so young. I was even younger but glad to be alive. I was overcome by the idea that for the first time in my life, I was actually happy. I'd found something I was good at and was associating with people who valued me for who I was.

I entered the apartment just as the grill was flaring out of control on the balcony. Bill saw it and ran from the kitchen with a pitcher of water. Linda and the Houston boys were laughing. I glanced at Bill. I thought laughing at him was the last thing I wanted to do. But, he was just as amused as everyone else. The steaks looked like charcoal briquettes so we decided to find a place serving something closer to medium-rare.

Floyd drove an old Chevy pick-up. Donnie rode shotgun. They followed us to a steak house. We asked for a corner table. Floyd was a talker; Donnie was more laid back. Bill had told them his name was Tom Donnely, Linda and I were Jay & Eva Colby.

Floyd ordered the biggest steak on the menu, probably because Bill announced the meal was on him. Donnie had something more modest. Meeting Donnie reminded me of my older brother, but not just because they shared a first name. But my brother was more quiet than shy, this Donnie was definitely overshadowed by the much older Floyd. As the evening wore on, I wondered if I could ever work with those two. I didn't think so.

Donnie said very little. He did let us know he was awaiting sentencing for writing bad checks and expected probation. Floyd had a pending court date for marijuana possession. He planned to leave rather than face the judge.

Bill sounded like a good ole boy during the whole evening. I thought it was strange. Linda and I sat together, mostly listening to everyone else. It was more than two hours before Bill finally told Floyd and Donnie he might have a way for them to make a few bucks. We walked to the parking lot where Bill thanked them for coming and said, "I'll call if we can deal." The Houston's were completely out of sight before Bill moved to the car. That's when he gave us his warning.

"It's important those two never know our real names. And I want them to think you and Linda are married."

Hearing that last comment left me stunned for a moment, but I could see the wisdom of Bill laying out a smoke screen.

Shrewd.

The next morning we found a new apartment in North Dallas with underground parking. Each bedroom had its own bath. We didn't have much, so moving was no big deal. The new place was rented under the names of Daniel & Joyce Winters.

Bill showed me his several sets of IDs.

"We need to get a couple of these for you and Linda. I have a connection at the DMV. For $200 you'll have registered drivers licenses all nice and legal. Each will have different names and birth dates with your photos."

The next time we returned to Gary's place, it wasn't a social visit.

Bill spoke first, "I'm considering the possibility of using the Houston boys on our next Appointment, but we'll have to work out a few details. This would normally take three people. So if we send in the two yahoos looking like amateurs, no one will ever trace them to us."

Gary laughed, "Like shakin' pepper on a hound dog's nose?"

Everyone cracked up laughing. I was still skeptical.

Bill laid out the plan. "After the Appointment and the usual exchange, you and Linda will head up here. Is that okay with you Gary?"

"Fine with me."

Bill went on. "Assuming all goes well, I'll show up with the brothers in the trunk of my car. They get their split and we say good-bye. But, if anything goes wrong or we feel they pose a threat, we might have to waste them."

I was stunned by that thought.

He added, "On my signal: thumbs up or thumbs down. Either way be ready."

Gary was quick to offer further help. "I keep a couple of busted safes under a tarp on my flatbed out back." He grinned. "They're for people who might need to retire. Grapevine Lake holds lots of secrets."

On the return home, Bill noticed I'd been too quiet. "Don't worry, John. More than likely nothing's gonna happen. This kind of Appointment will keep our M.O. scattered. We send the brothers in. They take the risk, offer diverse descriptions, and we share the take."

If that was supposed to reassure me, it didn't.

"John, remember, we'll make all the plans and put everything in place before calling the brothers. I don't want to let them in on how we do things. We need them to look like the fools they are."

Morning came with a trip to a used car lot. Our attention quickly focused on a fairly new Buick. After short negotiations, we were heading home with a second vehicle. That afternoon, Bill called a session to continue planning for the Appointment.

"We'll give the Houston's the bare basics, just enough to get the job done. We tell the brothers where the moneybags are and send them in. How does that sound, John?"

I shrugged my shoulders. "Sounds good to me."

"Linda, how do you vote?"

"It's fine by me too."

Bill dialed the phone and talked with Floyd. We met the brothers at a small diner for lunch. Once our food was served, Bill set the bait. "You boys interested in making a few grand?"

That got their attention. We went through the setup. "Show time is in one hour. The cash will be sacked up waiting. All you have to do is ask for it at the office."

The brothers looked at Bill in amazement. "That's it?"

"That's it. Drive your pickup to the east side of the store. Donnie, you stay in the truck with the engine running. Floyd, when you come out, go the opposite direction and circle the building so they think you took off on foot. When you round the east corner, the truck will be there. Get in and crouch down out of sight. Exit the parking lot at a normal speed. Got that, Donnie? Normal speed."

Donnie nodded, looked at Floyd and said, "Sounds easy."

Bill told them where to meet for the exchange. He gave them both sunglasses and baseball caps for disguises along with a small pistol for Floyd.

"What's your truck worth, Floyd?"

"Haven't got a clue. I stole it."

"Good, because I want you to leave it at the exchange. You'll have plenty for another once this job is done."

Linda and I waited at the Venue. Bill led the brothers to the exchange, then into the parking lot. Floyd went inside. Linda and I checked our watches. It was almost three minutes before he ran out the door with a large grocery bag. Floyd took off clockwise around the building as instructed, but being Floyd, he instead jumped into the driver's seat.

I blurted out "Crap. He's driving way too fast."

Linda was just as stunned. "What a power junky."

To make sure they didn't disappear with the money, Linda and I followed them to the exchange. They met Bill and climbed into the trunk as planned. The drive to Gary's place was tense, not knowing how Bill would call our next move. Neither of us looked forward to the possibilities. I didn't want to hurt anybody.

Gary sat waiting on the porch as we pulled in. He wore his usual grin, which made me nervous. Linda and I took positions at the rear of the car. Gary said something but I was so focused on what was ahead, I paid no attention. The look in Linda's eyes said she was ready. I wasn't.

We could see Bill coming our way, bouncing along through the brush and ruts. Somehow I imagined Floyd's face and thought maybe I could handle it. But when I envisioned Donnie I began to tremble. I moved to the bushes and hurled. A swipe across the mouth with my shirtsleeve, and I was back in place.

The Caddy pulled to a stop. Bill stepped out and smiled. He'd forgotten to signal. Linda pointed her thumb up then down. He signaled thumbs up.

Instant relief.

Bill opened the trunk and told the boys to leave the bags and gun and come into the house. Gary poured coffee. After we were settled and had taken a sip or two, Bill began debriefing.

"Floyd, we have a problem." - J.E.S.

Unlike last night, sleep was pursuing me. I had begun to nod off even before I had my journal stashed. Once my headphones were in place and my head hit the pillow, I faded out to the sound of Sugarloaf singing *Green Eyed Lady*.

CHAPTER FORTY-THREE

HONOR AMONG THIEVES

I awoke with a terrible cold and headed to the infirmary to see about getting some Coricidin. I sat there for over two hours before someone finally emerged with a couple of Actifed's. Not sure they would help much, I grabbed a box of Kleenex and headed back to my house to write.

Once the doors racked, I spotted yesterday's news taped inside my door, just below the window.

SOME NEWS from NEWSOME
1. 35 years ago today, Robert Johnson, famed blues guitarist died.
2. 25 years ago today, Babe Ruth, The Bambino died.

8th Journal Entry: Friday, August 17th, 1973 - 10:20 am

Bill's look was stern and cold as steel.

"News on the radio is reporting an eye witness gave the police a detailed description of you, Floyd . . . says he can make a positive identification. They say fingerprints on the exit door should help lead to a suspect. You two need to get out of town and let things blow over."

Floyd and Donnie nodded in agreement.

"After dinner we'll get you boys on a bus to Minnesota. No one'll be looking for you up there."

The meal was great as usual, but not much was said, except for Floyd who wouldn't shut up. I finished eating first and left to grab the bags from the car. Gary served pie.

We watched as Bill tallied and divvied.

"The take was $58,000 less the change. We have $6,000 in expenses leaving 52K."

Bill divided six ways: the two brothers, Gary, Linda, Bill and me. Everything that day had been weird. Nothing seemed right. Even the split was strange. The two brothers had a little over $8,500 each. They were very happy.

Bill gave Floyd a piece of paper. "I have a contact in St. Paul. Here's his number, he'll take care of you."

Floyd looked surprised and for the first time was grateful. "Thanks," he said.

Gary spoke up with a suggestion. "If you boys don't like bus rides, I have a fairly new Chevy Bel-Air outside, loaded with gas. I'll let you have it for $1,500."

"Sold."

Bill led them to the highway. Linda and I sat with Gary sipping beers and dumping quarters into coffee cans.

Over an hour later, Bill was back. Linda asked, "What took you so long?"

Bill laughed. "I drove every twist and turn around every dirt road for miles. They'll never find this house again. Now let's redo the split."

That's when things started making sense. Bill piled all the money back together, took $5,000 off the top for Gary and split the rest with me. I came out with $18,000.

Gary grinned and asked, "So, Bill what about this 'honor amongst thieves' thing?"

Bill just laughed, "Those boys weren't thieves, they were idiots and they're lucky they can still breathe."

Gary asked, "Do you think they'll make it all the way to Minnesota?"

"Who knows?"

Then I asked, "So, how big a threat is the witness you mentioned and what about the fingerprints?"

"That knuckle head probably left prints but there is no witness and I have no friend in Minnesota either. I did however get them on the right road to Oklahoma."

Gary traded his smile for an uncontrollable belly laugh. I was obviously missing something and asked, "Okay Gary, what's the joke?"

"That Chevy I sold them boys belongs to a friend a mine. He had it insured to the max, hopin' someone would steal it so he could get out from under the payments. I'm sure Ol' Floyd is thinkin' he really got away with something."

By the time he'd finished talking, Gary had tears streaming from his eyes he was laughing so hard.

Our carefree mood suddenly turned serious as we spotted an eerie light flickering in and out of the shrubs along Gary's road. A car was coming towards the house. Had the brothers found their way back? Was it the police? Instincts took over. We all threw down and waited.

As the lights came closer, Gary recognized the approaching car.

"It's some folks wantin' to buy handguns. I forgot they was comin' tonight."

We all holstered our guns and greeted them as Gary introduced us to Marty Leon Martin and his wife Irene. They were just as surprised to see us, as we were to see them.

We learned that Irene was from Germany, where the couple met and married. Marty had been stationed there for a few years while in the Army. They had four kids, but Texas Social Services had taken them away.

Irene definitely had a German accent, somewhat softened from years in the States. She was about 30 and fairly petite. I had always thought Germans were blonde and blue eyed, but not Irene. She had long, dark brown hair, green eyes, and no sense of humor. She was courteous and pleasant, but at the same time formal and distant. There was an honesty and sincerity about her. I sensed she could be trusted.

I was to find out Irene could have been the poster child for loyalty, like a Black Lab. I got the impression she was strong, yet for some reason I pitied her. The look in her eyes made me think, along with losing her children, she'd been through hell.

Marty, I guess I should say Marty Leon Martin, was like no one I'd ever met before. He was six two, weighed around 160, was clean-shaven, and had short, dark, wavy hair. Unlike Irene, he was not at all quiet. He spent a majority of the evening telling bad jokes and trying to be funny. Irene never even cracked a smile.

The guy was getting to me. So I thought I'd change the subject for him. "Hey, Marty, did you serve in Nam?"

"That illegal police action? America shoulda never stole that war."

That wasn't the shift in subject I had in mind. The more he ranted, the more I suspected he really wasn't all there. Marty was either suffering from the traumas of combat . . . or perhaps he was just suffering from the effects of being Marty Leon Martin.

Then Bill asked a question that calmed him down. "What do you do for a living?"

"I'm an inventor and an entrepreneur. I have a couple of ideas in the works."

I had no clue what an entrepreneur was, but I figured Marty couldn't possibly be one. He didn't seem like an outright liar, more like an exaggerator. After all he was from Texas, not Washington D.C.

Gary brought out a box of weapons and invited us to the back yard. Marty tried a few pistols and settled on a blue steel .38 for himself and a 380 auto for Irene.

When Gary pulled out a sawed off shotgun Marty flipped. "I gotta have this baby. I've never seen anything like it!"

My first thought was, *that reaction just cost you a few hundred extra.* I couldn't help myself and had to throw out another question.

"Hey, Marty, what does an entrepreneur need with a sawed off shotgun?"

Bill looked at me and cracked up.

Marty stayed serious, "I've got investments to protect."

I could tell by the way Bill was talking with Marty and Irene; he was sizing them up as possible Imports.

"I'd like your phone number, so we can stay in touch. Never know when I might need an inventor, entrepreneur or whatever."

Linda had been unusually quiet all evening and finally spoke up, "Bill, it's been a long day. Can we go now?"

On the drive home, Bill suggested a trip to Las Vegas for R & R. I had to ask, "R & R?"

"Rest & Relaxation."

"What's the difference?"

"You know John, I've never really thought about it. I have no idea."

"Sounds redundant to me." I thought my statement was impressive, especially by throwing in the word redundant.

Linda was curled up in the back seat. So Bill and I had another one on one about all sorts of things. We decided R & R actually stood for rest and recuperation.

"John, I'd like to branch out, widen our path to give us better cover. That means we'll be scouting new areas."

"How far do you want to go?"

"Not sure."

I was familiar enough with Bill's moods to know something was getting to him. I knew I could ask.

"Bill, you seem preoccupied. What gives?"

"Did you notice something very important that was out of order tonight?"

Wow, that was unexpected. Thinking through the evening, I had no idea what

Bill saw or heard that I didn't.

"No," I answered, "Except Marty. He wasn't just out of order, he was out of control."

Bill answered but kept his eyes on the road. "I was very disappointed with Gary tonight."

"Gary?" What did he do?

"He introduced us by our real names."

"Well thank God he only used our first names."

The motion of our car, gliding across a virtually empty highway, rocked me until my eyes fell shut. It was long past two in the morning before I woke.

We were somewhere in a Fort Worth alley. I was still groggy when Bill motioned me out of the car. He popped the trunk and removed the coffee can we'd filled with coins in Gary's kitchen. Bill tossed in a few bills. In a distant corner, the glare of our headlights had found a graffiti spattered red brick wall. A shadowy figure rose from a discarded mattress. I watched amazed as Bill walked forward and handed the can to an old lady.

Her low, congested voice inquired, "Coffee?"
Bill responded, "You'll see." - J.E.S.

I jumped to my feet to see what all the racket was coming from below. Two guys were fighting over a card game. Cards and coffee cups were scattered all over the floor. I watched as the Goon Squad entered and hauled them away. I glanced across the tier and saw Lerma shaking his head and smiling. "Pendejo Tejas, pendejo . . . No?" I just smiled and nodded back.

CHAPTER FORTY-FOUR

ON THE ROAD AGAIN

Dennis and another guy showed up as I was heading into my cell. He introduced me to Paul Stavenjord. We headed down to the tables on the flat and as I grabbed a coffee, Paul took tea instead.

He was from Alaska and was serving time on a state case but since they still didn't have full service prisons up North, the convicts were contracted out to the Federal System. So he ended up in California, serving a dime, like me.

We talked for a few hours. I shared a bit about my life and rather than talk much about his, instead, he shared about his faith. A mixture of Hinduism, Buddhism and Taoism. He said he spent most of his time reading, meditating and chanting. He gave me a couple of books and said, "If you get tired of writing and need a break, check them out: Upanishads and Bhagavad Gita."

9ᵗʰ Journal Entry: Friday, August 17ᵗʰ, 1973 - 5:15 pm . . . well scratch that. Apparently we're having a unit wide shakedown. All the cell doors swung open and in marched the Goon Squad again. We were all taken out to the main floor, patted down, and scanned with metal detectors while our houses were being searched. Seems the fight earlier produced rumors of a shank stashed somewhere in K-Unit. What a pain in the ass. Several hours later and no shank, they did however find a big paint bucket full of Pruno. One to the hole for perhaps a week. 10:00 pm count time, along with that all too familiar call from the loud speaker, "On your bunks for the count . . . En sus camas para la cuenta."

9th Journal Entry: Friday, August 17th, 1973 - 10:12 pm

It was tough getting out of bed the next morning. When I was presentable, I entered the kitchen. Linda's friend Virginia Manning was emptying her purse on the dining table. I arrived just in time to intercept one rolling lipstick tube before it hit the floor.

"Nice catch, John."

"Thanks Sis. Good morning ladies. What's going on?"

"Ginny is loaning me her purse. Isn't it cool?"

I flashed a glance at Bill who just rolled his eyes. The girls smiled and disappeared into the bedroom, talking fashion all the way.

Ginny had been a dancer at a big club in Vegas. She was being kept in a lavish, pampered lifestyle by her nightclub-owning-sugar-daddy. She was Linda's best friend.

Bill stepped up beside me and asked, "Are you packed?"

I hesitated before answering. "I can do R & R just fine right here. You and Linda don't need me tagging along."

"John. Are we family? Or what?"

I hardly knew what to say. The feeling of belonging, of being important and significant to someone was overwhelming. Bill gave me *the look*. I went to my room, chose my best clothes, packed a bag and went to find Bill.

"I'm ready."

Seconds later, Linda chimed in, "Me too."

Ginny swept the contents of her purse from the table to a large baggie. Bill opened the door and we all filed out. In the parking lot Linda and Ginny hugged and waved goodbye.

Somewhere between the apartment and the airport, we decided driving to Vegas would be more relaxing. I was comfortably spread out in the back seat. Our three way conversations were pleasant and at times humorous. It was great.

A few hours down the road, Bill announced, "Oh, by the way, we're making a quick stop in Albuquerque. I've always resented the way Linda's parents treated her. It's pay-back time."

Linda asked me to swap seats so she could nap in the back. Glad for the chance to sit up front with Bill, it wasn't long before we were sharing the most private parts of our lives.

"Bill, I'm curious about something."

"Like what?"

"How come you sing after every Appointment?"

"Because I enjoy singing. And it's even better when you and Linda join in."

"Thanks Bill. But I'm curious . . . why all the old Gospel songs?"

Bill didn't reply immediately. It was as if he was calculating his answer. "Well truth be told . . . I use to be a Pentecostal pastor."

Of all the things Bill could have done before his career change, pastor would have been my last guess.

"One Sunday morning I was standing behind the pulpit, looking at my notes. The sermon title was just two words but it screamed out for attention from across the page. STOP SINNING. I looked up at my congregation and the thought hit me, before I could tell those people to stop sinning, I had to deal with the sin in my own life. I laid my Bible down and walked out. Ever since then I've been on a journey to find out how to become a better man."

A long, dry silence followed before I asked, "But Bill . . . we're robbers."

Bill answered, "Well, I had to finance the trip somehow, didn't I?"

Funny . . . odd, but funny, still.

Linda directed us to the house where she'd grown up. Bill rang the bell. No one answered. With a pair of vice grips, he opened the back door and headed straight to the garage. Linda drove inside.

We loaded the trunk of our car with a collection of pistols, long guns, ammo, and jewelry. We threw family photographs in the fireplace. I found a large coin collection and bunch of sterling silver in the master bedroom closet. I hauled it all to the trunk of our car.

I was shocked as Linda started opening cans of food and dumping them everywhere. Soon Bill and I joined in. Seemed like a waste and made me feel as if we weren't just enjoying the thrill of stealing, we were flat out being mean.

Just before leaving, Bill turned on the gas in the fireplace. Back in the garage, three buckets of paint were emptied onto Linda's father's pride and joy . . . a beautifully restored '55 Chevy.

Bill said, "The pilot light from the stove should blow the house in about 20 minutes."

Actually, we heard the explosion within only a few minutes as we turned onto the freeway. Instinctively I jerked around to see the huge plume rising in the distant sky.

I felt sick but forced myself to laugh with Bill and Linda as we continued west.

I was ashamed. - J.E.S.

Jesus Lerma caught me as I was headed out to grab a shower.

"Tejas, come. Necesitamos un portero,"

CHAPTER FORTY-FIVE

VEGAS

"Portero. I had the honor of being, not only the lone gringo on the K-Unit fútbol team, but I was the official portero or goalie. K-Unit verses C-Unit. We won, one nothing. It was a good game, followed by an hour of cutting up onions and peppers and smashing avocados into guacamole. Then came celebrations, which included one guitarra and four Mexicans, sober, but singing like they were way into a bottle of tequila.

What fun.

10th Journal Entry: Saturday, August 18th, 1973 - 6:15 pm

Lobster? Never even heard of it. Avocadoes and Crab Louie. Wow, I was discovering things that were making me lose my craving for bologna and American cheese. Shrimp cocktails, fifty cents. Steaks . . . huge steaks, a buck fifty.

Incredible.

"Hey Bill, at 17 am I allowed in the casino?"

"If you look like you belong, you belong. And, if you win something, they'll ask for ID. When they find you're under age, they'll boot you out. But by law, they have to pay."

Bill liked Craps. My game was Blackjack. I discovered the hardest things to find in Vegas were clocks and drinks you had to pay for. Personally, I think they knew I was underage. The issue never came up. We left a few grand at the tables that week. I'd never had so much fun, ever.

Late one night Bill and I were sitting in a lounge, just the two of us.

"John, I've been wondering, what do you want?"

I wasn't ready for that one. "I'm not sure how to answer. Because of you, I have more than I've ever had. For that matter, more than my entire family has ever had. I can't think of anything I really want . . . or need.

"That's because you're not thinking outside the box,"

"What does that mean?"

"You still think like a poor man. In all your 17 years, you've never been allowed to dream."

"How do you know that?"

"Because I was raised poor and I see a lot of me in you. With bags full of Benjamin's, you still look at prices before you order a meal"

"It's a habit I can't seem to break. In my family, eating out was rare. Mom wanted to give us special treats, but it was always on a shoestring. We'd order the cheapest thing on the menu and shared. It was enough just to be there. Eating was a bonus."

"How well I know. But John, there must be something I have that you want."

"Maybe a girl friend?"

Bill laughed, "Well you can't have her."

"No, Linda's your girl. I want one of my own."

"Then buy one!"

Embarrassed, my face flushed. "I don't want a prostitute, I want a girlfriend."

"John, think about the logistics of bringing a girl into The Family. Now if the right one comes along, with the right chemistry and character, we'll talk about it. But, until then, buy one. Buy several."

I declined.

Tossing and turning and fighting a losing battle with my thoughts, I punched the pillows a few times as I mulled over what Bill had said. He was right. It really wasn't feasible to expect I'd ever have a girl in my life as long as I was a bandit.

An unexpected knock startled me. At 2:13 in the morning? I grabbed the monogrammed hotel robe and threw it around me as I swung open the door. There, on the threshold was a gift from Bill. She smiled as she walked in with a bottle of Champagne and a basket of strawberries. - J.E.S.

With that I closed my journal for the night and just sat looking out the windows waiting for the sunset.

Walter Dean Morrison

Jomes E. Rasor

(Walt)

Evelyn, Mom, Donnie, Walt

John, Tammy, David

Hitchiking
Gonzales
Louisiana

1969

Donnie
John
&
Billy
Shires

Mom
&
Evelyn

Donnie
&
Charlie

Headed to
Alaska

John
&
Charlie

At a motel
on the
way to
Alaska

Pvt. John E. Swanger
Platoon 1067
MCRD San Diego

CHAPTER FORTY-SIX

OUTSIDE THE BOX

I spent the morning reading Paul's books. I found myself curious and wanted to learn more. While I can't say I was really looking for god or anything, I enjoyed the books and they did get me thinking. There has to be something out there. Right? After all, we didn't just appear. For now, however, my job was to focus on the task at hand, my journal. However, by mid-morning we were summoned to the Auditorium. Once we were seated, the warden, Frank Kenton, announced that we were about to be entertained by The Beach Boys. Immediately everyone jumped up and began cheering. The curtains opened and *Surfing USA*, began to fill the air. Pure joy was soon stifled as one of the Wilson brothers told us they were recording a new live album and they started playing stuff that didn't sound at all like Beach Boys. Cheers became boos and hisses drowned out the concert. They quickly left the stage and we were sent back to our cells. About an hour later we could hear the jeers of the other half of the prison as round two of *Beach Boys Live* was attempted. Rumor was that a couple of the Wilson's were sentenced to several prison concerts for possession of copious amounts of weed. Really, it didn't matter if the music was good or not. People felt like the band was exploiting us cons for their own gain. I've since wondered if they managed a good recording at one of the other prisons.

11th Journal Entry: Sunday, August 19^{th,} 1973 - 2:10 pm

By the time the sun was breaking the horizon, Bill, Linda, and I were pulling into a small airport for an overhead tour of the city. I'd never been in a small plane. It made me queasy . . . no, I was scared stiff. But it only took a few loops before I became terrified. Bill laughed as I tried to retrieve the coins falling from my pocket.

"If I promised to think outside the box, will you make the pilot stop? Please?"

Bill laughed again. One look at Linda's white face and I didn't feel quite so bad.

The plane ride was only one of many new experiences on that trip. Every time Bill made a suggestion, it was for something I'd never done or ever dreamed of doing. We were going from one thing to another and I couldn't believe the money he was spending. Bill read my concern.

"John, your life is different now. We're on vacation."

He looked at his Rolex. "It's time to test our marksmanship."

After spending a couple of hours at an indoor range, trying out our newly acquired arsenal, we were back in the car, hungry, and ready for dinner. Barely a mile down the road, we picked up a hitchhiker. He was young, maybe a college student. We never asked. His clothes and backpack were grubby. He looked as if he could use help.

Once in the car, Bill asked, "Where you going?"

"Tampa,"

He was heading back home after venturing out to try life on his own. Next thing I knew we were at the airport buying him a ticket home. Still recovering from such an act of kindness and preoccupied with the gal writing his ticket, he never notice Bill stuffing bundles of cash into his backpack. We said our good-byes and waived him on.

Later, sitting in the airport coffee shop, we watched the guy's plane disappear into the clouds. We all grinned, knowing we'd done something really cool.

"Hey Bill, why didn't you just hand him the money?"

"That would defeat the purpose, John."

"What purpose?"

"It's not just about changing his situation. I want that money to change his life." Smiling, Bill concluded, "When he finds the cash, he might even think we were angels."

"Angels? I don't think so."

That night I added the word spa to my ever-growing vocabulary. After a swim and massage, I was totally relaxed. I slept more peacefully than I had in months.

The next morning, heading for breakfast, Bill stopped at a phone booth. I watched him tear out a few sheets from the white pages.

"Why'd you do that?"

"Could come in handy. I have pages from several cities around the country."

I didn't push for any further explanation.

During the trip back to Dallas, the Houston brothers entered our conversation. "Bill, I have to tell you, I really got up tight with the prospect of killing those guys. In fact, I don't like the idea of working with anyone outside our Family." I surprised myself for speaking up.

After what seemed like forever, Bill smiled. "That was good John. You're starting to use your head . . . seeing the bigger picture. It's like a game of chess. You have to think a few moves ahead." Bill paused and gave me a quick look. "Getting rid of Floyd and Donnie wasn't what I wanted either. But know this: in life there are thieves and there are marks. Everyone outside this Family is a mark. We import players for no other reason than to accomplish our end. If they suit our criteria, we use them; if not, we don't. I agree we shouldn't kill. It's not something I want to live with. Our weapons serve a purpose, but always remember the many reasons to keep your bullets in their casings. And, John, there truly is honor among thieves."

I sat speechless, trying to absorb Bill's words and the events of the last few weeks. My life had gone way beyond anything I'd ever known. It felt as if I'd moved into the twilight zone. If I had opened my eyes to find myself at Nanny and Pa's, waking up from a dream, it wouldn't have surprised me.

But this was no dream. - J.E.S.

It was nearing 10 pm and time for the count. But as the cell doors opened at final lock-in for the evening, I ran down to the office for an ink pen. Mine had started to skip. I darted back into my house just as the doors began to close. I had plenty more to write. But the bulb in my cell light flickered. I watched it die along with my hopes of papering any more words into the night.

CHAPTER FORTY-SEVEN

BACK IN DALLAS

As the morning sun began to move shadows of the bars across my wall, I sat in bed thinking back on my blemished adventures. When my wondering thoughts brought me to the edge of Lake Dallas, I recalled walking along the shore. Barefoot and in thought, I glanced back at my Olds. I reached for my journal.

12th Journal Entry: Monday, August 20th, 1973 - 6:10 am

Back in Dallas, we went shopping. Bill bought me a '68, powder blue, Oldsmobile 442, with a white convertible top. It was the nicest thing I had ever owned. Bill said we needed to change vehicles often, to add more confusion into the mix. But this time I had the impression he just wanted to do something nice for me.

Bill said, "Some people change cars when the engine starts to go bad. I prefer trading them in when the ashtrays get dirty."

We laughed.

The next couple of days were spent preparing for another Safeway Appointment. However, before that, Bill took a chance on an interim idea.

Dressed as a Coca Cola vender, complete with hand truck, Bill entered a Venue. I expected him to reappear with a grocery bag full of cash. Instead he showed up with a hand truck loaded with empty Coke bottle cases. He walked to the rear of the store where Linda was parked and placed the top case into the trunk. As Linda drove away, I pulled up. Bill yanked off the uniform shirt and jumped behind the wheel.

"What went wrong?"

"You mean what went right? Everyone was busy with customers so I walked into the office. Three bags were sitting there. I took them. This might be a world record. I just shoplifted about $50,000."

I was speechless, dumbfounded.

With a big smile on his face, Bill began singing *Just a Closer Walk with Thee*. Back home, we counted a little more than half of what Bill had predicted . . . still not a bad days work.

The next morning Bill woke me. "Linda and I will be gone for a few hours.

"Where you going?"

"I'll tell you later."

I spent the day watching TV and went to a café for lunch. As I entered the apartment, the phone was ringing.

"Meet me at the bottom of the back stairs. Linda's sick. I need your help."

"I'm on the way."

I slammed down the phone and took off racing as fast as I could for the stairs. When I shot out the back door, Bill was still walking away from the payphone. I opened the car door and Bill reached in for Linda. She looked terrible, pale and limp. The poor kid was about to throw up. We got her into the bed, clothes and all. Within minutes she was out like a light. I left. When Bill joined me in the living room; his face was contorted with concern.

"What happened?"

"Linda was pregnant and we had it taken care of."

"What do you mean, 'taken care of'?"

"She had an abortion."

I had no idea what he was talking about. Bill had to explain it to me. Suddenly I felt like Linda looked. Just the idea of it made me incredibly sad. I didn't want to question Linda's judgment, but at the same time I was shocked. How could anyone ever kill their own baby?

Later that evening when Linda was awake, I went to see her. My intent was to be supportive but I couldn't hold back my tears. I stayed in my room the rest of the night.

The subject was never mentioned again.

We spent the next few days with Marty and Irene at their house and in restaurants. Even though they seemed like a fit, we never invited them to our apartment.

Marty was having a hard time finding work and Irene was homesick. They were willing to do anything to finance their move back to

Germany. When Bill suggested a way they could more than cover the cost, Marty went for it.

We teamed up on several appointments. All seemed to be going well. They were making so much money, Marty decided to delay the move. We struck several venues around Dallas over the next few months. I was the front man with Marty as backup. Irene would drive. Other times Linda took the lead with Irene as backup and Marty would drive. We began to gel as a team, even hitting two or three appointments a week. On a few occasions two, even three stores in a single day.

We were playing way to close to the edge. Eventually Marty asked for a meeting, "Irene and I think we've been working great with you guys and we want to be part of The Family."

Bill didn't even have to ask Linda and me.

"No, Marty."

"Hey. Why not?"

"Separation is the reason we work so well together."

As Bill continued, I could tell Marty was disappointed but he took it well.

The whole idea of working with two more people got me thinking. I began to realize how little our activity had to do with money. It was more about the thrill of it all. But lately the rush had changed for me. While the first few Appointments were an exercise in conquering fear, the next few dozen were like a high, incomparable to any drug. But the more we perfected our technique, the less of a rush there was. It finally hit me: the thrill came not from success, but from flirting with danger and the unknown.

I had more money than I could ever use, which should have been a blessing. By my best estimate, I had nearly $400,000 stashed. Strangely I had nothing I wanted to spend it on.

One night as I lay in bed staring up at the ceiling, it occurred to me that my whole life had become a clandestine illusion. The greatest satisfaction I'd ever had was not during the commission of Appointments. In fact, while that adrenaline rush was waning, another more seductive feeling began to surface. It was the pleasure I experienced from giving coffee cans to bums and bag ladies. It was amazing to realize that we could take a relatively small amount of money and literally change someone's life. On average, each coffee can held only a couple hundred bucks. But to a person with nothing, it might be the difference between life and death, or just enough for a new start.

How many times could my Mom have used a can full of change? Another truth needed to be faced; I really wasn't much concerned about the poor people being helped by the money. It was about the pleasure of giving it away. It wasn't about being some kind of Robin Hood or anything. He fought injustice with a purpose. My motives were totally selfish. I lived for the rush it gave me. The subject came up a few days later when Bill admitted he felt much the same way.

Marty had a different opinion on the subject. "You're both crazy and it's not fair to me. You wanna give away money; that's your business. But when you take cash out before the split, you're takin' part of my money without my say-so."

Bill laughed. "Marty, you are such a crybaby."

That broke the tension. I tried to help change the subject by asking Marty how his inventions were coming along. He gave me a dirty look. Everyone else cracked up. Even Irene laughed. She was actually beginning to develop a sense of humor.

Then Marty brought up another subject. "I've been the backup on every Appointment so far. I can handle the lead."

Bill put the issue to rest with his usual tact. "Marty, I'm sure the right job will come along where you'll be the perfect one to take the lead position. But you won't tell us when that happens, we'll tell you."

Later, Bill, Linda, and I shared our unanimous view. We would never be at ease with Marty controlling the flow of a hit. Linda addressed the problem in a way that humbled me.

"John has a demeanor for the position that Marty doesn't." - J.E.S.

The Unit Hack stopped by to see how my writing was going and to let me know I only had about twenty minutes or I'd miss my window to hit the Commissary. I tossed the journal into my locker and hurried down the walk. One box of Hostess O's, a six pack of Pepsi, a carton of Camels, a bag of Doritos, toothpaste, two Pinochle decks and three avocados. Total? $8.60.

Not bad.

CHAPTER FORTY-EIGHT

LITTLE ROCK

The plan was to spend the afternoon working on my journal. Instead I found myself reviewing everything I had written so far. It became obvious, a dictionary would help. I also realized my writing was improving. On my way to the library to see if I could check out a dictionary, I ran into Mr. Kelly. "Nah. If you check one out from the library you'll have to renew it every three days and that could be a problem. You could get written up for not returning it and well. . . . I've got one in my office you can have and a thesaurus as well. How's it going anyway?"

"Working on it. The more I write, the more I re-write,"

"Well, don't re-write too much . . . they'll be plenty of time for that. Just get it all down,"

Back at my house, dictionary in hand, I spent the better part of the afternoon and evening checking spelling and changing my choice of words here and there. Finally, I found myself considering what I had written earlier in the morning.

I liked it.

13th Journal Entry: Monday, August 20th, 1973 - 8:10 pm

The sun was struggling to break the horizon when Gary called. It was five in the morning. Bill was annoyed at being roused so early. Instead of going back to sleep, he called Linda and me into the living room.

"We're heading to Grapevine. Gary says he has the Appointment of a lifetime."

It was still early when we pulled into Gary's long driveway. He was waiting and holding some kind of device.

We were still rolling into his yard when he yelled, "Kill the engine." He yanked the hood open and quickly slammed it shut again. "Ok, now drive."

Bill gave the engine a quick crank, threw it into gear, spun around and took off. About 100 yards later the engine died. Gary was laughing as he ran up to Bill's open window. Popping the hood again, he disengaged his gadget and showed us what he'd made. The apparatus had replaced the coil wire. With the flip of a switch on his remote, Gary had killed Bill's engine.

"I built it from a kit designed to control a model airplane. This here servo is 'sposed ta manipulate the plane's rudder. I made it into a kill switch to shut down your car." Gary was obviously pleased with himself and couldn't quit grinning. "Come on inside" he said. "I'll lay out the plan over breakfast."

We were always ready for a meal at Gary's table. While feasting on bacon and eggs and freshly made biscuits with homemade jelly, we listened.

"I've been spendin' a lotta time casin' a potential Appointment in Arkansas."

I shot a glance at Bill and Linda. We were all thinking the same thing. Turning to look at Gary, we revealed our thoughts, out loud, in unison. "Arkansas?"

"Hold on. Le'me esplain. Every month a man and a woman leave a bank in Little Rock with two duffle bags full of cash. They load'um in the trunk of a car and drive to a second bank. There, they meet two more women, transfer the bags to the trunk of another car and load in three more bags. The four people deliver the five bags in one car to the Air Force Base. They spend all day processin' the payroll."

After a moment's pause, Bill asked, "How much?"

"About seven to eight hundred thousand, maybe more."

"How far from Little Rock to the base?"

"About nine miles, more than half of it along a section of road with minimal traffic."

We sat dumfounded. Bill took input from us all and began to devise the plan. "First we needed to rent a house with a garage near the Venue. Agreed?"

We were all onboard. Gary spoke up next. "I figer' since their trans-port car sits idle most of the month, I'll install the kill switch the night before."

We brainstormed and came up with a plausible scenario. I joined in. "Ok. So on delivery day, the front man, probably me, will be dressed in an Air Force uniform, walking along the road. As the bank car approaches, the kill switch will be engaged. When the vehicle rolls to a stop. I, the Good Samaritan, will offer to help. I'll look under the hood and yell 'Bomb!' Then instruct everyone to run for cover. I replace the coil wire, drive the car loaded with payroll money to hide it in the garage of the rental house. I move the bags to a shadow car and meet Gary at the air-strip. He flies the money and me to Dallas. The rest of you drive back."

Bill was pleased with my synopsis. "Let's do it."

We decided to leave immediately for Arkansas to map out the sce-nario. Marty and Irene would go with us, but we wouldn't brief them til we reached our destination.

Gary flew himself down and met us at the airport outside of Little Rock. We rented two cars: one for the guys, one for the girls. Marty was dropped off at a hotel with our luggage. His job was to arrange for rooms and wait for us.

The girls followed at a distance as Bill and I scouted the banks. We found the delivery car parked in an easily accessible but secluded area, out of public view. Gary, Bill and I drove along the delivery route look-ing for the optimal location to make the hit. The girls were still following.

While checking out side streets, Gary spotted a house with a *for rent* sign in the yard. It was less than a mile from the proposed hit location.

Linda and Irene rented the house and paid two months in advance so the landlord wouldn't need to see them again. Back at the hotel, we met in Bill and Linda's room to brief Marty and Irene. Gary explained the Appointment.

Of course, Marty asked for the lead. "Bill, I was in the Army and know how to act military and be convincing."

Bill stalled. "We'll have to discuss it."

Marty's reaction was obvious frustration. Once more Bill proved his skill in soothing the situation. "I'm not saying no. But Marty, I don't act alone."

"Yeah, as long as John is a member of The Family, I'll never get to be the lead. Right?"

Marty was still pouting when Bill gave him a look, which immediately ended the discussion.

Over the next few days we prepared for the Appointment, reviewing the scenario and gathering things we'd need for the hit. Secure in our plans, we flew back to Dallas. Back home, Bill, Linda, and I held a meeting. We decided to let Marty take the lead. I wanted to drive the shadow car anyway, so I could intervene if anything went wrong. We'd make the exchange and head to the airstrip. Gary and I would fly the money to Grapevine. Irene would drive the Olds to Texarkana with Marty in the trunk. Bill and Linda would drive the Buick back to Dallas. Eventually we'd all meet up at Gary's house.

Bill looked satisfied. "With the details settled, it's time to call Marty and Irene."

Of course when Bill told him he had the lead position, Marty was ecstatic. From then on he took every opportunity to infer that I had been replaced . . . by a better man. I tried not to let it bother me. Our plans were coming together.

We arrived back in North Little Rock at four o'clock the morning of the hit. The sunrise was bright orange and beautiful, but there was an ugly tension, thick as a fog in the air. To minimize exposure, we didn't go to a hotel and we avoided the rental house. Irene was sent to unlock the garage and to see that nothing had been disturbed.

Linda reminded Irene, not to touch anything in the house. "Fingerprints become evidence. So don't leave any."

Marty, all decked out in uniform, was chomping at the bit, waiting for the clock to catch up with him. Bill and I went to the bank. He watched as I placed the remote on the engine of the delivery car. We drove to our position near the second bank.

The delivery car pulled into its parking area at 6:20, right on schedule. As expected, the tellers entered the bank through a back door. They were inside less than three minutes. All four tellers emerged with the extra bags and entered the car.

Suddenly, I was overcome by a feeling that something wasn't right. I couldn't explain it but I knew we should abort. I wondered for just a second if I should tell Bill. I looked at him and could see concern in his eyes too.

I whispered, "Bill?"

He lifted his hand to hush me and whispered back, "Something's wrong."

We arranged for everyone to meet us at the airstrip. Once we were all together, Bill explained how he and I both sensed trouble.

"We're pulling the plug. It doesn't matter how much money we could possibly haul in if we get caught or worst yet, any one of us or them get hurt."

Marty was angry. Gary was upset about losing his switch. Bill offered a solution.

"Marty, I'll pay a $1,000 if you retrieve Gary's kill switch."

Marty didn't want to do it but Irene convinced him they needed the money. Gary calmed down once he knew the remote would be returned. His concern wasn't so much about the contraption itself but the possibility of it being discovered. That might ruin any chance of using it in the future. We left the Buick with Marty and Irene. Gary flew his plane to Texas. Bill, Linda and I drove back in the Olds.

Except for songs on the radio, the trip home was quiet. Even though Bill and I were sure we'd avoided a disaster, our decision had stressed the bands of our team.

After several hours of mulling it over, I finally spoke up. Bill and Linda gave me plenty of time to vent. "I know Marty resents me. His attitude has always been a problem. But after today, I have a gut feeling he's going to make real trouble, maybe even try to split us up. I'd like to do something about him, and soon."

"You're right John. But I don't think he's a lost cause. Let's try to find a way to keep him happy but on a tighter leash. Marty has become an asset. He's filling a backup spot we couldn't cover before he arrived. What do you say Linda?"

"With Marty and Irene there's always a driver. Frankly, before they came, leaving the getaway car running with no one behind the wheel would make me a nervous wreck." - J.E.S.

I heard a bunch of racket from up above. Some guy was flopping around as medics and guards were holding him down. F-Tier was full of commotion as his seizures were drawing the attention of most of the residents of A, C and E-Tiers, as well as many of his neighbors that could focus their mirrors on the action. Poor guy. I felt bad for him as several idiots were calling out rude bull shit. My bunk was calling me.

CHAPTER FORTY-NINE

FLIRTING WITH DISASTER

Mail call brought a letter from Nanny. She said she was taking in extra sewing and could send me $5 each month. It felt like Nanny was the only person who knew I was alive . . . or cared.

It had been a few days since I had received anything from Dennis and in fact I hadn't even seen him around the unit. I was beginning to worry.

14th Journal Entry: Tuesday, August 21st, 1973 - 8:14 am

Back in Dallas, we began casing an A&P grocery store near Arlington. By the end of the week plans were set. Marty had been assigned as backup. Irene would drive.

Inside the Venue, everything went as planned until I entered the office with the manager. He suddenly turned around to face me. "I'm not going to open the safe. You can have the tills but the safe is off limits."

I swung my pistol at his face. "Open the safe or I'll blow your head off."

Still he refused. I took a step backwards, maintained my aim and cocked the pistol. "I'm only going to say this once. Open the safe or die."

I lowered the hammer and slapped him across the face with my gun. Blood flowed from his nostrils. The poor guy broke down. "If I open the safe, they'll fire me."

"If you don't open it, they won't have the chance."

By then the whole store was aware of what was going down. Marty was fully engaged. Within a few seconds the manager had the safe open and was filling a bag.

By standing on the threshold of the office door, I could watch the manager and yell out my instructions. "No one move. Clerks, empty your tills into bags and place them on the counter."

Marty told one clerk to gather all the bags and place them in a single bag. When we left the office, clerks and customers saw the blood on the manager's face. Some panicked. We sent everyone to the back of the store and made our exit.

Once in the car Marty started in on me. "You shoulda been outa that office sooner. What the hell were you thinking?"

My insides churned with his every word. I was about to lose it. Instead, I turned to him with a warning, "Shut up. Don't make another sound."

Back home, Bill could tell something was wrong.

"All right, Marty, what's the problem?"

"John blew it."

I looked at Marty with blood in my eyes. Bill knew I was furious.

"John, tell me what happened. Marty, you be quiet."

"I did what was needed to get the job done. As far as I'm concerned nothing went wrong; it just didn't go as expected. We've trained to adjust our actions as situations demand. I used all the resources available and we were successful."

Marty eyes were glued on me. "So, Mr. Hit Man, what if he hadn't opened the safe?"

Bill intervened. "Let's hope we never have to find out."

I was not pleased that we used Marty and Irene as much as we did. Practically every appointment involved them in some way. And I was getting sick of it. - J.E.S.

I had missed breakfast, so lunch was definitely on my agenda. Chili and salad. Cornbread and iced tea. Really, it wasn't all that bad. Seconds just about filled me up.

Nick wanted to hit the weights but I talked him into a Pinochle game with two guys from C-Unit. We took them two in a row so they couldn't afford another loss. I had the choice of $10 green or $20 Commissary. I took the green. Just as I was heading in to write, I spotted Paul.

"Hey Stavenjord, you seen Dennis?"

"Didn't you hear? He was raped and beaten pretty bad a few days ago. Still in the Infirmary. We should drop in and see him."

I was shocked and saddened. Of all the kids I looked after I should have known that even the older ones need help every now and then.

"If you want, I can go now. Will they let us in?"

"I don't know why not. Let's do it."

I ran to my house and grabbed some cans of Coke and a few dough-nuts. Paul met me back at the unit door. He had some rice and a jar of salsa. I looked at him, I guess kinda puzzled, so he said, "I'm vegetarian"

"But . . . I don't think Dennis is."

They didn't let us in to see him but we were able to leave the stuff for him. Paul headed to the yard to meditate and I headed back to the house.

CHAPTER FIFTY

BUSTED

I needed a break. Time to unwind. I was really upset and not sure how to sort out my feelings about what had happened to Dennis. The mingling of anger and sadness were a combination I had hoped to never experience again. But there I was, shaking my head, and contemplating the thickness of the sheet metal on the side of my locker. Dennis had managed to take my mind off of my own troubled life, and now I needed to grab my journal, to take my mind off of Dennis.

15th Journal Entry: Tuesday, August 21st, 1973 - 6:44 pm

Food Basket Market was our next hit. I was dealing with a heavy case of nerves because it was across the street from where Nanny worked and where she did all her grocery shopping. As it turned out, I casually entered the store, picked up the moneybags in the office and walked out unnoticed. It was close to $58,000. Shoplifted.

Sweet.

Things settled down for the next few Appointments, but soon Marty was at it again, pressing to take the lead. We decided to try him on a relatively simple hit.

The manager of a particular Venue habitually camped in the office during a three-hour period between the armored car drop and when customers began lining up to cash checks. Marty was instructed to open the office door, show the manager his gun and tell him to load up the canvas bags. Linda and I would be in the store as backups.

At a nearby apartment complex in north Dallas, we found a newer model, gray Monte Carlo. I hotwired it and headed to the freeway. Bill and Linda followed. The freeway was virtually vacant, except for a Dallas Police car up ahead. I slowed so as not to pass him. When I checked the rearview mirror for Bill, there was another police car behind me. I'd been had. By the time I pulled over and got out, eight squad cars surrounded me. A helicopter hovered overhead.

Overkill.

I stepped away from the car with my hands raised. As I was being cuffed they began to question me.

"And just why are you wearing surgical gloves?"

"I'm not talking til I see my attorney."

The policeman frisking me came up with nothing, not even an ID, just surgical gloves and empty pockets. I wouldn't give them my name.

"I'll tell you one thing kid, I'll for sure get your name once we're downtown. If not, I guarantee you'll rot in jail. We don't release anyone with unconfirmed identity."

I didn't respond. I'd never been arrested for anything serious. I wondered: *now what?*

The cruiser pulled into an underground garage at the Dallas County Jail. Not wanting to draw attention to Bill and Linda, I didn't know who to call for help.

As the officer escorted me to the desk, I heard the booking sergeant say, "Step over here Mr. Swanger. We'll need prints, a quick photo and you'll be on your way."

The arresting officer and I were both stunned. Bill and Linda rounded the corner with our Attorney, John T. McCullough, a man who had spent seven years with the D.A.'s office. He was loaded with connections. It took longer to arrest me than to book me. I was charged with grand theft auto and released.

On the way home, we wired another car for the hit . . . something less flashy.

Even though it was late, I couldn't sleep. My mind was racing, *was I on the verge of losing my freedom?*

The next day, the Appointment went smoothly. Marty was elated. Even Irene was smiling. I thought I was an adrenaline junky, but Marty was ridiculous. He couldn't stop talking about the hit. His actions were more irritating than ever.

Bill finally addressed it. "Look Marty, if you can't curb your ego, we'll have to reconsider letting you take the occasional lead."

"Occasional? What do you mean occasional?"

Bill was in no mood to explain and snapped back, "You start bitching about 'occasional' and we'll make it not at all."

That shut him up. - J. E.S.

Paul stuck his head in my door, "Our news boy is back,"

I dropped the journal and followed him to Newsome's house. He didn't look good. Back to staring at the floor and on the verge of tears. Yet when he saw that it was Paul and me at the door he slowly got up and grabbed a couple of pieces of paper from on top of his locker. "Sorry I didn't get these to you earlier. August 20th hasn't been a good day for Christians, or I guess I should say, Catholics."

SOME NEWS from NEWSOME
August 20th 1973

1. Time magazine asks: Can we trust Nixon again?
2. Giants beat the Expos 6-4 in Montreal
3. Pope John XIV Murdered August 20th 984 AD
4. St. Bernard of Clairvaux died August 20th 1153 AD
5. Pope Pius VII died August 20th 1823 AD
6. Pope Pius X died August 20th 1914 AD

Dennis began to cry and we tried as best we could to console him. He said he didn't think he could take it anymore. And then he asked, "Do you guys think you could pray for me?"

I was without words but thankfully, Paul began to chant a beautiful chant and told Dennis that god was within him. I found myself tearing up a bit and again wondering if this Eastern god was true or if Jesus, the God that Nanny always spoke of, was the real one. The call rang out for the last rack in of the night and we both headed to our respective homes. Any thoughts of my journal faded away as I couldn't help but dwell on Dennis, destiny, and God.

CHAPTER FIFTY-ONE

MARTY LEON MORON

That turned out to be our last Newspaper. Dennis was taken away during the night. As I sat with Paul eating breakfast he said that at about 2:30 in the morning he watched as Dennis was led away. He was either transferred to different prison or he checked into the hole.

We walked back to my house where I returned the two small books to Paul. He said, "Wait right here. I'll be back."

He ran off but quickly returned with three much larger and frankly a bit overwhelming books, *Tibetan Buddhism and Secret Doctrines*, *The Tibetan Book of the Dead*, and *The Tibetan Book of the Great Liberation*. Then in a really bad Chinese accent he said, "Ah butterfwy, are you weady to espan you enwitenment?"

I just laughed and shook my head.

16th Journal Entry: Wednesday, August 22nd, 1973 - 9:09 am

Over the next few months, Marty proved prone to be chronically cracked. His lack of common sense was dangerous. Once while he was driving Linda, Irene, and me to an Appointment, he made a left turn from the wrong lane, causing an accident in downtown Dallas. Although we were in a stolen vehicle, in full disguise, and armed, Marty stopped and was about to exit the car. I pulled him back and told him to drive off. Nothing came of it but his idiotic decision could have been disastrous.

There seemed to be no end to Marty's blunders and stupid actions. On one hit he pulled his gun and yelled orders at everyone in the store, preempting my position as the front man, increasing our already danger-ous situation.

Once, when Linda had the lead, with Irene as backup, Marty was the driver. He made a wrong turn, ending up lost for ten minutes while Bill waited for them at the exchange.

Another time as we were climbing into Bill's trunk, Marty tossed his sawed off shotgun in first. It went off, blowing a hole through the driver's side quarter panel. Then, as it recoiled, it bounced back and hit me in the face. That scared the hell out of me . . . not to mention Bill. My reaction was, well, use your imagination. I had a black eye for weeks.

Marty's serious instability called for a family meeting. Linda was the first to voice our common fears. "Maybe it's time to leave Dallas. We've hit so many places. I think we're over-taxing the market."

The next morning we visited the DMV for more licenses. Linda chose to be Lyn Bailey and Linda Sue Elliot. I settled for Jay Collier, Jerry Daniels, Joe Harper and Jeff Cox. While waiting, I discovered Linda was already using an alias. She told me her real name was LaDeanna Ruth Pringle. Bill's name was actually Billy James Headrick.

After the DMV, we met Marty and Irene for lunch. Bill told them, "Gather your things for a trip. We leave this evening."

On a quick excursion to Gary's place, Bill had him dress a couple of shotguns and removed the serial numbers from several others. As payment for his work, Bill gave him the rifles we had stolen from Linda's parents.

We left town as planned, with Marty and Irene following in their vehicle. By the next night we were checked into an El Paso motel and looking for something to eat. We ended up in the parking lot of an inter-esting grocery store. It was huge but not well protected. Specials were painted all over the front windows. There were no cameras and the safe was hidden in the office.

Bill signaled Marty and Irene to stay in their car while we cased the place. At the customer service desk Bill bought a roll of quarters. Because the office door was ajar, he saw a couple of moneybags just sitting on the floor beside the manager's desk. Linda and I wandered around pretending to shop. We were scanning the lay out, making mental notes of various details.

Once outside, Bill called us all together for final instructions. "There's no time to run around looking for a car. We'll grab one from here and make our exchange behind the lumber yard."

Marty threw on his stupid wig and bandanna. I put on a baseball cap and tinted glasses. We entered. I stopped long enough to take a paper bag from a checkout stand then walked toward the office. Marty thumbed through magazines. By now the office door was closed. I opened it and stepped inside.

The attendant reacted the moment she saw me. "Hey, you can't come in here."

I drew my pistol. "Look, I have a key." Handing her the bag, I said, "Fill this with everything you can lay your hands on."

She opened the safe and began removing its contents. Then she said something that almost made me laugh. "I'm sorry sir, but we're going to need another bag."

We walked together to a check stand. Marty was close by, I handed him the full bag. The girl and I returned to the office. She emptied the safe and took bills from a stack of cash drawers, then handed me the second bag.

I asked for the two on the floor by the desk. She gave me a funny look but complied.

We had no trouble leaving the store. Once in the parking lot, I spotted a lady opening her car door. I walked up and pointed my pistol at her. "Leave the keys on the seat and get out of here." She was shaking. I hoped she wouldn't scream. "I don't want to hurt you. Stay quiet. You'll be okay."

She stood dumfounded as I jumped into the driver's seat. I grabbed her purse and handed it to her out the window. Her expression was priceless. By then Marty was in. I drove away. We met for the exchange then headed back to the motel to pack and leave. On the way, Bill turned up the radio. I'm convinced, no matter what, they always think I said, 'This is a stickup.'

Our destination was Flagstaff. But we were all so tired; we couldn't make it past Gallup.

I don't remember much about the town except the freight trains sounded as if they ran through my room. I was finally in a deep sleep, when a loud knocking jarred me awake. Panicked and disoriented, I broke out in a cold sweat. Outside, Bill's muffled voice calmed my fears. I opened the door. The whole crew flooded in. Linda handed me a cup of coffee. I shut the door and slumped into a chair.

Bill dumped the take on my bed. The last two bags I'd insisted on having were full of checks and tally sheets. It explained the clerk's funny look when I ask for them. After 20 minutes of counting, Bill announced, "There's close to $85,000 here."

It would turn out to be the largest take we'd ever see.

Linda's curiosity took over so just for fun she counted the checks. "There's another $55,000 for a grand total of $140,000."

Bill said, "Great. Burn them."

Even with all the elation over the money, I was bummed and Bill picked up on it.

"John, I thought you'd be happy with those numbers; why the discouraged look?"

"No coins."

"Not so fast cowboy. Who needs change? Just give them whatever you want. I'll bet you can find empty coffee cans at the café next door."

Marty just shook his head. "You're both crazy."

Then Bill tossed me the roll of quarters he'd bought at the Venue the night before. He smiled and everyone headed to their rooms to pack.

Later, as Bill was checking out of the motel, I heard him in conversation with the guy at the front desk. "We left Portland two days ago and we're getting a little road weary."

The guy wished us well and never knew he'd been set up to believe we were traveling east. We continued west. Exhausted from the lack of sleep, our next stop was a cheap motel in Flagstaff.

As I tossed my bag onto the bed, a loud gunshot blast startled me. I ran outside and met Bill and Linda. Marty had accidentally dropped his shotgun . . . again. The discharge had blown a hole in the floor. We grabbed our bags and hit the highway. The next morning we were in Vegas.

After a few days of hanging out and resting up, we took a vote and continued west. Somewhere along the way between Las Vegas and San Francisco, we pulled into a parking lot. The neon sign said restaurant and bar. Bill took off his Rolex, tossed it in the glove box and replaced it with a Timex. I wondered, *now what?*

It only took a few minutes til there was a crowd gathered around Bill. He was buying drinks for eight strangers. That was out of character, but I was no longer surprised by whatever he did. The next thing I knew he was showing off with magic and card tricks. Everyone was amazed. I was too. Bill asked the bartender for paper and pens. He removed his watch and placed it under an inverted coffee cup. A wad of cash went under another cup.

"Now, we're gonna play a game."

Bill was slurring his words a bit and acting as if he was getting drunk. "Ok, I want everybody to write on your paper: give me your watch, or, give me all your money . . . one of the two."

Bill summoned the bar tender for an empty pitcher.

"Now, put all your papers in here and the one we draw out will be the winner."

Bill held the pitcher up for Linda to choose.

"Whose handwriting is this?"

An older lady raised her hand. The crowd cheered as Bill gave her the bundle of cash and put the watch back on his wrist. When everyone was gone, Bill pulled a plastic baggie from his pocket. He dumped in the papers from the pitcher.

When we read them later, each note said: Give me all your money. - J.E.S.

"Hey, you going to lunch?"

A tall thin guy, about four or five years my senior, with a huge mustache and an even bigger smile, was at my door.

"And who might you be?"

"The name's Alvin Glatkowski and I'm here to afford you the opportunity to enlighten your life and possibly avert a disastrous future."

"Well, Alvin, you sound like a salesman."

"Nope. What I'm offering is free and only requires an open mind and a desire to see things from a different perspective. Interested?"

"What is it?"

With that he shoved his hand through my window and offered me a little Red Book.

Quotations from Chairman Mao Tse-tung
Former leader of the Chinese Communist Party.

Although I had often heard of Communism, I must say I had never actually met anyone who believed in it. And there at my door stood an authentic, card carrying Communist. Smiling.

"Well Alvin, why are you here? At my door? I mean MY door?"

"I just received a shipment of a 100 of these books along with assurance from my attorney that I can distribute them without fear of being molested by the goons in this country, called the Constabularies."

Alvin Leonard Glatkowski Jr. was serving ten years for Mutiny on the High Seas. Seems he was the first in over 150 years to take over an American flagged ship. He and a buddy hijacked the freighter as it was sailing on a D.O.D. supply charter carrying napalm to the US Air Force base in Thailand for use in the Vietnam War.

They managed to give the ship, along with nearly 5,000 bombs weighing nearly 3,000,000 pounds, to Cambodia where they were given asylum. Unfortunately, the Cambodian government was overthrown a couple of days later and the new Pro-American régime promptly handed them over and sent the ship on its way.

"So you really hate America?"

"That is such a bourgeois question. Not at all sir. Quite the contrary. I love America. But I hate this opulent establishment. Do you not understand Totalitarianism? The Proletariat? What about Fascism?"

"Thanks anyway Alvin, but I think I'll pass."

"Hey one question before I go?"

"Sure, what?"

"Well, you and that Paul guy are studying god or something right?"

"And?"

"Well, if I don't believe god exists, and he knows I don't believe he does, do you think he will hold it against me?"

"You can bet your life on it."

He just chuckled and walked away still smiling. I was sure he would find others to take his books. I hadn't yet started on the books Paul had given me. I did however, decide to open up the dictionary and try to find some of the new words Comrade Glatkowski had graced me with.

CHAPTER FIFTY-TWO

GRAND THEFT AUTO

Lerma had given me a harmonica well over a year ago and wanted me to learn a few Mexican songs, so I could play along with the band after fútbol each Saturday. The band sounded like a mixture of Zydeco from New Orleans and Mariachi from Mexico. I know, weird. Right? Zydeco without an accordion? Lerma said. "That's why we need you on harmonica, Tejas."

Well, I hadn't picked it up in over three months. Truth be known my playing sounded more like the Blues than Zydeco. In fact, I had teamed up with William Dean, a black vocalist, and John Miranda, an incredible guitarist. Throw in a bass player and a drummer and we were beginning to sound pretty good.

But I really needed to either learn some of the not so bluesy stuff, or at least try, so I grabbed my harp and headed to the yard. Most everything I had learned was mastered while walking around the yard.

I tried. No, seriously I did. But I just couldn't stop myself from sliding down to the lower notes and bending them into a long drawn out cry. Over and over again. It was how I felt.

Dirty South & Gatemouth . . . Look out, here I come.

17ᵗʰ Journal Entry: Wednesday, August 22ⁿᵈ, 1973 - 8:22 pm

There is a cool California resort town along the Russian River called Guerneville. We rented three cabins and relaxed. Grilled steaks, wine, and stories filled our days and nights. It was like nowhere else I'd ever been. Guerneville became our hideout, so to speak . . . our favorite place to unwind. It was there I added another word to my vocabulary.

Cheesecake.

One morning I found my way to the river and discovered how nice it was to sit in green grass, under a blue sky and do nothing but listen to the song of water lapping over rocks. It was a different kind of music . . . calming and peaceful; a nice background as I reflected on the way my life had been changing.

The more Appointments we did, the less time we spent preparing. We were neglecting a vital part of what made us good enough that so far we'd been untouchable. Lately, every robbery made me more and more apprehensive. The idea of getting caught never left my mind.

What if some off duty cop is cashing his paycheck and we're robbing the place? Or we end up in a shootout. I don't wanna die. Worse yet, I don't wanna kill anyone.

The charge of grand theft auto in Dallas was still hanging over me. My life was getting complicated.

Thoughts of going to jail terrified me . . . taking its toll. Before every Appointment my stomach tensed into knots. Fear made me avoid stealing getaway cars. Excuses began to flow, either nothing was available or we would find a way to function without it.

Sitting by the river had helped me collect my thoughts, providing me with a better perspective. Still, I had a list of things that were bugging me.

Back at the cabins, I was glad to hear that Marty and Irene were hibernating. Linda and Bill suggested a picnic. I showed them my quiet place where we could talk. We all agreed Marty had become a liability. Once again, with his usual wisdom, Bill was thinking ahead.

"If we dismiss him, there's a chance he might turn on us. But keeping him around could get us caught anyway."

I had to unload. "That guy's been pissing me off since day one."

"Linda and I really appreciate the way you've maintained your self-control."

"Thanks, Bill. But how do we solve the problem?"

"By letting him stay we retain our options. Once the toothpaste is out of the tube, you can't stuff it back in."

We decided to keep a more watchful eye on Marty. I continued my list. "We've stopped following armored cars; we don't profile Targets any more. It's been months since we actually prepped for an Appointment."

"Well said, John. But remember, things did change when we decided to shift our attention away from the Friday armored car drops-offs to the more lucrative Sunday or Monday pick-ups. While part of the take includes checks that have to be disposed of, our average is almost always double."

I insisted, "That's true. But with the Marty factor thrown in, we should do more planning not less."

Linda shot me a sympathetic look and handed me another sandwich. "John, I think you worry too much."

Bill looked at her then at me and said, "Listen John, with wit and controlled intimidation, you've shown a natural ability to manipulate the Target."

I shot back, "And I cover for Marty when he blows it."

Bill was quiet, as if considering his reply. "Remember we've never even come close to being caught."

I blurted out, "No thanks to Marty."

"That's true, John, but so is this. If we get away from the Venue, chances are they won't come looking for us. There are sloppy criminals and more important things going on in this country. Authorities are too busy. The nation is still reeling over the Robert Kennedy and Martin Luther King assassinations. They are dealing with the Watts and Harlem riots, Attica, Viet Nam, peaceniks and war protesters. Kent State, plane hijackings to Cuba, and Charles Manson. There's Angela Davis, Timothy Leary, Black Panthers, the SDS, the SLA, not to mention landing on the moon. Compared to that, we are small potatoes, back page news."

"Bill, I get it. But my focus has shifted. Being arrested in Dallas really scared me."

"Don't worry. We'll deal with things one at a time."

"So, no more impulse hits?"

Linda jumped on that one, "Yes, please. No more."

Bill was quick to say, "Done. And while we're at it, we need to resume meeting the night before each Appointment to review details and make sure everyone's in sync. That should keep a bridle on Marty."

Before I could express my relief, Bill had one last comment, "By the way John, I've saved the best for last. McCullough has managed to have the charges against you reduced to a misdemeanor for Minor Joy Riding. You'll get 10 days in jail and a $500 fine."

I was pleased but I didn't want to go to jail. Bill knew there was something else on my mind. He could read me like a book.

"Ok, John, what's bothering you now?"

"Would paying a bigger fine make jail time go away?"

"Maybe. I'll ask."

Talking out our concerns had taken most of the afternoon. Back at the cabins, we parted company to change for dinner. Bill had decided it was time for a nicer than usual meal at an upscale place in town.

Totally wrung out from getting things off my chest, I flopped down for a quick nap. It worked. With a nice hot shower, I was revived and ready to enjoy the evening.

I was nearly at the door when Bill knocked and let himself in. "I spoke with McCullough, $1,500 and no time. We'll need to bring $3,000 for his fee and another $3,000 for fines and gifts for the judge, prosecutor and recorder. Your court date is three months plus a few days away. Linda has it logged on her calendar."

Amazed by all Bill continued to do for me, I stammered,

"No one has ever treated me. . . ."

Bill gave me a generous slap on the back. "Forget it John. Let's eat."

The next morning we drove north, up the California coast. At noon we pulled into Ukiah, a unique little town with Victorian gingerbread-laced houses, antique shops, and galleries. I was tempted to skip lunch and go roaming.

Inside the restaurant Marty couldn't sit still. He finally motioned for a huddle.

"I saw a Wards Drug Store on the way in. I think it would make a great hit."

Marty jabbered on. I expected Bill to say, no more impulsive hits. His reply took Linda and me by surprise.

"Marty, I'm impressed with how far you've come in understanding the mechanics of an Appointment."

Marty glared at me as he answered Bill. "Thanks, always nice to be appreciated."

"You're welcome. Now, let me ask you something."

"Okay. Shoot."

"I've been wondering how you feel about splitting the take with others when we have a big Appointment?"

"It always irks me to split with anyone."

"Well then, do you think you're ready to strike out on your own?"

"Never thought of that."

"You won't have to split if you operated by yourself or with Irene."

We all waited for Marty's reaction. Bill continued.

"We'd like to help you get started. We'll work with you on the drug store and call it good. What do you think?"

Marty turned to Irene who looked as if she might go for the idea. They both turned to Bill for his next comment.

"John has been thinking of moving on. Linda and I need a change. You and Irene might try L.A. It's an easy place to get lost in the crowd."

Irene, who had never said much since the day she'd arrived began to unload.

"Now that we have money, we can get our kids and go back to Germany. Let's give it a try Marty. I want my kids and I want to go home." - J.E.S.

It was late and I was tired. Postponing time to do some re-writing until the morning, I wondered how the hot August wind could blow so cold in the night. I fell asleep with my headphones on. Last thing I remember was Al Green singing *Tired of Being Alone.*

CHAPTER FIFTY-THREE

MARTY GONE WILD

Waffles and bacon, coffee and orange juice. Too bad I didn't get to finish them. Some big old defensive lineman looking dude slapped a guard and all hell broke loose. I spent 30 minutes laying on the floor until the Goon Squad hauled him away, followed by that annoying siren and announcement, *"Return to your Units and Rack in."* Great, now how long will we be in lock down?

18th Journal Entry: Thursday, August 23rd, 1973 - 8:52 am

Linda and I wandered around the store, pretending to be shoppers. Marty, wearing his usual wig and headband, entered and walked directly to the manager's office. The door was ajar. I was able to see Marty throw a bag at the manager, hitting him in the face.

"Fill this with cash."

The poor guy was even more startled when he saw the barrel of Marty's .38 only inches from his head. The trembling man crammed the bag full of bills.

Marty grabbed the take and left the office, but not as planned. Instead, he meandered around the store. Then, as if he'd forgotten something, he reentered the manager's office and pulled his sawed off Shotgun. Lowering it toward the manager's face he shrieked,

"Give me everything in your safe."

The manager turned white. I felt sorry for the guy as he fumbled to dial in the combination.

As Marty was about to leave again, I heard him say, "Now the reserve."

The man stammered, "I don't know . . . What? . . . What are you talking about?"

Marty jammed the shotgun against the man's head and repeated his demand. Removing a plate at the bottom of the safe, the manager gave up a few thousand more.

With cash in hand, Marty backed out the door. As a last minute ruse, he yelled, "There's a bomb in this store. Try anything funny and I'll blow you all to bits."

The store was noisy so there was very little reaction. A few people questioned if they had heard right. One lady left her cart and took off running.

Marty walked directly to me, grinned and asked, "Did you see that?"

I turned, muttering under my breath, "Idiot. You've gone completely insane."

Meanwhile, Marty stopped at the checkout stand to buy a pack of Virginia Slims. The clerk rang up the sale. Marty threw the bag on the counter and raked out bills.

The woman went all wide eyed and said, "Where'd you get that?"

"I just robbed your manager. Now empty the till into this bag and throw in a full carton of smokes."

I nearly peed my pants. Marty ran out the door and circled the building the correct way. But it was still anyone's guess if he'd end up in Bill's trunk as planned. Fortunately, he did.

Linda came along side with a shopping cart. We decided to stick around another few minutes. People began to panic as the word "bomb" buzzed through the store.

Linda asked, "Did Marty actually say there was a bomb?"

Yes, what an idiot!"

"John, that guy's so crazy,"

"Linda, I don't know if I can take much more of him."

Someone yelled, "Call the police."

Another responded, "Phone lines are dead."

People were high-tailing it out of the store, Linda, visibly shaken went with them. I followed the crowd out the door in time to see Linda get into Irene's car. Bill waited nearby.

I slid next to Bill and said, "Let's get out of here. It didn't go well."

As we were about to drive away, several Police and Highway Patrol cars entered the lot. We waited for a clearing then drove towards an exit. At the last second two cruisers cut us off, then parted going in opposite directions with spotlights flailing, searching along the highway. My knees were shaking.

Bill voiced what I was thinking. "Good, they're looking for a bandit on foot."

The mob of shoppers on the run made it slow going. We were lost in the confusion of a traffic jam, which was exactly where we wanted to be. Bill slowly turned left, heading north. In the rear view mirror, we spotted Linda and Irene following.

Half an hour later, Bill called to Marty in the trunk, "I'm pulling over so you can get out."

Marty yelled back, "No! I wanna wait til it's safer."

We drove on. Two hours later in Eureka, Marty still refused to come out.

"I'm not getting' out til we're across the State line."

It was well past midnight when we stopped at a roadside motel in Brookings, Oregon. We woke the night attendant to request rooms. I had no trouble falling asleep.

It was still early morning when Linda shook me awake.

"Grab a shower and meet us in the restaurant."

I grunted, "See you there."

It was just the three of us. Bill explained, "We'll finish our breakfast and go see Marty and Irene. It's time we sent those two packing. But we need to choose our words carefully, so follow my lead."

By the time we'd finished our meal, I felt better about everything. We left the restaurant with a tray of cups and carafe of coffee. We stopped to pick up the take.

When Irene answered the door, Bill was downright cheerful as he greeted her in German. "Gut morgan."

With a smile, Irene eagerly replied, "Guten tag."

Linda stepped in with the tray. "Thought you'd like to jump-start the morning."

Irene's smile faded, "Marty's in the shower."

Bill poured her a cup. "We'll just sit here on the bed until he's ready. Okay?"

Irene took her first sip and answered, "Okay."

Marty was annoyed when he discovered we were there. He seemed a little better when Bill dumped the take on the bed. We counted about 12,000.

Bill grinned and said, "Not bad for your first solo job, Marty." Then he scooped it all into the bag and threw it on the bed. "It's yours. Guess you'll be heading out?"

Irene smiled at Bill.

Marty grimaced, "I'm worried. I messed up last night."

"Marty, it went fine. You just over reacted a little. Otherwise, a good job."

"I cudda done better."

"It's over and you did fine. By the way, John is going back to Dallas. Linda and I will drop him off at the airport in Portland and head for Canada. We've been thinking about retiring up there."

I thought we'd pulled it off. Then all of a sudden Marty changed everything.

"We're going with you guys, at least to Seattle. Let us hang out a while longer. We'll go with you to see John off."

Bill grabbed the bag and counted out $4,000 and tossed it on the bed.

"Normal split then? Your call."

We left Marty and Irene and walked back to our room. Bill was the first to speak.

"Damn it. Let's drop it for a while and just keep moving." - J.E.S.

By 3:00 pm we were still in lockdown. Then our unit was flooded with staff. Around 20 guards entered and began a shake down. Tier by tier they ordered us out and searched our cells. However, this was a much quicker search and we were released as soon as each tier was completed. All in all it took just over an hour. Two were hauled off for shanks and a few shots were written for various other contraband.

CHAPTER FIFTY-FOUR

POINT OF NO RETURN

Nick offered to bring me dinner so I just headed back to my house to write. I found myself reviewing my manuscript for well over two hours and way past the roast beef and powdered mashed potato sandwich. I opened my locker to wash it all down with a warm Pepsi. I was ready to write.

19th Journal Entry: Thursday, August 23rd, 1973 - 7:05 pm

In the back corner of a Portland diner, Bill called a meeting. "Marty, if you're going to stay with us you'll have to start following instructions better and no questioning Family decisions. You will fill whatever role we assign without discussion. Understand?"

"Yeah. But with John leavin', can I be a part of The Family now?"

"We've asked John to stay. You becoming part of The Family will never be an option. Don't ask again."

Bill was beginning to sound like my Marine Drill Instructor. By the time Seattle rose into view, we decided to rent an apartment rather than stay in motels.

On our first day in town, Marty and Irene found a place south of Renton and bought a faded blue Volkswagen Microbus. Irene sounded like a commercial, bragging about superior German engineering. Marty was excited thinking now they really did look like Hippies. He painted a peace sign on the front.

We found a very nice two-bedroom at the Brittany Lane Apartments on 8th Avenue in Auburn. The complex had a pool, hot tub and sauna, exercise room and a pool table. Our unit was roomy, pleasant, and next-door to the property manager. Through him we learned about our neighbor on the other side.

"Mac is a good guy, young, single. He's a Washington State Trooper. He stays real busy. Gone most of the time."

That made us cringe but we were free to discuss things openly without Marty's constant nonsense. I was nearly settled when Bill called Linda and me into the kitchen.

"How's it coming, John?"

"I didn't have much to put away. This is a nice place. Feels like home already."

Linda agreed. "Nicer to be dealing with Marty and Irene on a limited basis."

I had to voice my concern. "That sounds good but we all know Marty would sell us out in a heartbeat to save his own skin. We've got to be careful." - J.E.S.

Nick and Paul both showed up at my door at the same time. Nick wanted to play Spades and Paul wanted to talk about a Guru who was coming to do a three day seminar.

"Shuffle up and deal."

CHAPTER FIFTY-FIVE

SHOCKER

I could smell the ocean air. It mixed with, and brought the scent of Eucalyptus through my open window. Ahh but no. I was still sleeping, and dreaming. But then the beams of sunlight finally crossed my walls and lit my face . . . I awoke.

I took a deep breath . . . no ocean air.

20th Journal Entry: Friday, August 24th, 1973 - 6:18 am

A few days later, Bill took Linda and me to meet his wife Mary, and daughter Donna. That was a shocker. I never knew Bill was married or had kids.

Mary didn't seem to mind that Bill was with Linda. In fact, everyone was getting along great. We sat in the kitchen of their small house near the town of Federal Way, munching on snacks and drinking iced tea. Eventually Bill took Mary and Linda into another room, which left me alone with Donna. I knew not to let on what we did for a living. I was to say we were in sales, but only if asked.

Donna was 15, attractive and easy to talk with, until Bill came back into the room. He mustered one of his glaring looks.

Donna's beautiful green eyes filled with mischief. "Pay no attention to daddy. I can watch out for myself."

Bill touched his daughter's shoulder, "I'm not worried about you honey. It's John I'm trying to protect. He's the best salesman I've ever had."

Donna and I talked about everything from the weather to her growing up in Oklahoma. Over all it was a pleasant visit. Something I wouldn't have expected. Later, when Donna began calling me, it was nice talking to a beautiful girl so close to my age.

Bill had a different opinion. "I don't think it's a good idea for you to be spending so much time with Donna, even if it's only on the phone."

One afternoon Bill called Linda and me to the dining room. "We're about to go big time."

Linda and I raised our eyebrows and gave each other a quick look. Linda giggled. Bill went on, "Time to get serious, my plan is for grownups only."

It was such a relief to be out from under the major stresses we'd just lived through. But one more look at Bill and we straightened up, put on sober faces, and gave him our undivided attention.

"Our next Appointment: the National Bank of Commerce."

We looked at each other again but this time we were poker faced and stunned.

"The branch is between Kent and Renton. I've been taking Polaroid's of the location, looking into the bank manager's habits and associations."

Bill laid out an intricate plan, brilliant in detail. Trying to absorb it all was like drinking from a fire hose. When stage one of our briefings was over, I took in a breath and let out a sigh.

"I figured that might be your reaction, John."

"It's not what I expected. My first question is: have you told Marty about this?"

"Don't plan to."

Part of me squirmed at the thought of switching to banks. But I was pleased to be once again spending time in preparation with Marty nowhere in the picture.

The next afternoon Linda and I played around with wardrobe possibilities. She put on a platinum wig, a heavy plaid coat with a big fur collar, and flashed a purse large enough to hide her pistol.

I looked at that thing and said, "Isn't that Ginny's purse?"

"It matches my outfit."

"I thought she wanted it back?"

"I'll buy her a dozen more."

I just laughed and watched in amazement as Linda made herself look 30-something. A sport coat and pair of horn rimmed glasses made me look older too. I took a lock of blonde hair and shoved it under my dark brown wig, with an inch or two sticking out. It had worked before with witnesses reporting a blond bandit in a dark wig. Linda had me install brown contacts.

With our costumes completed, Bill took us through the plan again. Satisfied that we were set and ready to go, we gave the familiar nod, signaling agreement.

Bill drove us to the parking lot of Valley General Hospital to find a car. I spotted an older white Falcon with a red hardtop. Within seconds I had it hotwired, Linda was in, and we were rolling. The Kent Branch of the National Bank of Commerce was less than half a mile away. Just before exiting the car, Linda grabbed my hand.

"Are you ready for this, bro?"

With a slight hesitation I answered, "You bet, Sis."

Once out of the car, tensions returned. Anxiety went straight to my gut and the pain was unbearable. For a second I thought I was going to pass out. I didn't want Linda to discover the real problem. I was scared sick. Panic was getting the best of me and I caught myself wanting to run. So while my fears were pulling me away, my need for approval pushed me on.

I told myself, if I can reach the handle of the bank door, I'd be okay. That became an icon, a point of decision. Until I reached it I could back out. But once I grabbed it, I was committed.

Walking across that parking lot seemed as if it took forever. I reached for the door handle, felt the hot metal in my palm. Anxiety and fear were instantly swept away. The decision had been made.

We were in. - J.E.S.

The guard stuck his hand into my cell and tossed a piece of paper my way. He disappeared without a word. The stench of ammonia was still fresh and the purple ink wasn't yet dry. It was a layout of the Unit and a diagram of the assault on Hernandez, complete with card tables and chairs. A dotted line showed the path the assailant took as he danced Hernandez around our table and then up against the wall.

I quickly got up and looked out to find the guard tossing papers into every cell. I sat back down and read.

> Place your name and number on top of the page and mark a clearly distinguishable X at the exact spot where you were during the attack.'
> Return this sheet to your Unit Officer before final rack in this evening.

I wrote across the bottom, 'I was in my cell and didn't see anything.' At the next rack I walked the paper back to the guard's office and dropped it in through the slot. Then exited the Unit and headed to the yard. I needed time to think.

I sat alone on the bench the furthest point away from the buildings as I could and turned to look out into the ring of trees. I was outraged at what had been done to Hernandez. I felt a mix of anger, sadness and fear. Knowing that at any moment, I could be Hernandez. Just knowing my life wasn't my own was hard to handle. My destiny was no longer in my hands. In order to survive, I had to watch my back, control my mouth and keep what I saw that day to myself. God help me.

A gentle breeze kicked up and I could smell the ocean air for real. I closed my eyes and took it in.

CHAPTER FIFTY-SIX

BRANCHING OUT

I sat there for several hours. I was only disturbed by the PA system calling out the ever punctual Count Time. I hurried back home just in time to rack in. Twenty minutes later I was out and went to see Paul.

"So who's this Guru?"

"His name is Maharishi Mahesh Yogi. He is the founder of Transcendental Meditation. Pretty much the top Guru in the world. He is also the Guru to The Beatles."

"So why would he be coming to a prison?"

"He believes that if he can just get 2% of the convicts meditating and following T.M., we can change the attitude of the whole prison, even everyone who works here."

"So when is he coming and how much of our time will he be spending with us?"

"Well don't sound too overly excited."

"Sorry"

"Next week. He will be here three days, but only needs a few hours with each person. Three hours in a classroom, then two hours one on one."

"Cool. When you sign up will you put me in also?"

"Consider it done."

I wasn't sure what to think about all of that but curiosity pushed me on.

21st Journal Entry: Friday, August 24th, 1973 - 6:15 pm

I'll have to say I looked spiffy, professional and confident as I walked toward the bank receptionist. On the corner of her mahogany desk the nameplate said, Margaret Allen.

"Good morning, Margaret."

With a sweet smile and lyrical voice she answered, "Good morning."

"I'd like to speak with your president, Mr. Bauer."

"Do you have an appointment?"

I almost laughed when she mentioned an 'Appointment.'

I gave her a quizzical look and asked, "Do I need one?"

"Not really."

"Is there a chance he might be free to see me now?"

"May I tell him the nature of your business?"

I leaned down and confided, "It's personal. Just tell him I'd like to see him this morning if he's available."

Margaret rose and motioned me to follow. We walked down a long, well carpeted hall to an office at the rear of the bank. She knocked.

Resounding from inside came a man's strong voice, "Please come in."

Margaret opened the door and announced, "This is your next appointment, Sir."

Mr. Bauer rose from behind a massive, manly-style command post. Margaret left and shut the door behind her.

"Mr. Bauer, this is a robbery."

As I continued speaking, I showed him I was armed.

"Please don't set off any alarms. Once we've secured the money, we'll be taking you with us. On the way out, if you give a signal to your security guard, teller . . . any one, I will kill you. If you want to live, Sir, do as I say. No alarms. No signals. Do you understand?"

Bauer stood behind his desk, looking stern and brave. Through his teeth clenched, he said, "To hell with you."

I took two steps back and pulled a sawed off shotgun from beneath my jacket and pointed it at his head.

"Are you ready to die?"

The tactic did exactly what it was designed to do. "Okay, okay. Please just don't hurt anyone."

I followed him to the lobby. He surprised me by yelling, "No alarms. They're taking me with them."

He looked at me. I nodded. "Go on, you're doing great."

"Ok, tellers, place all the money from your tills into bags, put the bags on the counter and step back. Oh, and no dye packs, please."

One by one they all complied.

Linda was standing near the middle of the lobby, with her hand on the gun inside her purse. An elderly man stood at the head of a teller line with two $100 bills on the counter. I gestured toward the bills.

"Sir, put those in your pocket."

The look he gave me was priceless.

As the tellers worked at emptying their tills, I began to explain our plan.

"We're taking your boss with us. If you want to see him alive again, wait until he returns. If we even see a cop car we will kill Mr. Bauer. Pray it doesn't happen."

I took Mr. Bauer by the arm. "Come with me, sir."

We walked back to the car. Linda got in. I quickly jumped into the driver's seat, leaving Mr. Bauer standing there alone and confused.

Linda scrunched down in her seat as we drove off. My last look in the rear view mirror showed Mr. Bauer frozen in place.

Linda admitted to being a bit puzzled. "You had me worried there for a moment. I didn't remember anything in the plan about hostages."

"I wasn't going to take him anywhere. I just figured it would buy us a few more minutes."

Back at the hospital I parked in a secluded area where Bill was waiting. We climbed into the trunk and headed home. We changed clothes somewhere between Kent and Auburn then crawled into the back seat. Bill asked how it went but we were on adrenaline overload. It took a few minutes before we could even talk.

Linda turned up the radio to check for news reports. We drove past the bank. The place was swarming with cops.

Back home we tallied. It was less than $4,000, but somehow it didn't seem to matter. We'd pushed our skills to the next level. The thought of our new trade brought with it a new thrill. In an instant, we had become Bank Robbers.

The next morning Bill flipped on my bedroom light. "Come out here, you've gotta see this."

I pulled on my jeans and stumbled to the dining room. Bill was sitting at the table. Big as life, right there on the front page, was a photo of Linda and me. The caption read: *Bonny & Clyde Style Hold Up.*

I hadn't realized that the bank camera could take such clear photos. There went our anonymity. Even though we were disguised, the thought of our faces out there for the entire world to see was scary. At the same time, it was thrilling.

We discussed laying low for a few days, but I felt more like pulling another job right away. Linda and Bill were just as stoked as I was.

Looking at the headlines brought back the emotions I felt before entering the bank, when I toyed with walking away. Fear seemed at odds with a new kind of pride. The long missed adrenaline rushes that had faded with each appointment had returned. We were back. - J.E.S.

I threw my journal back into my locker and just stood there. I could feel my heart pounding in my chest just. I closed my eyes and for a few minutes, I was back in Renton, just as if I was standing in the parking lot, trying to not throw up. I had to sit back down and hope the adrenaline would fade. I felt really good to have that rush again. At the same time I felt guilty about feeling good. How am I ever going to become a better man if I am so drawn to that feeling? Is there really a way to feel like that about something else? Something other than robbing banks?

I sat on the bed eating a meatloaf sandwich, which I paid a green dollar, for and tried to at least unwind enough to go to sleep. I had a feeling it wasn't going to happen.

CHAPTER FIFTY-SEVEN

HAPPY BIRTHDAY!

After battling my mind for sleep I think I finally dosed off around 3 am. I tossed around with terrifying dreams which I couldn't remember once I woke up. Not sure I could have slept past noon if it hadn't been for Nick pounding on my cell. With just one eye opened I jumped as I saw him toss something in the window. Instinctively I grabbed for it in self-defense. It was can of V8 . . . cold!

"Wow, where did you get this?"

"I have connections."

With a slightly tilted head and a look of 'cut the crap' I asked again, "Where?"

"Lerma is now working in the kitchen. He asked that I give it to you."

"Nice. So it's actually commissary, but cooled off in the fridges, right?"

"You got it."

I thanked him and sent him on his way. Two Hostess O's, a handful of Doritos and I was at it.

22nd Journal Entry: Saturday, August 25th, 1973 - 10:10 am

It was an unusually peaceful morning. No one was rushing to get anywhere or do anything in particular. Linda cooked breakfast while Bill and I sat with our morning coffee. On the table in front of us sat a box of birthday cards and the stack of pages that Bill had torn from various phone books from around the country. One by one we stuffed new twenties from the bank's bait pack into each card. A bait pack is a bundle of bills with red markings along one edge. Serial numbers from those bills are recorded and placed on a hot list.

"You're a savvy guy, John. You know what will happen when these twenties start showing up around the country."

I nodded. "I figure it's just another little something to confuse the Feds."

Bill smiled.

Of course we were wearing surgical gloves. As one last precaution we rubbed Vaseline over the area around the stamps so the postal cancellation wouldn't show where they were mailed from.

Happy Birthday . . . whoever you are. - J.E.S.

Crap. Another Shake down? I had just barely gotten into writing when the P.A. blared out, *Everyone rack in.*

It wasn't a shake down. About 15 minutes after all the doors came to a hammering halt, and a hush filtered through the unit, I looked out to see virtually everyone else doing likewise. We all just stood there waiting. Wondering.

Instead of the goon squad, two of the office staff entered and methodically began opening select doors. They handed a few garbage bags into each door and told the leaseholders to pack up their belongings. In all they walked out with 12 from our unit. A half hour later we were racked out. We found out 83 were gathered and released throughout the prison, everyone who was convicted of smuggling. Someone back East appealed the smuggling laws based on the "Do you have anything to declare" line. The Fifth Amendment says you cannot be compelled to incriminate yourself. So new laws immediately took effect, which outlawed the importation of items as opposed to criminalizing non-declaration. Sweet, every smuggler in the U.S. got a free walk.

Smart.

CHAPTER FIFTY-EIGHT

DEED IN A DIAPER BAG

Shits and grins were exchanged throughout the unit into the afternoon. Most were thrilled for the good fortune which had befallen our neighbors, but a few were outright pissed. Two were strutting around loudly proclaiming something about the white establishment and their racist moves to free only whites. As far as I saw, I think there were more Mexicans walked than whites or blacks.

The only other man upset about the whole thing had, perhaps the only legitimate complaint. One of the guys who walked, owed him green. Didn't say how much and no one was up to asking.

23rd Journal Entry: Saturday, August 25th, 1973 - 2:16 pm
During the next few months we stayed in the Seattle area, hitting more banks and an occasional grocery store. We used the *give me all your money* notes during a few Appointments. One by one, we tallied each take. The largest amounts were not from banks but grocery stores. I was amazed.

One afternoon, just for the heck of it, we decided to head to California. A young couple stood at the roadside, just South of Portland, hitchhiking with a baby. We stopped and picked them up, stroller, baggage and all. Once we exchanged names the conversation came easy.

"Actually, this is my brother. Mom sent him to rescue me and my baby."

Linda asked, "Rescue? From what?"

"I did a really stupid thing by running off with my boyfriend. When he found out I was pregnant, he dumped me.

Bill asked, "So, where are you heading?"

The brother answered, "Heading down to L.A. to try and find work so we can eventually make our way back home. . . . To New York."

Our conversation went on with more of their story. They were both in their early twenties, nice people, from a good home. They didn't have much money and were doing their best.

We turned around and headed back to Portland. Pulling into the airport, they were shocked to see we were going to buy them tickets home. While Linda held the baby, I went behind her and shoved $20,000 into the bottom of the diaper bag.

I can't explain my feeling as we waved good-bye. It really got to me, seeing how grateful they were for the tickets. Even the baby had a grin on her face. I would have loved to see their reaction once they found their buried treasure.

Having accomplished something good, we headed back to Seattle. - J.E.S.

I needed a break but it was a half hour before count so I just grabbed my headphones and kicked back. Midnight Ryder was blasting out. Great song. Then the D.J. announced, *"Today in Macon, Georgia, Allman Brothers drummer, Butch Trucks breaks his leg in an auto accident just a few yards from the exact spot where Duane Allman died in a motorcycle wreck two years ago."* Then he spun a song I had never heard of before but it was obviously The Allman Brothers. Nice.

"That was a brand new one by The Allman Brothers ironically released, today. Ramblin' Man."

Man I love those guys. I grabbed my dictionary to look up the word ironically. Interesting . . . here I am a writer and I don't know what ironic means.

Ironic.

Then the D.J. went on, *"Jerry Garcia of The Grateful Dead was arrested last Tuesday when Police search his car during a routine speeding ticket stop in New Jersey. They found a significant quantity of LSD."*

Ridin' that Train, high on Cocaine.

CHAPTER FIFTY-NINE

THE CATERING CAPER

Dinner sucked. Stew . . . sort of. Meat flavored gravy with peas & carrots. Soggy toast? Are you kidding me? For dinner? I didn't eat.

24ᵗʰ Journal Entry: Saturday, August 25ᵗʰ, 1973 - 8:12 pm

We kept Marty occupied with smaller jobs, just enough to keep him content. But as time rolled on, his animosity toward me grew. He was always looking for ways to show how much he hated me. Later, when the five of us were together, Marty began ignoring me. He acted like I wasn't even in the room with him. I finally asked Irene about it.

"Because Marty was in the Army, he thinks he should be in The Family and you should be answering to him. He's older than you."

But Marty failed on common sense and logic. Without that, he couldn't be trusted. The next day I mentioned Irene's comment to Bill and Linda. They just shook their heads.

Linda patted my shoulder. She was reminding me of my sister Evelyn again. "Be patient, bro. They'll be gone soon."

It was one of those lazy days that make you want to kick back and do nothing. An unexpected visitor showed up and destroyed the mood. It was Marty, with a plan that actually sounded like a substantial hit.

"I've been watchin' this catering outfit. They're runnin' 100 trucks. Late every afternoon they go to a little office and turn in their bags.

Three guys count the money and do book work 'n stuff. The back door is unlocked so drivers can get in."

Marty was becoming more animated the longer he talked. "All we have t'do is wait til the last guy reports in. We get the money and leave. Simple, right?"

Bill was intrigued and began calculating. "If each truck brings in at least $500, I estimate the take might be somewhere between 50 and 100K. It makes sense to hit on a Friday. Payday might bring in more cash."

We staked it out for a few days to watch before deciding to take the Appointment.

It was about seven in the evening when Marty and I entered the office. The three men checking in trucks were shocked to see us walk in with guns drawn. They were easily convinced to step into a closet and allowed themselves to be locked up.

We found two large canvas duffel bags. Each contained dozens of smaller zipper bags. Marty grabbed one, I took the other. As we approached the back door, I heard a muffled snicker coming from the closet.

I drove our stolen car through the gate, right past a slightly plump guard who was trying to run while yelling for us to stop. From the rear view mirror, I saw the poor guy fumbling to extract his weapon from its holster. It was comical

The exchange was easy. Lying there in Bill's trunk we had ourselves a good laugh talking about the three men locked in the closet. I marveled at how extremely well everything had gone. In fact, this was the first time in months that nothing had gone amiss during an Appointment involving Marty.

Almost.

Back home, we found every last bag empty. Not a dime. Nothing. Nada. That's when the snickering I'd heard coming from the closet made sense. They were probably still laughing.

We'd been had.

Not funny . . . at all. - J.E.S.

Just as the doors racked for the 10 pm count, Lerma ran to my cell and handed me a ham sandwich. Complete with all the trimmings.

"Hey Tejas, couldn't get chips but I grabbed some leftover peas & carrots too. Man they're good bro."

I tried not to laugh, or gag. I hate peas & carrots. But obviously, he loved them. I just smiled and thanked him. I watched as he entered his house then flushed the mushy veggies. The sandwich was amazing though.

Nice.

CHAPTER SIXTY

....

WILL STEAL, DETECTIVE

Paul showed up at my door just at the 8 am rack, "Come on, let's go to church."

"What the hell? Thought you were Buddhist? Or something?"

"Ha, who cares? Besides, it beats sitting in this smelly old house. Come on, grab a shirt and let's go."

"No thanks. I think I'll pass. I got a bunch more writing to do."

As he walked down the tier, I looked around my house and sniffed the air. Smells? I headed to the office for the cleaners, a bucket and a couple of old rags. The next hour was spent making sure Paul was joking. Walls, floor, toilet, sink, everything. Even the windows. Then I stripped the bed and flipped the mattress over. I gathered everything up just as the doors rolled open. The boss man gave me a chit to the laundry where I picked up fresh bedding and my shirts, Khakis, sox and underwear. By 9:30 I was sitting on a fresh bunk, journal in hand.

25th Journal Entry: Sunday, August 26th, 1973 - 9:33 am

One morning while Bill, Linda and I were sitting in a small diner in Renton. Bill spotted an article in the paper about a grocery store in Belleview that had been robbed over the weekend. It said the bandits got away with an undetermined amount of cash and checks. Bill wrote down the names of the store manager and detective in charge.

After finishing our meal, we went shopping and bought Bill a sharp suit and a nice tweed hat. Linda fixed him up with a false moustache and horn rimmed glasses. His wallet contained a badge that he'd gotten from who knows where. Bill entered the store featured in the article, asked for the manager by name. When he introduced himself as one of the detectives assigned to the case, the manager led Bill to his office.

"Where do you keep the money?"

The manager didn't hesitate to show him.

That's when Bill calmly drew his .357 and said, "Bag up the cash, all of it."

The manager was shocked but did as he was told.

"Now, carry it and escort me to the main entrance."

As they walked, Bill gave more instructions, "Wait five minutes, call my office and tell them Detective Will Steal just left with some new evidence."

I'm not sure if Bill really gave that outrageous name or if he was B-S-ing. Either way we thought it was pretty funny.

The bag contained $30,000. - J.E.S.

I was hoping to run over to J-Unit but the noon count was taking longer than usual. A bad spades player over there owed me $10 commissary from last month. I stood waiting at my door, peering out, then came the call, *'Count is not clear. Repeat, not clear. Stay in your cells and come to the door for a standing count.'* All of the doors opened and everyone stood at the threshold as officers counted again.

Escape.

That was the only reason they ever ran a Standing Count. Fifteen minutes later we were told to back in, and the doors reclosed. We waited. Then we did it all again. Not a glitch. For real someone was missing and two recounts couldn't rectify it. Finally we were cut loose at 2:10 pm.

CHAPTER SIXTY-ONE

UNINVITED MESSENGER, UNWELCOME MESSAGE

I ran to J-Unit and was met at the door by my debtor with a box of commissary and a bunch of apologies for taking a month to pay. I just smiled and said, "No worries. We should do it again sometime. Give you a chance to win back your box."

I ran back to my house just in time to make the rack. I love Hostess O's.

26th Journal Entry: Sunday, August 26th, 1973 - 1:33 pm

A few nights later, everything was ready for grilling steaks. We were looking forward to an evening meal and the final discussion concerning an Appointment planned for the next day.

Marty showed up uninvited and drunk. Irene looked irritated. Bill was annoyed with him but hid his displeasure. Typical of Bill, he simply pulled a couple more steaks from the fridge. Then he quietly said to Linda and me, "Tomorrow is off. What the hell, might as well make a party of it. "

Bill called Mary and Donna to join us. The evening seemed to drag on forever. I found myself just wishing it was over.

Then Marty made an obnoxious observation, "I have a wife, Bill has a wife and a girlfriend, but John doesn't have anyone."

Donna jumped to my defense, "Yes he does. I'm his girlfriend."

That shocked me, and Bill. But it didn't stop Marty. For the next couple of hours he was on an endless rant. Finally, he passed out. Irene took him home.

All was quite. We sat for a while in dead silence, until Bill finally spoke. "You know, eventually we're going to have to kill that son of a bitch."

I had never heard Bill speak with such anger. Shock turned to surprise, as a part of me was actually pleased with Bill's statement. I also wondered if I might one day provoke Bill's anger. Neither Linda nor I said anything. Instead, we called it a night.

Unable to sleep, I was realizing, for the first time, I wanted out. I wanted to leave. Being accepted by Bill and Linda, as a trusted member of The Family, was satisfying. Being close friends was wonderful. Our activities were thrilling. But I couldn't shake the growing fear of getting caught or being shot. I loved Bill. He was my Dad, my role model and mentor, but I was also a little afraid of him. The 99% of me that needed his love was being overpowered by the 1% that thought, *if I walk away, am I dead?*

Trapped. That was it. I felt trapped. Marty's words stirred my emotions, 'But John doesn't have anyone.' He was actually right. I needed someone I could trust with my fears, someone to assure me I'd be all right, like Nanny used to. Thoughts of Donna came rushing in. She was a friend. But could I trust her? She had no idea we were bandits.

Somehow I managed to fall asleep. By morning I was in a better frame of mind and glad Bill had postponed the Appointment. - J.E.S.

As the 4:00 pm count cleared, Nick was begging me to join him to take on the Borovsky brothers in a three game set of pinochle. Valery and Boris were busted for illegally importing diamonds into the country. I had never heard of a man named Valery and found it amusing. He didn't. Nick called them Val and BB so I did too. We beat them two straight. But it seemed like forever. Val spent the whole time bragging about the superiority of chess players in Russia.

"You know, they even teach chess in schools back home."

Perhaps they should teach pinochle.

CHAPTER SIXTY-TWO

THE OFFERING

I kept winning so much commissary I was running out of room in my locker. Wasn't a big fan of Ginger Ale, but Oreo's and Camels?

Nice.

27th Journal Entry: Sunday, August 26th, 1973 - 7:32 pm

One morning without notice, Bill said, "Linda, John, let's go to Disneyland."

My answer wasn't very enthusiastic, "Sure, why not?"

Bill invited Marty and Irene to go to Southern California with us. He hoped they'd be attracted to the free love, hippie scene and lured into staying.

The next morning, before leaving, we went ahead with the grocery store hit. There I was again, with more money than I knew what to do with . . . or where to hide it.

Early Sunday morning, our two-car convoy had made it to a cozy mom and pop diner somewhere in Oregon. We were eating steak and eggs. Bill was reading the local paper.

"Hey, listen to this. A little church has been fund raising to buy the building they're leasing. The truth is they don't even have enough to pay the rent."

Marty and Irene responded with blank stares. Linda and I weren't surprised when Bill left the table. Within moments the cashier handed Bill a phone directory.

Marty watched as Bill and I counted $50,000 into a grocery bag. We drove to the church, placed the bag on the front steps and took a position close enough to observe.

Marty just shook his head. "You guys can give away money if you want, but I'm not that foolish. In fact I think I just found 50k sitting on a step down the street."

Bill glared with murder in his eye. "Don't even think about it Marty or I'll shoot you dead on the spot."

Everyone gasped. Bill smiled and started laughing. We all joined in, but Linda and I knew he wasn't joking.

A short time later the minister arrived, picked up the bag, unlocked the door and walked inside. Moments later he came rushing out, looking around to see who may have left the bag. He didn't notice us watching from the car. He looked up at the sky, obviously praying.

That was so cool.

We took Marty and Irene to their Van and continued on. - J.E.S.

Paul stopped by just before last count. "You ready for tomorrow morning?"

"What's up?"

"Maharishi Mahesh Yogi. Remember?"

"That's tomorrow? What time?"

"Eight o'clock, bright and early."

Surrendering, I mumbled, "See you then."

Wasn't really looking forward to it, but I promised Paul so . . . I was in. I decided to call it a night and just kick back and doze off with my headphones.

I nodded off to Deep Purple's newest . . . *Smoke on the Water.*

CHAPTER SIXTY-THREE

MISTAKEN IDENTITY

I was up and ready. Not knowing what to expect but I decided to go at it with an open mind. Paul showed up and we headed to the classrooms. After filling out forms with name, age, race, number, home town . . . etc, we sat on the floor in a cross legged position called *'the Lotus'* for well over two hours just listening to the Guru chant and meditate. He talked about emptying ourselves of thought and emotion.

He then began talking about mantras and the power of meditation and prayer. Most were dismissed to smaller rooms where some of his helpers entered and shut the doors. Paul and I stayed with the group in the main room. The Guru spoke briefly about secrecy and how our mantras would lose their power if we ever said it out loud or write it down. We were to chant it in our minds only, and to never tell anyone our mantra. Each mantra was unique and given by god especially for us. I thought . . . *cool*.

Then one by one he sat in front of each one of us and whispered into our ears. He came to me and gently said, "A-em". I repeated it in my mind . . . over and over.

Once he passed everyone in our room, he asked us to remain in the lotus position for the next 30 minutes. He then told us, "Empty your minds of everything sacred and unsacred. Nothing except your mantra." With final instructions to chant 20 minutes each morning and evening, we were dismissed.

28th Journal Entry: Monday, August 27th, 1973 - 1:35 pm

As we approached Ukiah, it had been six hours since breakfast. We stopped for lunch. Bill, as usual, grabbed a newspaper. Suddenly he hushed us all and read.

"Local man convicted of robbing Wards Drug Store is sentenced to 20 years in prison."

The guy in the paper looked shockingly like Marty. He and Irene began to laugh, but Bill wasn't amused.

"We can't just stand by and let this happen."

Bill motioned us out and we drove to the drugstore, where he instructed Marty to put on his wig and headband.

"Hold the newspaper against your chest so we can see the headlines."

Bill took several pictures with a Polaroid camera until he had one that clearly showed Marty's face, the newspaper, and the store sign. Back at the coffee shop, Linda wrote a note stating they had convicted the wrong man. We mailed the note and photo to the newspaper and continued south. - J.E.S.

So I thought I'd try the meditating thing. I sat on my bed and began repeating the mantra over and over in my mind. *A-em . . . A-em. . . .* Actually it sounded more like what you say when you're talking time. Like 9:00 am.

After a while it all became a blur. He never said how fast to say it or how slow. So for a while it was like A-em, A-em, A-em, A-em, A-em . . . . Then A-em . . . A-em . . . A-em . . . A-em. Neither seemed to do anything for me.

I don't know. I really felt I did better with the Buddhist chant 'Nam Myōhō Renge Kyō' that Paul taught me. While chanting I began to draw a Buddha sitting in the lotus position holding a flower and a pot of incense beside him. I drew A-em, A-em, A-em, coming out of his mouth. As soon as I did I realized I had violated the code and my mantra would lose its power. I thought, *Oh well. . . . Didn't seem to work anyway.*

CHAPTER SIXTY-FOUR

COURT DATE

Mail call. Another letter from Nanny. She sent pictures of some of my cousins. She also wanted to know why I stopped writing to my Aunt Toni. I began to think, *I am different from most others in here. They may like lots of letters but truthfully, I don't. Every time I get a letter I feel obligated to write back. There isn't anything worth writing about in here so after a while all my letters sound alike. Same thing over and over. Then I think they feel obligated to write back to me. So we do it again. They tell me how great it is out there and I tell them how bad it is in here.*

I hate it.

29th Journal Entry: Monday, August 27th, 1973 - 7:05 pm

Two days later instead of Disneyland, we were resting and recuperating in the cabins at Guerneville. Bill and I talked over breakfast about going fishing. Linda was looking through her calendar.

"Oh, no, John's court date in Dallas is tomorrow."

We grabbed our things, loaded the cars and took off. It soon became obvious we couldn't drive the distance. I'd have to fly. We made one stop before heading to the airport.

We pulled into Hayward California as the sun was just breaking the Eastern sky. The bank was situated in a strip mall adjacent to a grocery store. The plan was: hit the bank, exit the front door, make a quick right, enter the grocery store, hit the office and leave by the back door.

While we had occasionally hit two Appointments on the same day, two at the same Venue was a first.

With the newspaper photo of the man wrongly convicted in the Wards robbery, we decided using Marty as the lead at the grocery store was a good idea. Two robberies with two different leads would equal two sets of descriptions. It could throw the Police way off. Who'd be crazy enough to do such a thing? Investigators would have to be confused . . . at least for a while.

Linda and Irene would create confusion by blocking anyone from leaving after us.

It was a little past 11 when we stepped from the heat and humidity outside, into the air-conditioned lobby of the Hayward branch of Wells Fargo Bank.

In seconds, Marty took over the lead, pulling his gun and announced, "This is a robbery,"

I was speechless but pulled my pistol too and made everyone back away from the counter. Marty went from one teller cage to the next gathering the contents of cash drawers. I reminded him not to take dye packs or the last $20 from any drawer.

I looked around in time to see the manager standing near the open vault with a large bag in his hands. I pointed my gun at him and instructed, "Bring me the bag."

"It's only receipts." He opened the bag to show me and said, "The $20's rack is open."

I hesitated, wondering why he'd want to tell me that, but quickly entered the vault with him. Several large bricks of twenties were stacked in a rack behind an open door. Knowing I couldn't carry more, I only took three bricks, which filled the bag. I returned to the lobby and glanced back just in time to see the manager take another brick and place it in a file cabinet.

Across the room, Marty grabbed a teller. "We're taking her with us."

Marty's arm was around the woman's neck, holding her close to his side. I watched in disgust as he lowered his hand to grab her breast. Pulling the horrified lady with him, Marty backed to the door, yelling, "John let's go!"

For a moment I thought, *just shoot him right here.* I was furious because he yelled out my name. Mostly, I was outraged at the site of him fondling that terrified woman.

As we backed out the door Marty grabbed the woman's hair and pulled her to him. He kissed her on the neck then shoved her back into the lobby so hard she fell.

Following Marty out the door, I insisted, "Forget the store. There's no time."

He ignored me, entered, and headed to the office. I waited by the front door, watching for cops to arrive at the bank. Marty showed up with a bag filled with cash. Together we headed out the back. No one followed us. Linda and Irene performed as planned. By the time we made it to Bill's car the wail of sirens was coming closer.

It was as freaky as it gets. Cops everywhere. Bill saw the girls leaving the store as he slowly drove away. I removed my dark glasses, moustache and beard, placed them in my hat and bundled everything together in my coat.

I was in hyper mode, mad as hell, and could hardly wait to unload the details of what Marty had done. The guy was a maniac, out of control and dangerous. He was going to get us all locked up or killed. I wanted him gone.

By the time we reached the interstate, the girls had caught up with us. Once in Sacramento we headed to the airport only to find I'd missed the last flight to Dallas. The ticket agent let us know there was an early morning flight out of Reno. We grabbed a few burgers. Linda took her place next to Bill and we drove to Reno with Marty and Irene behind us.

I tried to be calm as I told Bill how Marty hijacked the Appointment. "He grabbed a teller and started yelling, 'we're taking her with us,' and called me by name. I could have shot him."

When I discribed how Marty had mistreated the woman, I thought Bill was going to pull over and confront Marty right there on the highway. Linda talked him down.

"John, Linda, I promise you, when we get this court thing out of the way, we're going to Disneyland and Marty will be history."

"Bill, there's something else."

"Like what?"

"The bank manager was a little too helpful. Without my asking he led me into the vault, with bricks of twenties. And, get this, he took one of the bricks and put it in a file cabinet."

"That's easy. The robbery was a great cover so he could steal a brick for himself."

I'd never thought of that. - J.E.S.

I was just getting ready for bed when I heard the alarm blaring in the camp. I looked out my window. The sky behind the industry buildings had become bright orange. Fire had consumed several acres around the camp. I grabbed my mirror and watched as fire trucks rolled past the gun towers toward the fire. Two long lines of inmates from the camp were sitting beside the road that encircled the prison and several guards stood by and keyed microphones on their radios. I sat for hours just watching.

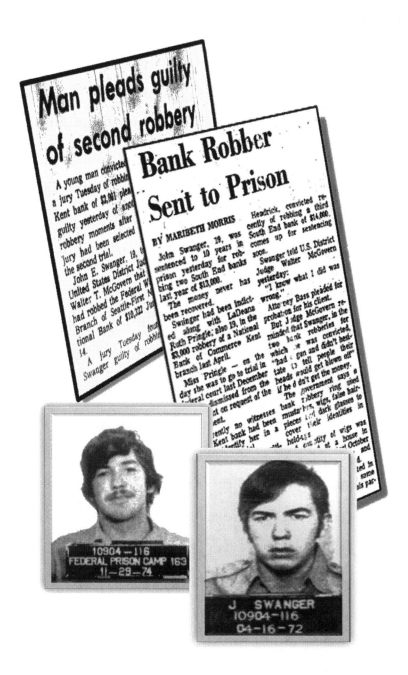

Man pleads guilty of second robbery

A young man convicted
a jury Tuesday of robbin
Kent bank of $9,961 plea
guilty yesterday of anol
robbery moments after
jury had been selected
the second trial.

John E. Swanger, 19, t
United States District Jud
Walter T. McGovern that
had robbed the Federal W
Branch of Seattle-First N
tional Bank of $10,322 Ju
14.

A jury Tuesday foun
Swanger guilty of robbin

Bank Robber Sent to Prison

BY MARIBETH NORRIS

John Swanger, 19, was
sentenced to 10 years in
prison yesterday for rob-
bing two South End banks
last year of $13,000.

The money never has
been recovered.

Swanger had been indict-
ed along with LaDeana
Ruth Pringle; also 19, in the
$3,000 robbery of a National
Bank of Commerce Kent
branch last April.

Miss Pringle — on the
day she was to go to trial in
federal court last December
was dismissed from the
nt on request of the
ent.

ently no witnesses
Kent bank had been
dentify her in a

Hendrick, convicted re-
cently of robbing a third
South End bank of $14,000,
comes up for sentencing
soon.

Swanger told U.S. District
Judge Walter McGovern
yesterday:

"I know what I did was
wrong."

Attorney Bass pleaded for
probation for his client.

But Judge McGovern re-
minded that Swanger, in the
two bank robberies for
which he was convicted,
"had a gun and didn't hesitate to tell people their
heads would get blown off"
if he'd d't get the money.

The government says a
bank robbery ring used
mustaches, wigs, false hair-
pieces and dark glasses to
cover their identities in
held-ups.

A quantity of wigs was
at a house in
t October
and
ted in
same
his par-

Bandit Robs Food Store

A small man believed to be in his early 20s robbed the Safeway Chapel Wednesd...

Police tered the walked cage an manager during money change."

The g a .38 cal mat su...

$58,000 Taken Robbery f Grocery

armed men held up the r, Friday afternoon and with $8,350 dropped off at store minutes earlier by an red car.

lice said their getaway car...

Food Store Robbed

Fort Worth Bureau of The News

FORT WORTH—Two youthful bandits sprayed tear gas on clerks and shoppers while taking an undetermined amount of cash in a robbery of Strick's nia.

Bonnie and Clyde-like holdup nets $2,991

By Marlowe Churchill

A man and his stylishly dressed platinum-blonde accomplice robbed the National Bank of Commerce at East Valley Highway and South 180th Street between Kent and Ren-

belt. He told Bauer not to set off the bank alarm and handed a white cloth bag to Bauer. "Fill the bag up and nobody will get hurt. We are taking you with us," the robber told Bauer.

The Daily Review

Vol. 78—No. 226   783-4111   *Serving Southern Alameda County*   Hayward, California, Friday, May 21, 1971   10 Cents   40 pages

$11,500 taken in robbery

HAYWARD — Two armed robbers failed to get into the vault, but fled with more than taken from tellers d

the two employes were too frightened to work the com binations in the vault, and the robber stalked away after snatching an obscenity.

"We are going to take you with us until we get away and to police we are following," one

THE TWO FLED as fast through a grocery store next door to the bank.

One man was described as

Bank robbers get $25,000 in Magnolia

Two men with pistols escaped with more than $25,- to about 10:30 a.m. today er robbing the Magnolia nch of the National Bank ommerce, 3400 W. Mc St.

e said the men, 35 to the money from three ages before fleeing r-model car later doned near Fort

t Robbed; en Escape

one carrying a 12 un, held up the Safe market, 2303 Lake th an undetermined money.

F. T. Farmer told of the men remained store while the other at gunpoint to han from the

Bandits Hold Up Mart Grocery

bandits held up A-Mart ry, West Davis at Plym at 9:40 p.m. Saturday, four victims in a cooler escaped with a grocery ull of greenbacks.

said clerk Leonard rds left the locked store as marched back in at oint by two strangers 25 and 30,

Lompoc
California
1971 - 1975

CHAPTER SIXTY-FIVE

BUNDLES & BADGES

❖ ❖ ❖

The smell of smoke had me coughing and wiping my eyes all night. Not much rest. Finally, unable to deal with it any longer, I got up. It was 5:15. Only then did I notice my cell door was locked open. I looked out to find they all were. Confused I walked down to the ground floor where I found several inmates in the TV room. The Unit Hack said, "Since K-Unit is the closest to the camp and the smoke is still pretty thick, the A.W. gave us a reprieve for the night. Everyone can just hang out."

"Any chance I could head to the library?"

"Nope. Not til the morning count clears."

I ran back up and grabbed my journal then sat watching a rerun of the very last episode of The Mod Squad. I was in love with Peggy Lipton.

30th Journal Entry: Tuesday, August 28th, 1973 - 6:26 am

In the back seat, I had just enough room to change into a suit. As we pulled into the airport, Linda stuffed bundles of twenties into my pockets. I had no idea how much I was carrying. She wanted to make sure I had enough.

I had less than 30 minutes to catch my flight. Walking, perhaps faster than I should, I couldn't avoid several badges standing around a large piece of equipment.

One of the officers motioned me forward. I asked about the machine. They told me it could reveal metal objects such as guns and knives. As I stepped forward I began wondering, *what if it can also detect large amounts of cash?*

While I appeared composed on the outside, inside I was scared to death. I thought; *Oh crap, I'm going to jail.*

I walked through the detector and the officer said, "Thanks, have a nice flight."

I tried to act cool and continued to my gate. Once on the plane I settled, exhausted, into my fist class leather seat and ordered a Vodka Collins. I quickly downed my drink and fell asleep.

The stewardess woke me from my two-hour nap. "We're about to land, Sir. Please return your seat to the upright position."

I took a cab to a hotel about five miles from the courthouse. I must have set a record for showering, shaving and dressing in suit and tie.

The cab driver plowed as fast as he dared through insane Dallas traffic. I tried to gather my thoughts as the driver earned a good tip by arriving at 4:30 pm as planned.

McCullough was waiting on the courthouse steps. I followed him to the restroom. After checking the stalls, we locked the door. I began handing him bundles of cash. After counting out $6000, I realized it barely put a dent in the stash I was carrying. One by one we tore off the paper bands and flushed them.

McCullough said, "I know the cash you guys bring is either headed to the bank or coming from one. Something looks different this time, right?"

I just smiled and nodded my head.

"Don't tell me. I don't want to know anything else."

McCullough unlocked the door and motioned me through.

When the Judge entered the courtroom, he didn't waste any time giving us a *show me the money look*. McCullough handed him $1500 and another $50 for the court recorder.

The Judge passed $500 to the District Attorney and said, "I guess we need to make this thing legal. For the charge of Minor Joy Riding, Defendant John Edward Swanger pleads guilty. The fine to be $1500."

A transcript was typed. The Judge handed me a paper to sign. We went upstairs to visit the cashier. One set of fingerprints and two photos later, I was free to go. I thanked McCullough and left the building.

I looked for a cab and found none. I chose to walk down the street just because it felt good to be free of my fears. I did not go to jail.

Walking on, I noticed, Dallas looked different. Thoughts of my family rushed in. *They don't even know I exist.* Walt's words condemned me again, *When are you gonna stop screwin' around and start makin' something of yer life?* The sense of loneliness was terrible.

My thoughts shifted to the present. *I could stay and let the city swallow me up or I could go back to being a bandit. What should I do?*

I answered myself out loud, "It really doesn't matter; who cares anyway?"

For a moment I let myself grieve at the thought of Mom. One thing was sure, I knew Bill and Linda cared. They'd proven it by the many things they'd done for me, the kind way they treated me.

But, I was in Dallas, again. Even with all the memories I tried to put behind me, this was still the closest thing to home. Dallas represented a childhood filled with rough circumstances and tons of pain, over which I'd had no control. Those memories came at me like rockets, hard and fast, dragging me down.

I walked aimlessly, past high-rise office buildings and upscale stores. The leather soles on my shiny new shoes made an unfamiliar noise against the concrete sidewalk. As I passed a huge store window, I saw the image of a prosperous looking young man who could have been on his way to a fancy office somewhere in the city. Who would have guessed the man in that reflection, wearing a $500 suit, had once been that poor Swanger kid?

During the long cab ride to Mom and Walt's house, the driver tried to engage me in small talk. My limited response let him know this would be a quiet ride. I wasn't all that sure what going home really meant.

The Cabbie stopped at the curb and I froze. He pulled just enough past the house that I could see into the back yard. There sat Tammy, playing. She looked so innocent. Somehow that innocence screamed out to me. For the first time ever I felt utter remorse. I realized that I had walked away from my last ounce of innocence and I could never go back.

I no longer belonged in Dallas, or anywhere for that matter. When I'd been given a choice, I had crossed the line, stepped over a threshold that couldn't be reversed.

The driver's voice startled me. "Hey Buddy, meter's still running. You gonna' pay up?"

"I changed my mind. Take me to Love Field." - J.E.S.

I could have stayed in the library writing, but a Biology class was starting and they had enough overheads and flip charts to keep me distracted all day, so I returned to my 'Smokey Smokehouse'. Our doors were still locked open. The Hack said they would remain that way at least until the 10:00 pm count.

Paul stopped by and we talked about the books on Buddhism he had given me the week before. I really hadn't had much time to get into them but promised him I would as soon as I finished the journal for Dr. Bliss and Kelly.

He then happened to notice my Buddha drawing and looked shocked. "What the heck is this?"

"Yeah I know. I'm not supposed to write my mantra down. I messed up. I didn't even think about it until it was already done."

"Exactly. But . . . well to be honest with you . . . It's the same mantra they gave me."

"Are you kidding? So much for everyone gets a unique mantra, just for them. Given by god? Well that's a joke. No wonder it didn't work."

"Wow Tex, I'm bummed."

"Tell me about it Pablo. Believing is one thing. Believing a lie is another."

"Nam Myōhō Renge Kyō?"

"Nam Myōhō Renge Kyō, brother."

CHAPTER SIXTY-SIX

....

NOWHERE TO GO AND FOREVER TO GET THERE

We hung out and talked about faith and religion for the next three hours. I told him about my grandmother and how she used to take me to church with her. He told me how he had come to believe that the earth was the god of all and we are to serve and not abuse her.

"Her?"

"Yeah her. I think the earth is called her because of the term 'Mother Earth.' But either way we need to nurture the earth as the earth nurtures us."

"What about everything else? If the earth is our god, then who is god over everything else? Like the planets, the sun, stars? And the Universe?"

"Don't know. I haven't got that far yet."

"Well I'm not so much interested in 'our mother, the earth', but really want to find out who is the mother (or father) of the earth."

Paul laughed "Whatever,"

31st Journal Entry: Tuesday, August 28th, 1973 - 4:42 pm

Scanning the departures boards, it showed the next flight to Seattle wouldn't be until the following morning. I had no schedule to keep and no desire to be in Dallas. Approaching the counter I said, "A one way ticket to Chicago, please." When we landed at O'Hare, I walked from the plane to the ticket counter. "When does the next flight leave for New York?"

"Not til midnight, sir."

"How about Atlanta?"

The next three days took me to Milwaukee, Baltimore, Nashville and Orlando. All for no good reason other than I didn't really want to be anywhere in particular. I was tired. But I was running on empty so I headed to another ticket window. . . .

"Seattle."

I took a taxi to our apartment, not knowing if Bill and Linda would even be there. They weren't. I lay down for a short nap. Twenty-four hours later I filled a bowl with Wheaties and about lost it when the milk came out of the carton in one big lump. I flushed the disgusting mess away and headed to the store. My intent was to buy a few groceries and go home. But the smell of bacon detoured me to a nearby diner. Breakfast was decent however my thoughts were anything but. I couldn't stop thinking about Marty. I was both angry and appalled, recalling how he mistreated the teller by fondling her as he drug her around the bank. I was honestly at the point where I thought I could kill him. My only consolation was I hoped to never see him again.

I sat for hours at home, drinking coffee and trying to sort out my life. During the past several months, each Appointment had brought me closer to calling it quits. It was time to tell Bill and Linda I wanted out. I needed out. I hated the idea of disappointing them. My thoughts were colliding with each other. In the end, I'd have to find the right time to tell them.

A few days later, I happened to looking out the window when Bill and Linda drove up in a new, powder blue Cadillac. I met them at the door. "Hey, nice wheels."

Bill answered, "She talked me into it."

Linda laughed. "We bought it in California. I told Bill it would be nicer to drive home. So we just meandered up the coast along my favorite highways. You know how I love the 101 and the 1."

Bill added, "There's a lot of beautiful scenery between San Francisco and Seattle. But enough about that. How did it go in court?"

"It's all taken care of, thanks to you getting me there on time and . . . well, thanks doesn't really cover it, for everything you two have done."

Bill interrupted my blubbering. "Hey, Linda made it happen. I was ready to go fishing, remember?" Emotions were getting pretty sappy til Bill gave me a hardy slap on the back. "Come on John; give me a hand with the luggage."

It took two trips to unload the massive trunk. Bill did all the talking. "Linda did a little shopping on the way home. That's the only problem with taking a road trip."

I had to comment on that one. "Was buying a new car part of a little shopping?"

Inside, Linda did what she does best: made coffee.

"Sit down boys. Time for a break."

We looked at each other through the steam rising from our mugs. I spoke first. "Glad you're home. I really missed you guys."

Bill looked at me with his eyes of steel, "I think I missed you too."

We all smiled. Everything seemed okay but I knew something wasn't right. Then everything went quiet. Linda saw the questioning look on my face and I saw the disappointment on hers. "I'm sorry John. Bill and I tried but the Disneyland, California hippie plan didn't work. Marty and Irene are still with us."

Resentment over Marty's latest stunts boiled up in me. I felt my anger rise and my heart sink. "I'm not sure I can take any more of him."

Bill offered the only solution. "I feel the same way, but let's shelve it until we can think things through."

Linda came to my aid. "Come on Bill, how many more times are we going to keep putting off this Marty problem?" - J.E.S.

I decided to knock off early and write back to Nanny.

> *Nanny,*
>
> *I received the letter from you with pictures of Annette and Johnny and everybody else. Thank you for the pictures and thanks for writing.*
>
> *There isn't much going on around here. They had a fire in the camp (outside the Joint) and they were fighting it all night long.*
>
> *You asked me in the letter why I stopped writing Toni. Well, she stopped writing me. I figured since Rusty was back with her and she owned the beauty shop, she probably didn't have much free time. So I just thought she was too busy to write. I didn't want to write her and make her feel obligated to write back.*
>
> *I do appreciate her writing and sending money when she does. I just thought she was too busy. I will write her tomorrow.*
>
> *How are things with you? Are you working hard? When do you get to take a vacation? They ought to let you take a couple of months off. You work too hard.*
>
> *Did you know I have been in for almost two years now? The 6ᵗʰ of October will make two years. In another year and a half I can go to the parole board.*
>
> *Well I'm going to go to sleep now. I will write again later. Be Cool*
>
> *John*

CHAPTER SIXTY-SEVEN

OVER THE EDGE

❖ ❖ ❖

I woke up and began exploring the odd shapes on the wall that the sunlight made as it filtered through the bars of my window. I sat there for a couple of hours just thinking. I knew I was approaching an emotionally difficult part of my story. Putting it into words would be hard, not just what happened, but how I felt. Reliving it would be tough, but I was committed. I had to continue.

32nd Journal Entry: Wednesday, August 29th, 1973 - 8:48 am
Monday - June 14th 1971

One of the countless things Bill taught me was the difference between supper and dinner. I'd always thought dinner was also called lunch and supper was the evening meal. But Bill said supper was mostly about eating and dinner was more of a spectacle. It was about entertaining. He said, "Supper is just a meal, but dinner? Well that's an event."

Coming back home from an errand, the wonderful smell of sautéed onions and mushrooms let me know we were having dinner. Bill was prepping the grill for steaks. I found Linda in the kitchen, poking a fork into a boiling pot of corn on the cob. A bowl of steaming mashed potatoes sat next to a pan of burgundy gravy. The sights and smells before me would have made any chef jealous.

"Linda, this is looking like a feast. What's the occasion?"

"I'll let Bill tell you."

"Okay, so what's up Bill?"

"Marty and Irene are coming over tonight to discuss final plans for tomorrow."

My first thought? *What a way to ruin a good meal.* "Bill, wasn't this supposed to remain within The Family?"

"Well, I've been thinking, we need more than the three of us on this one." Bill went on to justify the evening meeting. "We need to go over the plans, make sure everyone is comfortable with their duties, finish off with a storyboard, and walk through the sequence on paper."

That didn't help. Having Marty and Irene invade our evening was unexpected and I wanted to know why. I tried to keep my voice calm. "After the way things went down last time, I'm not sure I'm ready for another round with Marty."

Bill remained quiet and stirred the charcoal before giving me an answer. "We do one last job, pack up, head south, and not tell Marty we're going."

For a moment I wanted desperately to spill the beans on what I'd been wrestling with. No, this was not the time. Instead, I replied, "That's cool."

When he arrived, it didn't take a psychic to discern Marty had been drinking. You could smell him from across the room. Within seconds, he was leaning on Bill.

"You know I should take the lead tomorrow. You know I can do it."

After listening to as much as he could stand and more than I could stomach, Bill ended the tirade. "Nobody's taking the lead. Tomorrow's Appointment is cancelled. Marty, you know the rules. We don't allow drinking within 24 hours of a job."

Marty laughed but Irene pleaded, "We've got to do it. We need the money."

Irene wasn't upset with us but she was furious with Marty for breaking the rules. Bill poured us all a glass of Merlot. Linda called Mary and Donna to join us.

Dinner seemed to drag on forever. Though having Donna there helped make the evening tolerable. Nevertheless Marty soon started in again.

"Hey, Bill, are you in love with Linda or Mary?"

Immediately the room became dead silent. We all wondered who would dare speak next. Personally I was curious to know what Bill's answer would be. He didn't say anything, just broke into a rather labored laugh and poured another glass of wine.

Linda served dessert before Irene was even finished with her steak. Marty had wolfed down his meal and whined, for all to hear, that he wanted to watch TV.

Bill had had enough. He whispered into Irene's ear, "Finish your dinner quickly and take him home."

Twenty minutes later, they were finally out the door.

Much relieved, Bill and Linda settled onto the brown leather couch and sipped cognac while Mary nursed a cup of coffee in the matching chair.

Donna and I decided to take a quick swim. The pool was only about a 100 yards away. It had closed at 10:00, but we figured no one would mind. After quietly thrashing around in the cool water for half an hour, I climbed out to grab a towel.

Suddenly a strange feeling hit me . . . like I knew something was wrong. The hair stood up on the back of my neck. A quick motion to Donna got her out of the pool.

"What's wrong?"

I held a finger to my lips and whispered, "We need to get back to the apartment."

She followed close, but asked again, "What's wrong?"

"I'm not sure. I just know something isn't right."

The sliding glass door was shut but the curtains were parted. I peeked in. Marty had returned and was sitting on the couch, waiving two sheets of paper in the air and talking to Bill. I tried to catch a few words. Marty was explaining something. When he finally settled down, I saw the glint of blue steel. It was his pistol, resting on his lap.

I froze. Realizing that if he turned his head even a little bit, he might be able to see me. Finally Marty glanced away. That gave me the chance to back off. My heart raced.

The thought occurred to me: we're all about to die. - J.E.S.

I wasn't ready to stop but I couldn't continue on. My heart was racing. I grabbed a washcloth and ran cold water over it. I wiped my face and decided to give it a rest. I slipped my harmonica into my shirt pocket and headed to the yard.

Two or three laps around the track should do it. I made it around to the farthest side and once again sat on the bench just staring off into the eucalyptus trees. I blew a long drawn out cry on my harp and listened to the soft echo as it rattled through the trees. My music goes beyond the cage. I wish I could.

As much as I didn't want to go back to my journal I knew I had to. Not just for Doc and Kelly, but as hard as it was I really felt, bit by bit, I was being healed of my past. Writing was more than therapeutic, it was as if writing it down was releasing me. Setting me free from the shackles that had bound me from birth. Somehow I knew that the physical chains and walls that restricted my movements paled in comparison to the shackles that held my heart. Each word put another dent, another scratch, another nick in my restraints. I knew that bit by bit they were eroding away and someday I'd be free. Then, I would more clearly see how to loosen the shackles that held my body.

All in due time.

CHAPTER SIXTY-EIGHT

CAPTIVES

I sat there for a couple of hours just thinking and occasionally dispatching a long note or two so I could listen, as each sound escaped through the fences and faded into the desert. I was beginning to love my harmonica. But when it was time, I returned to my journal.

33rd Journal Entry: Wednesday, August 29th, 1973 - 2:44 pm

At my bedroom window, we could see Mary. I lightly scratched on the screen. Seeing Donna and me, she quickly let us in.

I whispered, "What's going on?

"I don't know. When I heard Marty coming back into the apartment, I didn't want to see or hear any more out of him. So I hid in your room.

"Where's Linda?"

"I haven't seen her."

"Donna, you and your mom wait here."

I disappeared into my closet and put on a suit. My shoulder holster was packed and ready under my jacket.

Mary and Donna gave me a quick thumbs up as I quietly left the room. I crept down the hall to where Linda was hiding at the corner, trying to hear what Bill and Marty were saying. She turned. I whispered in her ear, "Go to my bedroom. Keep an eye on Mary and Donna. I'll try to help Bill."

I waited until Linda was in my room with the door shut. Only then did I take my first step into what could be the last conversation of my life. Marty saw me coming from the hall. He slammed his hand down to cover his gun. I planned to play the friendly card.

"Hey Marty, what's up?"

Before he could answer, Bill handed me the two papers. "Check these out: Letters of commendation. One from the Army and the other is from where Marty used to work."

I glanced at the letters. "Wow, that's cool Marty."

"See. I used to be a good person. That was before I took up with you guys."

Then I lied. "You're still a good guy, Marty."

"But I used to be a straight citizen. Now I'm just a common criminal. Who wants to hire a thief? I'm stuck robbin' banks the rest of my life."

Bill beat me to it and said what I was thinking. "No one is making you stay Marty. You can quit anytime."

I quickly added, "Bill's right, if you need to leave, no one's stopping you."

"Hell, I can't quit, not before I kill you guys."

Bill's voice was calm as he asked, "Why is that Marty?"

"Because I pulled my gun on you, now I have to kill you or you'll kill me."

I'd about had it. But since he was holding a gun on us, controlling myself and being nice was the course of wisdom. "Come on Marty, go home and sober up. All will be forgotten in the morning."

"No, John! I have to kill you guys or you'll kill me. Right Bill?"

To my surprise Bill said, "That's right Marty."

I was shocked. What was Bill thinking, or was he up to something? I tried to analyze my next move but had no idea where to start. One thing for sure, with the apartment manager living on one side of us and a State Trooper on the other, we had to defuse the situation before Marty started shooting.

We had a sawed off shotgun and a Thompson in the closet. Bank bags and bundles of cash with bank wrappers still on them were stashed everywhere. In short, several life sentences could be found in our apartment. We had to get Marty out of there. How did we ever let ourselves become mixed up with this armed lunatic? I thought of the girls, hoping he'd forgotten about them. Then Marty started in on me. "John, you're just a punk kid. I should be the lead on all our jobs. You know what else? You're gutless. You don't have the nerve or smarts to handle tough situations. If it really comes down to it, you don't have the balls to throw down on someone."

The desire to throw down on him was surging in me and when I saw Marty's hand wasn't on his pistol, pure instinct took over. I snapped my .38 from its holster, had it cocked and in his face before either of us could blink. I never intended to shoot. I just wanted to scare him and get his mind off murdering us. Of course he drew on me.

Bill jumped in and reached for both our guns.

"Now boys, knock it off."

I relinquished my gun to Bill. In all the confusion of keeping his eye on me, and reacting to his paranoia, Marty didn't see Bill let my gun slip to the floor and shove it under the edge of the couch with his foot.

Marty had never been able to handle liquor or stress. Now he was under the influence of both. Bill and Linda and I had feared the day when he would lose it and go off the deep end. As I looked into Marty's eyes, I could see, today was that day.

Bill was a master at defusing tense situations. This was the ultimate test. "Come on Marty, let's have a cup of coffee."

"I don't want your damn coffee, Bill. Now sit down!"

Marty seemed startled by what had just come out of his mouth and began apologizing. When Bill sat, it gave Marty a feeling of power. His tone shifted again. "I've gotta say it Bill, you're such a wimp. You can't even make up your mind between Linda and Mary. If you were half a man you'd hide your girlfriends."

Bill's control was admirable. He stifled his desire to rip into his accuser. "Look Marty, you may have a valid point, but Mary and I are separated. Linda is my only woman."

"So why do you keep Mary around? Does it make you feel macho to hang onto her? It ain't right."

"Mary is free to do what she pleases. But she's the mother of my children and I want the best for her. And naturally, I want to see my kids." Bill never stopped looking at him, drilling him with his eyes of steel. "You have kids so you can understand my feelings."

"Throwing my kids up to me isn't a great idea, Bill, especially since I'm the one holding a gun." Marty became even more upset.

By then Marty was standing, shifting his weight from one foot to the other, breathing hard, his eyes darting around the room, and a fierce expression on his face. My heart was pounding double time and my mind was rampant with the thought: *we're dealing with a total lunatic capable of killing us all.*

A chill ran through me. How this would end was anyone's guess. If the moment came I was determined to die fighting.

Bill was calm and controlled, choosing the right moment to continue his side of the conversation. "Marty, of all people, you understand what it's like not being able to see your children. My kids mean everything to me. I'm sure it's the same for you."

That's when the unexpected happened, Marty began crying. Bill moved toward him to offer comfort. Marty jumped back and swung around, pointing his gun at Bill.

"You think I'm some kind of stupid idiot? Back off or I'll kill the both of you." Waving his gun, Marty gestured toward the kitchen. "Now sit."

Marty grabbed a chair and straddled it. In one motion, both his gun and his gaze were pointing straight at Bill. Bill was so cool. Nothing seemed to knock him off balance. He waited a moment before calmly asking, "What do you want me to do?"

Marty pulled a pack of Virginia Slims from his shirt pocket and shook out a slightly crinkled cigarette. Turning it over and over, not saying anything, Marty appeared to be playing some sort of intimidation game. He finally placed the cigarette between his teeth, pulled out a Zippo lighter, and snapped it open. He stared at the orange flame for a long time. Finally, he torched the tobacco.

As Marty exhaled one long, drawn out plume of smoke, he never took his eyes off Bill. When he finally spoke, it was shocking.

Marty said, "Pick one." - J.E.S.

It was like I couldn't get out of my house quick enough when the doors racked. I walked over to see Paul but he wasn't in his house. I ran down to see Nick and he was gone. Finally I saw Brinkerhoff walking across the floor and called out. "David, want to play some Spades? Hearts? Pinochle?"

"Sorry Tex, I'm headed to the library to return some books. Maybe when I get back?"

"That's cool man. Catch you later."

All of the sudden it was like I was living in a ghost town. I just needed to be with somebody, but no one was around. I headed to the TV room and turned it on.

Are you kidding me? As the World Turns? All My Children? Days of Our Lives? In just one episode of D.O.O.L., I learned that Susan Martin was in an affair with Peter Brown and I watched while Julie stands by her dying husband Scott, as her father, Dr. Tom Horton, tries desperately to save him.

Puke.

CHAPTER SIXTY-NINE

TO CHOOSE WHO LIVES

It sucked. But it did what I needed. A calm heart and a fresh run at what was the worse night of my life. Twenty more minutes sitting on my bunk, two cans of coke, and I was ready to go again. God help me get through this. Please don't let me lose it.

34ᵗʰ Journal Entry: Wednesday, August 29ᵗʰ, 1973 - 6:14 pm

I couldn't imagine what Marty was talking about. He was in a frenzy, over the edge.

"Pick one. Decide right now which one you love."

Bill and I glanced at each other. *What now?*, had to be written all over our faces.

"Pick one. Linda or Mary? When you decide, I'm going to kill the other one."

Bill leaned forward and folded his hands on the table.

"I'm not going to do that, Marty. I care for them both. I love Linda as my soul mate and I'll always have feelings for Mary as the mother of my kids. I can't choose.

"Fine, I'll pick for you. John, go to the bedroom. Tell them both to get out here. One of them is about to die."

Before I could move, Marty cocked his pistol and jammed it to my head. "Get 'um. Now!"

I dared only move my eyes. Bill nodded for me to go.

"Ok Marty, I'm going."

Marty pulled away and I hurried down the hall. Inside my room, three pairs of eyes screamed out for answers. I motioned Donna and Mary to the window.

"Marty is totally whacked," I whispered. "Make a run for it and don't look back."

Mary climbed onto the window and straddled the sill. "Should I call the police?"

Linda and I answered in hushed yet stern unison, "No."

I pleaded, "Go home and lock yourselves in. We'll call when it's safe."

We lowered Mary, then Donna to the ground. When they were out of sight I took a deep breath and whispered, "Linda, come with me. But watch Marty's every move, I'm afraid he's ready to snap."

Linda was visibly frightened. I wanted to comfort her, but what could I possibly do or say in such a vile situation? My only option was to warn her. "Marty is so unpredictable. For now, we do what he says. But first, where's Bill's gun?"

"In the hall closet."

"Where's yours?"

"In the car."

The look of despair on Linda's face and the tears on her cheek were too much for me. I had to avoid eye contact. Emotionally drained and fearful, I sucked in a huge breath and tried to act brave. "If Marty catches any hint that we're afraid, it might give him a reason to finish what he came here to do." I reached up and brushed the tears from Linda's face.

As we walked down the hall, we heard Bill saying, "Marty, Linda is pregnant. You're the first to know."

We entered the kitchen in time to see the expression on Marty's face. He looked like a kid who'd just been told his dog had died. Bill had managed to break Marty's focus and shift his attention. I wondered, *is it true? Or something Bill made up as a diversion?*

When Marty saw us coming, he ordered me to sit down at the table but allowed Linda to stand near Bill. "Crap Bill, why didn't you tell me before now?"

"I tried calling you the other day but no answer."

Either Bill was the smoothest liar I'd ever met, or it was true. From out of nowhere I was remembering Linda's last pregnancy and abortion.

At that moment Linda turned slightly, our eyes met for a split second. She quickly turned away. The thought of another baby dying was breaking my heart. I was on total overload.

Marty was buying it and asked, "Have you picked names?"

Linda was fighting back tears. She moved closer to Bill as she answered. "If it's a girl we want to call her Eve. If it's a boy, Shane."

Marty softened for a moment.

Bill added, "Marty, Linda hasn't been well lately and look at her, all this stress could cause a miscarriage. Just to be on the safe side maybe we should take her to the hospital. What do you think?"

Marty looked sympathetic, but suddenly his eyes flashed with contempt and darted around the room.

"Where the hell is Mary?" An evil look crossed his face and his voice changed. "I see what you guys are doing . . . trying to confuse me." Marty began waving his gun around again. "John, get her in here."

Marty squinted his eyes then jerked his head in Linda's direction. "You bitch. You're probably not even pregnant." He cocked his pistol and swung it around in my direction. "I said get Mary. Get her now or you're dead."

I rushed down the hall thinking, *I hope Marty has forgotten about Donna.* Back in my room, I looked at the open window. It gave me the perfect chance to leave. The thought of Bill and Linda dying, without me doing everything possible to prevent it, held me back.

The tension in the air was unbearable. Marty's voice boomed through the apartment so loud I thought, for sure the Trooper next door would be showing up any minute. My mind scrambled for options: *distract Marty, catch him off guard.*

I ran back to the kitchen. Marty sat opposite Bill, with his gun pointed for a shot through the heart. I tried to keep my voice low but frantic. "She's gone. I can't find her anywhere."

Marty stood up so fast his chair slammed to the floor.

Bill took the cue, "Oh, my God! Now what?"

Linda joined in, "Did you check the bathroom?"

Hanging onto his pistol, Marty ran down the hall yelling, "Try under the beds!"

The thought of an accidental shot going off was causing as much anxiety as the fear of an intentional one. Of course our search was futile. Marty herded us back to the kitchen and growled. "That's it. Find her."

He motioned Linda, Bill and me into the parking lot. To buy time, we went through the charade of searching behind each vehicle. Finally Bill approached Marty, asking in a hushed whisper, "Don't you think we should get back inside before someone spots us?"

"No. Keep looking."

After another 20 minutes of wandering around the complex, Marty finally ordered us back into the apartment where he cut loose. "It's your fault John, you let her get away."

In a sudden lunge, Marty swung his weapon, pointing it directly at Bill's heart. "Well Bill, looks like John made the decision for you."

That's when he spun around and pointed his pistol at Linda. He slowly walked up and shoved the muzzle into her mouth. He grabbed the back of her head and pushed harder, literally cramming it down her throat. Linda was gagging. Marty's superior strength made it impossible for her to break free. Bill and I were helplessly watching her squirm and choke. Any move on our part and Marty could decide to just pull the trigger. - J.E.S.

"Hey." Nicks simple greeting startled me. "I'm sorry man. You Okay?"

"Sorry. I was just in a tough place in my journal."

"Need a break?"

"Well yes. I suppose I do."

We sauntered out to the walk and just sat down on the floor. Nick began telling me about his life and how he ended up inside. He had been dating the same girl since junior high and wanted to marry her. She was 14 and he was 16 when they first began dating. When he turned 17 he enlisted in the Army with his mother's waiver. Two years later he came home on leave and asked her to marry him. She said yes but her father said no. He took her from Georgia into Alabama and they got married. But when they returned, he was arrested for statutory rape because she was still only 17.

The Army said he could be tried for rape in Georgia and face 20 years, or if he pled to lewd and lascivious behavior, he would just serve eight in a federal facility.

"As you can see, I took it."

"What about your wife?"

"A judge in Atlanta set it aside. And the Catholic Church did an annulment."

"Wow. That sucks."

He pulled out a stack of letters and showed me. "She writes twice a week. We are going to get married as soon as I get out"

"In seven years?"

"No, I was sentenced to seven under 5010c.1, The Youth Act. That means I serve two years inside, then two years on parole. If I stay totally clean for the remaining three, it all goes away. Like Bam! It never happened."

"Sweet."

CHAPTER SEVENTY

TORMENT

I laid there in my bunk for well over an hour trying to sleep, wanting to turn it off. But I couldn't. I didn't want to think about the past anymore. I guess I needed to get it out. But finally, near midnight, I sat back up and grabbed my Journal . . . again.

35th Journal Entry: Wednesday, August 29th, 1973 - 11:52 pm

I decided it was my turn to try talking him down. "Marty, remember there's a State Trooper living in the apartment next door. We've been making so much noise. . . ."

Marty yanked his gun around and turned it on me. Linda slumped to the floor. Bill started to move toward her. Marty sprung back, aiming his gun at Linda. "Stay where you are Bill or I'll shoot."

Convinced he was back in control, Marty began looking around, surveying the apartment. His head jerked back and forth along the adjoining wall. "Where do you think that Trooper sleeps?" Marty stopped flailing and pointed his pistol. "If I shoot right here, do you think I'll hit him?"

We watched, not saying a word, as Marty calculated the perfect shot. Once satisfied that he'd figured out exactly where to shoot, he cocked the .38 and aimed.

As calmly as possible, Bill broke the silence. "You shoot and we all go to jail."

Marty snapped around and shoved the pistol into Bill's mouth. "I don't think so. They don't arrest dead people."

Pushing the chrome dining table aside, and arranging three chairs into a line, Marty shouted, "Sit down, stay put, and no talking."

Rotating between us, Marty stopped and crammed his pistol into each of our mouths. Occasionally, he'd slap us with it, all the while laughing and making insane comments, enjoying his position of power.

"If I shoot you all right now, how long would it take you to reach hell?"

His laugh was evil, like a man who'd lost his mind. He looked down at us, three silent sitting ducks. Marty had nothing better to do than to cock his pistol, lower the hammer, cock it again, lower the hammer, cock. . . . His cruel laugh made a perfect accompaniment to the reality of our nightmare. Cock, lower the hammer, cock. . . . But in rhythm with the sound, I heard a different lyric playing in my mind, *Just shoot me Marty, I'm not taking this anymore.* I became roaring mad. . . . *Grab the gun. Grab it. . . . No, not yet.*

Marty's torture and threatening went on until after four in the morning. I decided to stand up and walk out the door. I would tell him, *Shoot me or not, I don't care.* I leaned forward in my chair to execute my plan when Marty made an announcement.

"I'm tired. This can't go on all night."

He gave no hint of having changed his mind. Was he just to going kill us and go home? The next sentence out of his mouth was almost incoherent. He was crying again. "Bill, I'm sorry I threw down on you. If I knew you'd let me go, I'd walk out right now. But I know you won't." He reached up, wiped his eyes on his shirtsleeve and tried to gain composure. "Get your gun Bill. I want this to be fair. We're going to have a shootout and may the best man win."

Bill just sat there looking straight ahead.

"Do it!"

Bill took his time getting up. He walked towards the hall, stopped and opened the closet door to retrieve his .357 from the floor. Marty kept his eye on Linda and me as he followed right behind Bill, practically on top of him. Before Bill could grab his weapon, Marty cocked his pistol and jammed it into the back of Bill's head.

Sparks flew off in my mind. If shots were fired we'd all be had. For an instant Marty took his eyes off me. I lunged for his .38 with my right hand and curled my left into a fist. I swung up into Marty's jaw. I felt a sweet connection, the sensation of skin-to-skin, bone on bone. I have no clue what happened next. I blacked out. When I came to my senses, I was sitting on Marty's chest beating his face with both fists. I desperately wanted to knock him out, to shut him up. But the harder I hit him the louder he screamed.

Linda crammed a red velvet pillow over Marty's face. Bill moved in with duct tape, binding his legs and arms. Marty was still squirming when I spotted my pistol, under the couch where Bill had stowed it hours before. We'd both forgotten it was there. I reached for it, thinking I could knock Marty out with one blow.

Bill grabbed my hand. "You can't shoot him, John."

"I wasn't going to. I just want to knock him out."

Bill whirled around and pulled a brass lamp from an end table. Linda yanked the pillow away and Bill struck Marty three or four times on the head. Nothing happened.

Linda slapped the pillow back on Marty's face to muffle his foul language. I removed my socks and stuffed them both into his mouth. Bill was at the ready to tape them into place. When that roll was gone, he ran down the hall and returned with more tape and a baseball bat.

When we were finished with him, Marty looked like a mummy. He kept making muffled sounds. I no longer wanted to shut him up. I wanted to silence him for good. I grabbed the bat and got in a couple of blows before Bill intervened.

"You really want to do this?"

I was hyperventilating. My heart was about to jump out of my chest. I felt so weak; all I could do was stare.

"Hey John, get a hold of yourself. Think. Mistakes now could cost us later."

As I backed away Marty groaned. Amazing. He was still conscious. His eyes had swollen, like a frog. I was covered in Marty's blood and he was lying in a puddle. Suddenly I was enveloped in one of those points when time stands still and sounds become acute and clear, when all movement is in slow motion. It was a moment when everything made sense, while hanging on the edge of madness.

I was standing at another crossroad. I was so consumed with anger and hate; I wanted to kill the lump lying on the floor. Suddenly I was dizzy, like I was waking up from a horrible nightmare. I balanced myself against the wall glanced down. Marty looked like he was all dressed up ready for Halloween. - J.E.S.

Exhaustion overtook me but sleep eluded me, so I just laid there. I reached for my headphones.

Grand Funk Railroad, *'I'm your Captain, I'm your Captain. Please return me, my ship.'*

Made me think of Glatkowski.

CHAPTER SEVENTY-ONE

THE VOTE

Can't tell you when I fell asleep but my dream was crazy. I was stuck somewhere in the ocean rowing a boat. It was full of everything I wanted to eat with plenty of water and juices. I was listening to Credence Clearwater Revival sing *Bad Moon Rising*. I kept rowing the boat while yelling "I'm Free! I'm Free!" But when I looked up at the full moon then looked around I saw nothing. What good is freedom, if you are alone?

I brushed my teeth and had a healthy breakfast of Doritos, chocolate doughnuts, an avocado and . . . coffee, thanks to Nick.

36th Journal Entry: Thursday, August 30th, 1973 - 7:16 am

The sound of Bill's voice startled me. "Time to vote." I must have given him one of those confused puppy dog looks because he added, "And we need another pot of coffee."

Linda was on it. Then one look at me and she said, "Sit down John, before you fall down."

I sat, numb, in an emotional fog, aimlessly tracing the marble pattern of the Formica table with my bloody finger. Bill set out clean cups. Linda poured as he spoke. "We need to assess our options and vote on what to do."

My hands were shaking so badly I barely managed to pull a cigarette from the pack. Bill steadied my hand and lit the smoke. "Take a deep breath, John. You'll be okay."

Linda came over, wrapped her arms around my shoulders and gave me a hug. I was a wreck. I couldn't stop shaking and didn't dare lift my cup so I just stared into the steam, feeling the soothing warmth of it.

For about five minutes we just sat there, lost in our thoughts. No one said a word. Once the shakes subsided, I lifted my cup.

Linda spoke. "Well, if you ask me, I think we'd be foolish to let him go."

I nodded in agreement and Bill assumed his role as our leader. "We really need to look at this thing carefully and systematically . . . the whole picture, not just what we're up against here. Our decision has to be based on logic."

Bill leaned back in his chair and turned to me. "John, you go first. What's on your mind?"

"Well, I'm sure Marty will go straight to the cops if we let him go. Even if he doesn't, that fool will eventually get busted and turn us all in. I say we make sure he never has the chance to burn us."

Bill's look assured me his attention was on my every word. But as he paused before answering, he seemed troubled and chose his words carefully. "As I see it, we have two options: we let him go and take our chances, or kill him. Only one of those will guarantee he can't bite us later." Bill took a sip of coffee and turned to Linda. "Do you have anything to add?"

"Only that I agree with you both and I'm ready to vote.

"So how do you vote?"

"I say, kill him."

"John?"

"I agree."

As if sealing the deal, Bill said, "Well, I guess that's it then."

"No. It isn't." Linda's voice was strong with conviction. Her look was firm. Had she just challenged Bill? That was so unlike her. "You can't say the majority rules and not vote. Tell us, where you stand?"

Bill looked down at his hands neatly folded on the table. He seemed to be searching for the right words. "Point well made. I shouldn't leave you two holding the bag. It's not an easy thing, deciding to take a life. It's something we'll have to live with forever. Truth is, Marty can't be trusted. So my vote? We kill him. But, there's one more thing." Bill paused. He looked at Linda and then turned to me. "Killing Marty means killing Irene too."

Linda and I gave each other a quick look. Neither of us had thought of that. Bill went on, "Marty is an orphan and Irene is from Germany. Texas Social Services have their kids. I see no obstacles. The key is to make sure their bodies are never found. If we can accomplish that, we're home free.

"John, drive to their apartment, tell Irene about Marty's drunken tirade and bring her here. When she's inside, we'll tie her up, put them in Marty's van, drive to Lake Washington, shoot them both and run the van into the water."

I was surprised that Bill sounded so matter-of-fact, so cold and impersonal.

"Hurry, it's after four and the sun will be coming up soon. Go get her. We'll take care of things here."

Linda began loading our stuff into the new, blue caddy. I washed up, changed clothes and left. When Irene came to the door, it was obvious she'd been awake all night. She motioned me to come in. "There was no way I could stop him. He worries me til I can't sleep when he takes off in one of his moods."

"It's not just a mood, Irene, he's drunk and out of his mind. You need to come get your van and drive him home so he can sleep it off.

"Is Bill mad?"

"No, not yet, he's more disappointed. If you don't come . . . well, who knows."

Irene grabbed a jacket and we were out the door. I tried to avoid conversation but she sensed something was up. She had questions and I had only one-word answers.

Once we reached the apartment, I held the door for her. I was shocked to see Marty, unbound and huddled in a corner. Bill stood over him, baseball bat in hand.

When he spotted us, Marty yelled, "Irene, get a knife. Help me!"

Irene turned toward me. "What's going on?"

I didn't answer but Marty cried out again, "Get a knife Irene; they're going to kill me!"

Instantly Irene was at his side, asking quietly, in a motherly tone, "What did you do?"

"I pulled a gun on Bill. Now they're going to kill me."

"You messed up, Marty. You shouldn't have broken the rules."

"But they're going to kill you too."

Irene looked up at Bill with pleading eyes then turned back to her husband, "I know Marty, that's the way it has to be. You screwed up."

She looked at Bill again and asked, "What do you want me to do?"

"Just sit down on the couch and be quiet."

Irene did as she was told and Bill handed me the bat. I stood guard. Marty continued to whine. Bill went outside to the car. Moments later he returned with Linda's .380. He placed a silencer on the weapon, walked directly to Marty and pointed the pistol at him.

"Marty, say one more word and you're dead. The longer you stay quiet, the longer you live."

Bill tossed me a pair of cuffs for Irene. He cuffed Marty, then asked, "Irene, are we going to have any problems with you?"

She shook her head.

Bill motioned to the kitchen chairs. "We need to talk."

Linda and I sat. I knew instinctively that Bill and Linda had been moved by Irene's submission. I was both angry and outnumbered. Bill's words showed his compassionate strength.

"We can't do this. There's no way I can take her out."

Determined, I said, "I'll do it!"

Linda put her hand on my arm. "I'm sorry John."

I waited for the words I knew were coming next. "You've been out voted."

"Damn it. So, what now?"

Bill ended the conversation. "We send them home."

I was stunned, unable to move or say a word. Linda released Irene and the two women emptied out the apartment. In 15 minutes we were packed. Marty stayed handcuffed as I helped load him into the van.

Bill handed me four Reds. I made Marty drink them down but nothing changed. Adrenalin had made the guy strong as an ox. Bill gave me more. I ran back into our apartment, cooked up a dose and drew it into a syringe. Back at the van I shot it into Marty's arm. Within minutes he was out.

Bill walked Irene to the driver's side and held the door for her. She climbed in as he gave instructions. "Take him home but don't let him out til you hear from me. Understand?"

"Yes, I understand."

"Okay. Get going." - J.E.S.

It took three deep breaths before I could feel oxygen begin to hit my brain. I didn't realize that I had stopped breathing. I was shaking but also relieved to have made it through. What an emotional ride. Thank God I was nearing the end of it.

Lerma dropped by and asked me to come hang with the band. He said, "Bring your harmonica, Tex."

I told him I didn't think I was good enough to play along with the band. He just shot me a half smile, waved his arms and said, "Órale, Tejas, Órale"

He walked off but before leaving he said I should do my best to catch dinner. Meatloaf and mashed potatoes and corn. "Con Carne, de verdad, Tejas!"

"Real meat? I'll be there."

CHAPTER SEVENTY-TWO

ONE & DONE

Lerma was right. Dinner was almost like eating out. The meatloaf was nice. Even nicer? As I was going through the line one of the servers said, "You're Tex aren't you?"

"Yeah why?"

"Lerma said to load you up."

He threw an extra slice on my tray and then gave me a little paper wrap with bread, lettuce, tomato and mayo. I was blessed. Midnight snack, here I come.

37th Journal Entry: Thursday, August 30th, 1973 - 4:45 pm

We poured bleach on the bloody carpet and sprayed a thin coat of cooking oil on every surface. It was a great way to blur or destroy fingerprints on the stove, tables and chairs and refrigerator. Every window and sill, every door, every knob and drawer pull, sinks and faucets . . . even the handle that flushed the toilet got a once over. At the front door, Bill rubbed cooking oil on the key, stuck it in the lock and broke it off.

Relief and exhaustion hit all of us as we drove to Mary and Donna's house. They were still awake, wired, and wondering if we were dead or alive. Mary cooked a great breakfast but no one was very hungry. We gave them a short version of Marty's attempt to kill us. They were shocked but not surprised. Mostly they were grateful for the chance to escape. We just hung out, trying to forget the past several hours.

It was still early morning, around nine o'clock when Bill said, "John and I need to run a quick errand."

Acting as if I knew where we were going, I left with him and soon discovered I had guessed right.

"I've been saving this one for a rainy day. It looks pretty stormy right now."

Bill drove into the back parking lot of the Federal Way Branch of Seattle First National Bank. I pulled on a wig from a stash of stuff in the back seat and was ready.

Walking across the blacktop, the stress of recent Appointments was gone. The bank was a small temporary facility. Actually, it was a double-wide trailer.

I walked through the door, pulled my gun and for the first time ever, I announced, "This is a stick up,"

The bank manager emptied both tills but I could see the safe standing open behind the counter. "Fill the bag from the safe."

He did as told and handed me the bag.

"Now get the reserve."

"I don't know what you're talking about."

"I said, get the reserve or I'll kill you all."

He lifted a plate from the false bottom of the safe, withdrew more bills, and stuffed them into the bag. I snatched it from him, turned and walked out the door. I circled the bank. Bill was in place, waiting for me to jump into the trunk. Once the lid was pulled shut, we were gone.

Mary, Donna and Linda welcomed us with more coffee and small talk. I excused myself to freshen up and change clothes then slipped out the back door. Two blocks away, I pitched the bag which held my disguise into a dumpster.

There was a pool hall across the highway. I went in to score a jar of meth tabs. It only cost $70 for 1,000 tabs. I stashed them inside my leather jacket.

I was standing near the counter, just about to leave, when two F.B.I. agents walked in. They made the rounds, showing photos and asking questions. Rather than risk suspicion by leaving, I sat down at the counter and ordered a cup of coffee.

One agent came over and asked, "Have you seen this guy around here?"

The photos were from the security camera at the bank I had just robbed. The counter man squinted, as if trying to remember something before answering. "Reminds me of some guy that was hangin' around a few weeks ago. Haven't seen him lately."

I looked at the photo and just shook my head. When they had cleared the parking lot I paid for my coffee and hiked back across the highway.

Mary and Donna were standing in the front yard talking with Bill and Linda.

Bill welcomed me and said; "Now that John's back we can tell you more."

I couldn't imagine what was coming next.

"Mary and Donna want to know what we do for a living."

At that point I no longer cared, so I shrugged my shoulders and said, "Tell 'um."

Bill reached into the car and pulled out a small overnight bag. He opened it to reveal roughly $50,000 and said, "We rob banks."

Mary's hand flew to her mouth as she gasped in shock. Donna burst into tears.

"We want you to have this."

They refused. Bill could not persuade them.

Linda said her good-byes. Donna and I promised to write. Bill pulled both women against his chest for a long hug. Reluctantly they pulled away and let him take his place behind the wheel. I watched Donna and Mary wave us out of sight.

That's when I asked, "Bill where are we going."

His answer was weighed down with exhaustion, "South." - J.E.S.

I decided to lay in bed and listen to the radio until I heard a song that fit the day. So after suffering through Ricky Nelson singing *Garden Party* and Stevie Wonder's *Superstition*, I finally settled down when Chicago began to sing *Feeling Stronger Every Day*.

CHAPTER SEVENTY-THREE

EXODUS

War! What is it Good for? Absolutely nothing. Say it again! I shot up from my bunk and realized I had fallen asleep with my headphones on. I like Edwin Starr but geezz don't scare the crap out of me. I laid back and listened to the rest of it. But then came *Puppy Love* by Donnie Osmond? I don't think so.

I grabbed my cup and ran down to the coffee pot by the TV room and filled it up. On my way back I admired the nice crust that was forming around the brim. You could buy plastic cups in the commissary and it was kind of like a status symbol how crusty your cup got. No one washed their coffee cups. It was unheard of. Almost like you could tell how long a con had been in by his cup. Mine? Nearly two years.

Nice.

38ᵗʰ Journal Entry: Friday, August 31ˢᵗ, 1973 - 9:19 am

I remember lying down across the back seat, listening to the sound of tires on the highway beating time to the song Bill was singing, *Gimme that old time religion, gimme that old time religion. . . .*

In my dream, I was standing in a bank waving a gun in the air. No one was listening to me. The bank manager told me I'd have to wait in line, like everyone else. Then a cop walked through the door shooting, not at me, just randomly all over the place. Next, I was sitting in jail reading a newspaper with a picture of me on the front page. The headlines said I had died in a shootout while robbing a bank. I heard myself yelling for the guard to unlock my cell. "I gotta get outa here. I have to go to my funeral."

A guard approached. He was yelling, 'Ain't gonna happen fella. Calm down and stay put. Yer not goin' anywhere.'

Voices took on an echo, reverberating in my head. I was freaking out, shouting, 'I gotta get outa here. I want out.'

I woke up, wringing wet, confused, not knowing where I was. Pulling up to a sitting position made my head spin and sent shivers through my whole body. My bed was by a window. I looked out. The sunlight hurt my eyes. When I could focus, I heard myself say, "No way." Was this still a dream? No. It was true. I was back at the cabins in Guerneville.

My head had just crashed back onto the pillow when I heard Linda's voice, "Bill, I think he's awake! Hey John, you descent?"

My voice cracked as I invited her in.

She stuck her head around the door and smiled. "How you doin', bro?"

I pulled up onto one elbow. "What happened?"

Before she could say anything, Bill answered as he put a cup of coffee on the bedside table. "You fell asleep in the car and we didn't have the heart to wake you."

I must have looked really confused because Bill added, "Care to guess how long you've been out?"

I just shook my head. "I haven't got a clue."

Linda walked up, patted my shoulder, "Three days."

I blurted out, "You've got to be kidding me."

"Really. Three days."

"How'd I get into bed?"

Linda giggled while Bill answered, "Don't worry, I tucked you in. When you feel like entering the real world again, I have something to show you."

They both left the room. I took a sip of the hot java and lay down for another 10 minutes. I was still an emotional basket case, trying to sort out how to let Bill and Linda know I wanted out. Not that I was anxious to leave them, I just didn't have it in me to pull another robbery.

The thought of disappointing Bill wouldn't let go. I told myself, *once and for all, I have to stop. No matter what, I'll tell them today. I'm done.*

Hot steamy water covered my aching body. After being out for so long, it took a while to make myself presentable.

The smell of bacon cooking made my mouth water. Linda was in a good mood, smiling, pouring my refill.

Walking past the window, I noticed a beige Cadillac parked in the driveway. "There's a strange car outside. Are we expecting company?"

Bill tossed his newspaper aside. He walked over and put his hand on my shoulder. "That's what I wanted to show you. Let's go."

As the three of us approached the car, Bill handed me a pink piece of paper. It was the title to the Caddy. My name was on it. I must have looked puzzled.

"We bought this for you while you were sleeping. Come on, take a look."

Inside were boxes, all wrapped with bright paper and ribbons.

Linda couldn't wait, "Open them John."

It was hard to believe: an expensive new watch, a beautiful gold ring, several items of clothing and a brand new chrome plated Smith & Wesson .38 Special. The whole back seat was loaded with gifts.

"Bill, Linda, I don't get it."

"Look at your hand."

I hadn't even noticed the bandage. I pulled back the gauze to revel three stitches. "What am I missing here?"

"You saved my life, John."

Saved Bill's life? I couldn't imagine how.

"When Marty told me to get my gun for a shootout, I reached into the bottom of the hall closet. Remember? Marty jabbed his gun into the back of my head and you grabbed it at the very moment he pulled the trigger. Your finger somehow landed between the hammer and firing pin. A quarter inch, either way, and I'd have been a goner."

Trying to visualize what Bill was saying, left me totally confused. "I don't remember any of that. How'd I get these stitches?"

"A doctor friend did that while you were out. This car and gifts, well . . . it's our way of saying thank you."

I was speechless.

Linda suddenly gasped and ran off, frantic words trailing behind her. "Oh. No! The bacon."

Bill patted my shoulder. "Let's go inside. There's something else."

Linda was still working on our meal as we walked in. "Sit down boys. Give me a few more minutes." She handed me a glass of grapefruit juice. "Drink this. It'll help rebuild your strength."

I was getting nervous, anticipating what I needed to say. How would Bill and Linda take it, especially after the incredible gifts?

"John, you know Linda and I have liked you from the first time we met. Can't quite explain it but there's just something about you. Young as you are, you're smart and loyal, and you've never refused to do what I've asked. But it's more than that. . . ."

For a moment, I thought I saw the beginning of a tear in Bill's eyes.

Linda stood behind Bill. She smiled at me and said, "You're the brother I always wished for but never had."

Then Bill nailed me. "You've become my son. I love you, John."

My emotions were running wild. I'd never heard those words. 'I love you' was something rarely said in the south, especially one man to another. I started to cry. Not just a few tears, but uncontrollable sobs. To know Bill actually cared for me collided with my intensions to leave the only genuine family I'd ever known.

Linda came from behind me, put her arms around my shoulders and snuggled her face next to mine. "John, it's okay to cry."

"No it's not. I feel like such a wimp."

"Only real men will allow themselves to cry. It's what makes you so special."

Linda's kind words shook me up even more. Before I could gather my senses, Bill stood up then vanished. He returned with the take from the Federal Way Appointment. "Okay John, let's tally it up. Maybe this will lift your spirits a notch or two."

Linda turned the bag upside down, spilling its contents onto the table. We began our usual routine of separating the bills into stacks: ones, fives, tens, twenties. I tried to pay attention but was preoccupied with gathering courage to face my predicament. We counted nearly $10,000, which we divided into bundles of $500 each.

Linda brought breakfast to the table. "Finally, gentlemen, here you go."

Bill shoved the money aside and we began to eat. No one spoke during our first few bites. I couldn't believe how hungry I was.

Bill leaned back in his chair. "John, we want you to have the entire take."

I looked up from my plate. Again, my face registered disbelief. "I don't get it."

Bill was looking straight at me. "Did you know you talk in your sleep?"

What in the world could I have said? I shut my eyes.

"John, we knew this day would come. The money a going away present."

All of the sudden I felt both grief and relief. On the one hand I was leaving with their blessing but I still felt guilty, as if I was letting them down. An unexpected pain set in like fingers squeezing my heart.

"Bill, are you disappointed that I'm leaving?"

"I'm sad because I'll miss you. But understand me when I say, I love you . . . because of who you are, not because of what you've done for us. Leaving is what you need to do, so leaving is what we want for you."

Tears were falling again. I was a wreck. Linda handed me a tissue. Trying to pull myself together wasn't working. It didn't help that Linda and Bill were being so kind.

"There's no rush. Maybe we can go fishing one more time. Then, when you're ready, get on the highway and go."

Linda gave me a photo album. "This is so you'll remember us."

It was a picture diary of the last year and a half.

I turned the pages . . . Vegas, Guerneville, the three of us. I grabbed another tissue.

We spent the evening swapping stories and reminiscing about the incredible journey we'd just concluded. We talked into the morning. By the time we said our last good-byes, a couple of days had come and gone. I was rested and reassured.

Leaving Bill and Linda was the most difficult thing I'd done in my life, so far. Watching them in the rearview mirror, waiving, I thought, chances are we'll never see each other again. But I'll never forget them for as long as I live. - J.E.S.

Just a few minutes after the doors racked mine suddenly reopened. I stuck my head out to see the guard motioning me forward. I held up a finger signaling I needed a minute and his nod approved my securing the journal within my locker. I met the officer at his office and he handed me a chit to the Wardens office.

"What's up boss?"

"I have no idea Swanger. But you better get a move on you're due there in five."

I hurried down the walk to the administration wing and gave the guard at central command my number. He buzzed me in.

I have to admit I was both baffled and a bit scared. What did I do that the top dog wanted to see me? I gave the chit to the executive secretary and waited while he announced my arrival.

Five minutes later Brinkerhoff exited Kenton's office and they called me in. Seated inside were Warden Kenton, the A.W. Thomas Koehane, The Head of Counseling C. Scott Moss, and Burton Kerish the Staff Psychologist.

Now I was really worried. I was offered a seat on one side of a long table while the four of them sat on the other side. A rather large tape recorder was recording everything. Warden Kenton slid a sheet of paper towards me. It was the same mimeograph sheet we had to fill out earlier in the unit about the Hernandez stabbing.

"Now Swanger, don't try and bull shit us. We have reliable information, double sourced, that you were indeed on the floor during this incident."

I glanced at the black ball point pen sitting just to my right. I picked it up and moved it to the left of the sheet. What the hell am I going to do? I sat there for a couple of minutes just searching for a way to avoid the inevitable. I had to do something. I picked up the pen and stared at it, '7520009357135 US Government' . . . I rolled it over and read the other side also . . . *Blue*. I clicked it several times. As I pulled the sheet closer towards me, Kerish, Moss, and Koehane all got up from their chairs and leaned across the table.

I looked at the sheet and my eyes followed the bloody trail the victim and his attacker followed as the dashed line circled my table where blood sprinkled upon our cards and our Khakis. Convict code requires I don't give up anyone. My heart was pleading for justice for Hernandez, but my brain was in preservation mode. I looked past the bloody scene and followed the tables as far as I could to the last one by the windows and bars at the end of the unit. I reached down and placed an X on the chair facing the windows and away from the crime scene. As my mark hit the page, the full assembly sat back in their seats, each with a look of disgust.

Warden Kenton spoke, "That's your story? You are going with that chair?"

"Yes sir. I was there but didn't even know anything was happening until everyone was running around. I just went to my house and locked in."

"Swanger..." you could actually see the veins pulsating near his temples. "Swanger, there are 123 inmates in K-Unit. One was stabbing, one was getting stabbed, and damn it, I have 121 sitting in the same damn chair as you."

"Well no wonder no one could see anything."

Koehane spoke up, "You watch your mouth young man. You think this is funny?"

I was excused with orders to return to my cell and not speak with anyone in the waiting area or along the walk. As I exited the Wardens office I saw Watkins, the next to be grilled.

CHAPTER SEVENTY-FOUR

FINDING MY WAY BACK

I was glad to be back in my cell. I sat there and thought about Hernandez. I was angry about what had happened to him. But there was no way I could testify against the attacker and stay alive. I decided to walk away from it and save my life. It was what I needed to do to keep being an air pump.

39th Journal Entry: Friday, August 31st, 1973 - 6:33 pm

When the gravel road ended, I steered for the highway with no thought of where I should go. It really didn't matter. Reflections of the last 18 months haunted me. *Shake it John, I told myself. Leave it behind.* It had been nearly two years since I'd vowed never again to be a burden on my family. But I wasn't that person anymore and for sure I wasn't a kid any longer. I'd grown up fast and lived hard, been more places and seen more things in the past year and a half than most people do in a lifetime. B e y o n d that, I'd experienced something very rare, the reality of being loved. For the first time in my life I knew what it was to have someone truly care about me. I'm not saying Mom or my family never loved me; I'm just saying I didn't feel it. Several emotions and mile markers later, I decided to give Reno a try and just hang out for a few days. I had nowhere else to go and was in no rush to get there.

Evening lights were just beginning to outshine the setting sun when I turned onto Virginia Street. Crossing the Truckee River was something

I'd done several times before, but this time was different. Strangely enough, at that moment, all my future plans, all my hopes and dreams were summed up in a few words: find a hotel and call room service.

I fell asleep somewhere between the champagne and the cheesecake.

The sound of a latch rattling and my door opening suddenly shook me from my sleep. I rolled to grab my gun from the nightstand. A frightened maid was backing out the door pulling her cleaning cart with her.

She cried out in broken English, "So sorry. So sorry."

Looking around the empty room only added to my growing loneliness. There was no reason to stay. I threw my stuff into the trunk of my fabulous car. Rummaging through the things in the back seat, I couldn't find the photo album Linda had put together for me. I'd left it in the cabin. Filled with disappointment, I considered going back. Instead, I pulled out of the parking garage and went looking for The Mustang Bridge Ranch to buy a little R & R.

The Mustang is a world famous brothel near Sparks, a little town outside of Reno. Seventy dollars later, I didn't feel any better than before. It did nothing for the emptiness that plagued me. If anything, my loneliness was more acute.

Meandering down to the Interstate, I picked up four hitchhikers. Each was heading to a different place. Small as it was, I had a purpose again.

A few hours later we stopped for gas at one of those little mom and pop stations where the sign says: *Last Gas for 115 Miles*. As my passengers bought sodas, I headed to the bathroom to fix up. Water dissolved the two baby crisscrosses in my spoon. I drew the evil broth into a syringe and bought myself a few more hours of driving time.

Rounding the corner into the service station I asked the attendant, "You got a drinking fountain?"

"Nah, this water ain't fit to drink, too much alkali."

I thought my heart was going to stop right there. If the water is undrinkable, I was probably in trouble. Somehow my sinister soup had just become a little too sinister. Oddly enough, I soon forgot my pending doom. I was still alive.

The next 10 days took me across the Midwest. I would drop off one traveler and pick up another. My Good Samaritan adventure had turned into a chore. I was tired.

El Paso was where I dropped off my last passenger. But running solo wasn't working either. I didn't want to be alone. When I spotted another dusty traveler holding a sign saying, Destination: New Orleans, I stopped and offered him a seat. He was about my age and said he was heading back home after spending a year in California.

His story was interesting, "Hangin' out with friends doesn't put food on the table. I'm going back home. Maybe I can stay with my Mom while I look for work,"

That got me thinking about my situation and asked, "Do you really think your Mom will let you stay with her?"

"Heck, moms will always take you back."

Hoping that was true, and after a thoughtful silence I said, "I'll take you there."

His comment had made its way directly into my heart. I remember thinking. *Moms may take you back but what about a guy like Walt?*

We spent the day trading stories. My recent past kept me from being as open with him as he was with me. Just talking about it seemed to help him.

"Bottom line is, things in California didn't go as expected. I don't know what I was thinking to let myself get so messed up."

"You? Me too," I said. "I totally understand."

"Thanks, man. It's gonna be tough tellin' my Mom she was right. But that woman is a great lady . . . loved me enough to let me move out and be a jerk. She'll take me back with hugs and tears. You know, the prodigal thing?"

At that moment, I truly envied the guy. We had a few things in common. The difference was: he knew where he was going. I was lost as a ball in tall weeds.

We were driving through Dallas when I looked up and saw: Galloway, Exit 1 mile. That was Mom's exit. Without thinking I jerked the wheel and was off the road.

"Hey John, why are we stopping?"

Sitting there, looking at the exit sign, made me realize how tired I was and how much I needed to see Mom. "I've decided to go home too. This is as far as I can take you, man."

I popped the trunk. He was visibly disappointed. I handed him his stuff and we said our good-byes. He turned to leave, but I called him back, "Hold on a second." I reached into my duffle and pulled out a couple of bundles of cash. "Here, stick this in your pack."

His eyes got real big. "Where the hell did you get all that money?"

"I'm a Bank Robber."

As I spoke, I exposed the shoulder holster under my jacket. His eyes got even bigger. "Do us both a favor, take the money and go. Don't look back or try to read my license plate. Just walk away and have a good life."

I slid into the driver's seat and watched until he was out of sight, then slipped the Caddy into gear and headed home. - J.E.S.

I stood up just before the doors were being closed, after the 9:00 pm rack and made my way out the door. Someone I had never met was walking towards me and it was obvious I was who he was looking for.

"You Tex?"

"Who wants to know?"

"Hey, I'm Stump. Just came in on a chain from El Reno, Oklahoma. I've got a Kite for you."

He handed me a crumpled up sheet of paper. I opened it up and read.

SOME NEWS from NEWSOME
1. I'm okay.

I wasn't sure if I was going to cry or laugh. But for sure it was a good thing. I leaned over the rail of C-Tier, smiled and whispered, "Yeah, me too."

CHAPTER SEVENTY-FIVE

REUNION

I slept way past chow and felt like I really needed it. I had made it through an emotional part of my life and was drained. I dug through my locker and found a banana and a bagel. From somewhere up on the third tier I could hear Buddha's radio blaring *In the Summertime* by Mungo Jerry. Not my thing but it was cool. The guard went up and told him to turn it down.

40th Journal Entry: Saturday, September 1st, 1973 - 10:15 am

Mom came blasting through the screen door when she realized I was standing on her porch.

"Johnny! Is that really you?"

Our hug lasted a long time. Mom just kept hanging on. It made me realize how much I'd missed her and that she'd missed me too. When she finally let go, she held me at arm's length and just looked.

"Somebody pinch me. I can't believe you're here. Walt's out pickin' up cars. Is he ever gonna be amazed to see you."

"I'm sure he will, Mom." The thought didn't thrill me so I changed the subject, "Where's Tammy?"

"I think she's at a friend's house. Coffee's on. Let's get us a cup. You can tell me all about where you been and what you been doin."

Walking to the kitchen Mom kept up a steady stream of questions. My mind was racing, fabricating . . . I couldn't exactly tell her the truth.

"Why didn't you let me know you were comin'? Never mind, you're here now. Sit down, Sweetie. Still take your coffee black?"

"Yeah, thank you."

Mom planted two full cups on the oilcloth-covered table and sat down. She reached for the sugar and retrieved less than a half teaspoon into hers. With a big sigh, she gave me a smile that shot straight through my heart. I almost lost it when she put her hand on mine and started with words so tender and loving, "Where do we begin? I've missed you so much. I can't even tell." That's when she slapped my hand and changed her tone. "Do you know how worried I've been? A phone call woulda been nice."

She squeezed my hand and we had a good laugh. That and Mom's strong coffee helped me relax.

"I'm really sorry. I didn't mean to make you worry."

"I guess it's a mother's job, but here you are and all that worry was for nothin.' We've got a whole lot of catchin' up to do."

"Well . . . I, ah . . ." What could I say? I had to come up with something . . . "I, I started my own repo business . . . in Seattle. In fact, I just sold it."

Looking back, I think it was a pathetic story coming from a teenager, but she bought it. Well, at least she acted like she did. Either Mom was smart enough to not question me or maybe she wanted to believe her son had been successful. Ignorance is indeed bliss.

"Mom, I've been wondering, what do you want to do?"

"I know it's early but I'm fixing to get a jump on cookin' up a special dinner. You are staying aren't you?"

"Yes, I'll be staying."

Mom took another quick sip of coffee, left her chair and began yanking things out of the fridge, peeling potatoes, and going in all directions at once. During the entire time, she kept dreaming up things to say and ask.

"What a relief to have you back home. You can't imagine what all went through my head, trying to figure out where you were and if you were okay."

"No news is good news, Mom. If something had gone wrong, you'd have been notified."

"Notified? Now see, its talk like that gets me so nervous."

"I'll do better next time. Back about my question, tell me what you'd like to do with . . . like, with the rest of your life?"

She turned to me, with the faucet running and her wet hands dripping.

"Honey, I don't rightly know. What a thing to ask in the first 20 minutes of you bein' back home."

She turned off the water, dried her hands, and came back to the table. "What in the world's got you going on with a serious question like that?"

Mom was astonished when I opened the duffle and showed off my stash. We counted roughly $130,000. It was less than I thought I had. But then again, I'd given a lot of it away, perhaps too much.

"I have money, so think about it and let me know."

"Johnny, I haven't got a clue but I sure will think about it. My goodness, I'd have never guessed in a million years that you would be so successful, so young."

"While you're thinking, I know what I want. Put dinner on hold and let's go."

"Where to?"

"You'll see."

We took off in my car.

Big Town is a mall between Dallas and Mesquite. I took Mom into a music store where she helped me pick out a drum set that I thought looked really sharp. It was a blue sparkle Ludwig kit with two toms and a floor tom. I didn't know anything about drums. I just knew I wanted them.

On the drive back home, Mom couldn't stop talking about my purchase. "Johnny, I can't believe you just walked in there and bought something so expensive and paid cash."

"Well, now I want to do something special for you."

A look of stress covered her face. We sat in silence for a few minutes, both of us thinking. My mother had a way of somehow turning a good thing into something bad. You could offer her all the gold in Fort Knox and she'd figure out how it was going to cause her problems. I thought if I coaxed her she would have to think of something.

"Tell me what you want and I'll buy it for you, a car, a house, anything."

Her voice was sad and fearful. "I don't know Johnny."

The look on her face spoke volumes. To her, having money was in some ways harder than not having it.

"No pressure Mom. When you figure it out, tell me."

I was setting up my drums in the living room when Walt walked through the door. A glance in my direction didn't even slow him down as he headed for the kitchen. As he walked past me he asked, "What the hell is that?"

I was not impressed with his greeting and didn't answer. I figured it had to be obvious, even to Walt. A few seconds later he showed up again with a glass of iced tea.

"Just what the hell are you doing here?"

"Well thanks Dad, I'm glad to see you too."

He flopped down in his chair and watched me finish setting up. "Where the hell did you get enough money for those?"

Before I could answer Mom walked in, turned and gave Walt a sarcastic look. "He's got more than you ever had."

Mom handed him my bag and I thought he was going to come unglued. It took him a while to recover from the shock. Then for some strange reason his attitude changed and I became his best friend.

He spent a moment lost in thought, then jumped from his chair and said, with a much more civil voice, "Wait here."

He disappeared into the bedroom and returned with a small catalog full of real estate listings, mostly of farms in the Midwest. The pages were worn, with ragged edges. Some were dog-eared and had obviously been thumbed through time and time again. Several pages were heavily noted and some ranked for preference. The catalog was several months old.

"Can you get a newer one of these?" I asked.

"Sure John. Let's go."

Walt yelled over his shoulder at Mom on our way out. "Dot, we'll be back soon."

With that, we were off on a mission to the 7-11. Somehow it didn't matter that Walt was schmoozing me. The only important thing to me was the chance to buy Mom a house. I wanted to make certain she never have to pay rent again.

After grabbing a fresh copy of the catalog we drove to the Mid-Continent Truck Stop for a cup of coffee and a chance to talk. Walt and I looked through the ads and circled a few. Then with a half grin he sat back. "Ok, John, what gives?"

"What do you mean?"

I knew exactly what he meant but I wanted to savor the moment and stay in control, keep him guessing. Maybe I wanted him to be proud of me. That seemed ridiculous since he'd kicked me out at such a young age.

Yet, he had taught me a lot, letting me work with him. Ours was a hurtful and confusing relationship.

"Listen John, you can B S your mother, but that dog don't hunt with me. You're only a kid. Drivin' around in a caddy? And, where the hell did you get all that money?"

I just laughed.

"You wanna take a guess?"

Just as I noticed a bunch of cop's a couple of tables away, Walt gave his answer, a little too loud for comfort. "Well, I don't think you have what it takes to pull a robbery."

"Dang Walt, not so loud!"

"I must have struck a chord."

"You hit the nail on the head."

Walt put both arms on the table, pushed his face close to mine and with a grin larger than his head, he whispered, "You're kidding me."

"No, Walt, I'm not."

His eyes were as big as Texas. Just then the waitress decided to refill our cups. The moment she left, we were back at it.

"What do you mean I don't have what it takes?"

"I don't know. I guess I'd always figured you'd end up turning cars. So you pulled a robbery. What did you hit?"

"Banks, grocery stores . . . mostly stores. We were hitting a couple of times a week for about a year and a half."

"We?"

"Just a couple of people I know. After 18 months we called it quits . . . didn't want to push our luck so we dissolved our association. Figured it was best to split before something happened."

Walt hung on my every word, then asked, "Can they come back and bite you?"

"Maybe, but I don't think so . . . at least I hope not."

"John, that's crazy you know."

Walt looked at me as if he was really concerned. It was a nice thought, even though I knew he didn't mean it.

"Well, kid, maybe it's a good time to get out of town."

We spent the next hour or so searching the publication for suitable properties. Mostly we looked at farms around Wisconsin and Minnesota.

As we arrived back at the house, I asked Walt if he knew where David was.

"He's staying in that motel up on I-30."

"Thanks. Tell mom not to wait dinner, I'll have leftovers when I get back." - J.E.S.

A general announcement blared out on the Intercom: *'Tom Laughlin will be in the auditorium for a presentation of the hit movie Billy Jack. Units H through M report if you care to watch. Units B through G will be called later this evening.'*

I had heard of the movie but never seen it. Paul rushed over to my cell and said, "Man you gotta see this. It's about oppression and defeating the crooked cops."

I grabbed a couple of Cokes, a bag of Doritos and we headed out.

CHAPTER SEVENTY-SIX

GRAND THEFT AUTO . . . AGAIN?

Wow. Great movie and funny too. I never saw a movie that was both funny and powerful. Howard Hesseman was hilarious. Mr. Laughman gave a short speech before the flick and took questions after. Not bad . . . *One Tin Soldier Rides away.* . . .

41st Journal Entry: Saturday, September 1st, 1973 - 7:00 pm

I was surprised when a pretty young girl opened the motel room door and greeted me by name. Marsha said we'd met before but I couldn't remember. I was also surprised to see Tammy there. David emerged from the bathroom and after a couple of where you been's, it was just like old times.

At one point during the night I brought in a stash of uppers and my rig. After telling Tammy to watch TV, David, Marsha, and I headed to the bathroom where I showed them how to fix up. Neither of them had ever done anything other than pot but I was fading fast. I figured I ought to share if I was going to fire up in their room.

Almost the minute I closed the bathroom door, Tammy called out, "Don't think I'm stupid. I know what you'll are doin'. I saw you had a spoon."

I don't know if I was angrier because she was aware of what I was doing, or because she actually knew what it took to shoot up. Either way we didn't let it stop us.

About a week after arriving in Dallas, the ignition switch in my Cadillac went out, but being the resourceful repo man I was, I simply hotwired it. For a couple of weeks I drove around neglecting to take the time to have it repaired. Walt gave me a special wire he'd made that runs from under the hood through the door so I could start the car and turn it off without having to raise the hood.

Late one day Mom asked me to run an errand. Somewhere on the way back to her house, I checked my rear view mirror and noticed a police car behind me. As my attention returned to the street, another squad car blocked my path. I stopped, put my car in park and shut it off. By then several more police cars filled the residential street.

My hands flew up as they came running to surround me with guns drawn. One officer reached in through the open window and grabbed me by the neck, pulled me out of the car, and shoved me to the pavement. In a heartbeat, the cop was on me with a knee planted in the small of my back, a .38 Special to my head.

All kinds of thoughts buzzed through my mind. *If I'm getting busted, why in this state? Going to the Pen at Huntsville is scary. And how the hell did they find me so fast? Bill, Linda, had they been caught? Did Marty rat on us? I'm keeping my mouth shut til I can call McCullough.*

Once the handcuffs were on, they yanked me up, dragged me to the nearest cruiser and shoved me in the back seat. There I sat wondering, *am I facing Federal Bank Robbery charges or State charges from one of the grocery stores.*

I finally asked the question, "What's the charge?"

"Grand Theft Auto."

Was I being arrested for stealing getaway cars? I was a confused. "What car was I supposed to have stolen?"

He turned and looked at me as if I was stupid. "The one you're driving, dumb ass."

Just then another officer pulled the hotwire from under the hood and lifting it up for all to see, he announced, "Yep, it's wired."

My jaw dropped open and it was all I could do to keep from laughing out loud. "Check the glove box. You'll find the title and registration in my name. He checked, but blew it off. I had a feeling I was going to jail no matter what. Apparently, some lady's Cadillac had been stolen only a few blocks away. Fifteen minutes later, I drive by. How convenient. It made no difference that my Caddy was a totally different color, different model and the serial numbers didn't match. Somehow, this was about a kid driving a hotwired Cadillac.

I decided to ask a few more questions, "Listen, how could I paint the car and change the serial number in 15 minutes? Take my keys, they fit and if you turn it, you'll see the ignition switch is defective. That's why it's wired."

The cop was quick to tell me, "They'll get this all straightened out at the station. If what you say is true, you'll be out in no time."

Then it came to me, when the police ran my license he probably saw I had a prior for joy riding. All they could see was a kid with priors in a hotwired Caddy, so of course I was guilty.

Shrewd.

At jail I was booked, printed, and mugged. The familiar setting of the Mesquite Jail was not a welcome site, but I was still almost giddy, knowing I wasn't headed to the big house. By late afternoon I still hadn't been questioned. I was so hungry I didn't mind eating the despicable, overcooked TV dinner they served with a half pint carton of lukewarm milk.

The night passed as did the next day. No visit from the detectives, no interrogation, nothing. By the third morning I was beginning to think they'd forgotten me. Then, without warning, I was released.

They handed me my personal belongings. "Here's your stuff. We keep the hotwire. Those things are illegal, you know? And here are the directions to the lot where your car has been impounded."

I walked home, grateful to have dodged that bullet. When Mom and Walt heard where I'd been, Walt grabbed his keys and we took off to reclaim my car. At the Impound, I was handed a towing and storage bill for close to a $100. We were both fuming but Walt got real vocal.

"Don't pay it, Johnny. Cops made the mistake."

"I don't need any more trouble, Walt. I want my car so I'm gonna pay the bill."

The next couple of weeks were spent hanging out with David and Marsha getting high. But one night David started asking questions, "Man, you've paid for our motel and the meth. Where you getting all that money?"

I went out to the car and brought in a newspaper. The front-page article showed pictures of Linda and me with the caption: *Bonny & Clyde Style Hold Up.*

David didn't believe it was me. "That's one of those phony newspapers, like they make up at carnivals."

He changed his tune when I brought in my bag full of cash. It was a dumb thing to do. My brain was saying, *keep your life of crime a secret.* But I loved David and trusted him. It had always made me feel good to know he thought I was cool, that he was proud to have me as his brother. I wondered, *what does he think of me now?* - J.E.S.

I sat there on my bunk questioning, *what had I done to my little brother? He meant more to me than any other person in the world.*

I had spent my whole life trying to protect David and keep him out of harm's way. Yet, I was the one who had introduced him to drugs. I turned off my light and fell back on my bunk as the tears of remorse flowed. I asked God to forgive me.

CHAPTER SEVENTY-SEVEN

MY LAST BUCK

Paul came by my cell and said one of his favorite authors had died. J. R. R. Tolkien. His passing really seemed to upset him.

As best as I could, I tried to console him, "So sorry Paul, I've never heard of him"

"I figured so. Here I brought you a couple of his books."

He handed me *The Hobbit* and *Lord of The Rings*. I decided I would wait until I finished journaling before reading them.

42nd Journal Entry: Sunday, September 2nd, 1973 - 7:20 pm

Everybody was energized, getting into the act, packing up the U-Haul for our move to Minnesota. Even Walt kicked in to help me clean out my trunk, tossing stuff til it was totally empty . . . at least I thought so. After pitching the last load of trash, I returned to Walt who shoved a small canvas bag full of drugs and syringes at me.

"What the hell is all this?"

I tried to act shocked. "Where did it come from?"

"The trunk of your car, John."

I shrugged. "It must have been in the car when I bought it."

Walt wouldn't buy any of it. He'd already decided I was a junkie and there was nothing I could do to convince him otherwise. Then he nailed me. "Let me see your arms."

Like an idiot I held out my arms, thinking the track wouldn't show.

"Geez John! What the hell am I going to do with you? Is this how you've been spending time with David?"

I whispered, "No one knows I'm using."

"Better not let your Mom find out."

He walked to the trash and threw everything away. By the time we were ready to leave for Minnesota, my trunk was loaded with Mom's treasures. Donnie decided to come along. David stayed behind with Marsha.

The trip was long but pleasant. When we arrived in the little town of Mizpah, I bought Mom a forty-acre farm, a foreclosure. It cost me $55,000.

Heading down country roads, we were all excited about rural living. When we arrived, there was someone in our field, bailing Alfalfa and hauling it into the barn. Our new neighbor came over to greet us. We'd been told this neighbor owned the forty acres on either side of us and had wanted to purchase our land. But we beat him to the punch. He was not happy about that but at least cordial on our first meeting.

"I didn't know when you'd be here but figured you wouldn't want that field to go to seed. The usual deal is one third comes to me as payment for putting up the hay."

Walt could smell money a mile away and asked, "What would you give for the other two thirds?"

"Eight thousand."

"That's a deal."

Walt was real pleased with himself. We hadn't even moved in and he'd already made his first profit as a farmer. He said "It feels good to have money, so I don't have to use your loot all the time."

Within a couple of weeks I decided to go back to school. I had already enrolled when I was hired at the local sawmill where Walt worked. I drew an evening shift. Mom was thrilled to be staying at home fixing up her own place and we all began settling into life on the farm. I couldn't resist being a little proud of myself for making it happen.

Walt helped me put together a suitcase full of clothes, a wallet with my fake ID, about $50,000 of my remaining cash, a good pair of boots and a jug of water. We wrapped it in a big piece of plastic and hid it in a safe place. It contained everything necessary if I had to make a run for it. There were several locations nearby where a person could sneak across the border, undetected, into Canada. Walt and I kept my hidden get-away suitcase as our little secret.

"If it hits the fan John, just run back here, grab it and take off."

Everyone was so pleased about having a place of our own that we'd forgotten to check for certain basics. As it turned out, the old house didn't have indoor plumbing. How hard could it be to build a bathroom?

There really wasn't a suitable location anywhere in the house, so we moved the outhouse onto the back porch. I'm not kidding. We figured out how to install the plumbing and within a week we had a shower flowing and began the drainage system for a toilet. In the mean time we would simply make do in the great outdoors. Tammy was especially annoyed at having to go behind the barn.

Donnie had a weekend job gathering wild rice with some local Indians he had met. I went with him a couple of times. It was fun, floating along in canoes, gathering the rice in burlap bags. We took the harvest to a local dealer who paid by the pound.

Working at the mill was really hard on me. Working my butt off for a couple of dollars an hour was a drastic change from my previous employment. I told myself it was not about the money. I wanted to become part of the community.

Blending into my new environment meant sneaking out to the gravel pits outside of town for weekly parties with the local kids. I was 18. Some were a little younger, a few, like Donnie, were older. He had his eye on a girl named Nancy. Everybody called her Clutch.

Hanging out by the bonfire drinking beer with eight tracks blasting Rod Stewart was the in thing to do. There was only one cop in the area so we didn't worry about going to jail for drinking underage. One night Donnie drove up to the campfire and saw Nancy with me. I couldn't tell if he was pissed or just bummed. He was over it in a few days. But it was more than the Nancy thing. I could tell Donnie was restless, so I wasn't surprised when he packed up and headed back to Dallas.

Tammy was having a hard time too. Life in the country wasn't what she'd expected. Mom liked the change of pace. The peace and quiet was good for her. I enjoyed playing my drums and the contentment of sitting on the porch listening to the birds. What a contrast to my days of crime.

On the rare occasion when I did think about what I'd done, I couldn't believe the guy in those newspaper headlines was actually me. Out on a farm, in the middle of nowhere was exactly where I needed to be. I was a totally different person, enjoying a completely new life.

The trouble started when Walt decided we should go hunting to save money on our food bill. The poaching laws stated if you were caught killing a deer, the game warden would come onto your property, seize your car, guns, knives and anything remotely associated with processing game. Walt thought rules were for everyone but him.

The hunt was to take place on the backside of our neighbor's forty acres. We waited until long past dark, then headed out. I lay on top of my Cadillac with a .308 British Enfield rifle. Walt drove over bumps and ditches then turned on the headlights. About 150 yards ahead was a 10 point Buck. I emptied the clip but wasn't sure I hit him because the buck just stood there.

Walt was furious. "Dang John, I thought you could shoot."

"You try taking a bead on anything when you're bouncing across a plowed field."

As Walt left the car the buck tried to run but stumbled.

"Tackle it John."

"Forget that. I'm not going near him."

The Buck struggled to stand. Then the poor thing staggered again and fell. Giving me a dirty look as he passed by, Walt pulled out a hunting knife and cut the animal's throat. Seeing a buck sprawled on the hood of my Caddy as we headed for home was a strange sight. Walt gutted him and hung the carcass in the garage to let him bleed out.

The next morning at breakfast, Walt was preoccupied with real concerns. "I'm worried the guy next door will find out we've been poaching on his land. He's no dummy."

That got me worried too. "What happens if he calls the game warden?"

Walt snarled back, "Don't ask me. I just moved here."

"But Walt, they need a warrant to come on our property and poke around, don't they?"

"Maybe. I hadn't thought of that. And if he does come around without one, we can tell him to leave. By the time it takes for a judge issues one, we'll get rid of the buck."

Thinking back on it, we were pretty stupid, car tracks, blood . . . that's what happens when there's no plan. By then Walt was marching around giving orders. "We'll need a guard outside to make sure nobody goes into the garage."

We kept watch all day. But as sundown neared, it was overcast and it looked like rain. We were beginning to slack up a bit on guard duty. Walt and I were sitting at the kitchen table playing Chess and that's when all Hell broke loose.

I was arrested, went to trial, and . . . so here I am. In Lompoc Penitentiary. - J.E.S.

CHAPTER SEVENTY-EIGHT

FINISHED

I had committed to and accomplished my goal of writing every day with a one month target for completion. Emotionally it was an unpleasant trip through bitter memories with occasional reasons to laugh. Tears, heartache, regret, depression and despair all mingled into my tragic past. As for the writing, I had actually looked forward to that part of my chore. Kelly told me to write it all down. So I did, just like I would have said it.

I was hopeful that writing would help me understand my past and lead to a better future. Dr. Bliss said it was possible. I knew it would take time for her and Kelly to read what I'd written. I desperately wanted to know what they thought of my "less than jubilant journal,"

My appointment with Barb was brief.

"Welcome back. Did you have a good vacation?" I asked.

"Vacations are over rated, but the conference was great. Look at this mess." Barb pointed to the stack of papers on her desk. "There's my penance for having a great time and enjoying our family reunion."

Those words stung. I wondered what it would be like to attend a reunion with my family.

Barb's next words fractured my thoughts, "I have to say, I missed our sessions John and I look forward to reading your journal."

She promised to make a copy for Kelly and give it to him as soon as possible. I knew their schedules were tight. Waiting around would be gruesome.

Patience has never been my friend.

CHAPTER SEVENTY-NINE

THE CRITIQUE

I received word from Barb and Mr. Kelly. They had read my journal and wanted to meet. I could hardly wait. Kelly and I both arrived at Barb's office at the same time.

After taking our seats, Barb began. "Your Journal is a remarkable piece of work, John. And by adding the childhood years, we've discussed in our sessions, your Journal could even be a movie."

I was humbled and pleased with Barb's evaluation.

Kelly took his turn, "Doc is right. It's like reading a crime mystery novel. But true."

Barb nodded her approval. "John, you are a very talented communicator."

"I concur," said Kelly. "Your descriptions of what went on during your days as a bandit are unbelievable. Your writing tells a lot about yourself and I'm more convinced than ever that when the time comes, we have a good case for parole."

"Mr. Kelly, I'm happy to hear you say that, sir."

"Well when we first met, I said I felt you were salvageable and I meant it. There have been a few hiccups along the way, such as visits to the hole." Kelly gave me a knowing look. "But overall, you're making progress."

"Thank you sir."

Barb looked at me with those terrific eyes of hers and said, with all sincerity, "Your Journal has given us a lot of insight on how to proceed with your rehabilitation. But more than that, I think you should seriously think about writing the rest of your story."

"You mean like writing an entire book?"

"I do. You have the skill and you certainly have a story worth telling."

"Wow, I never expected my writing would cause this kind of reaction."

Kelly added his support. "Your story could help other young people think twice about taking similar paths."

Back in my cell, I had to lie down. What I'd just heard was beyond belief. Two people, in a prison of all places, had given me encouragement like I'd never experienced before. It was humbling.

I looked inside my locker and found there was another notebook. I grabbed it and quickly tore the cellophane wrapper off. The ocean air brought the scent of eucalyptus into my cell. After staring beyond the bars and into the darkness of the night, I began to write:

CHAPTER ONE

CAPTURE

Shadows of the Minnesota sun lengthened as daylight gave way to dusk. My little sister sat tracing raindrops . . .

THE AFTERWORD

SUMMER 2012

Even if you can't see them yet, you know they're coming. Twenty-four bikers, tearing down the highway, have their own unmistakable sound. I was right in the middle of them as we rode into the yard of Colorado's Sterling State Penitentiary. The irony of it all made me smile.

In 1972 I entered a similar facility. At barely 19 years old I was a convicted bank robber in shackles. I remembered how desperately I wanted to get out of prison. Now, forty years later, I had become a pastor and servant of Jesus Christ and I could hardly wait to get back in.

The 110 mile ride from Denver gave me time to reflect on being paroled and my attempts to change and become a better man. Nothing happened until I met Jack, a young seminary student, who told me about Jesus and gave me a Bible. God's first proof to me of His existence was to completely take away my addictions to both drugs and alcohol.

I was saved on a Tuesday and by Wednesday I'd written two gospel songs. Thursday Jack took me into McAlester, Oklahoma's State Penitentiary, where we met with dozens of men. They told me their stories, I told them mine. I could identify with those guys and desperately wanted to return as a minister, to let them know someone cared. There was paperwork to be filled out and sent in. The following week my background check had been reviewed. My request was denied; over time, many others were, as well. Finally, the doors have opened and I am somewhere between terrified and thrilled.

The roar from two dozen sets of Harley pipes ricocheted off the prison buildings, calling the convicts to the yard. Riders in black leather rolled past cheering prisoners who were shouting their approval. They couldn't believe it. As far as they knew, this had never happened before . . . motorcycles cruising through prison gates into their territory.

A stage had been set up at one end of the yard. We played and sang. When the time came, members of the band left the stage, all except for me. I slipped the blues harp into my pocket and took on my role of ex-con minister . . . the pastor with a past.

I told them about when I had attended such events. How it meant little more to me than another excuse to get out of my cell for a few more hours. I told them, "The guard in that tower is there to keep you from escaping to freedom. But you can fire the guard you placed in your heart and find liberty by letting Jesus Christ take over."

I spoke to the "naturals," prison lingo for those doing life without parole. I said, "Everyone else here will someday parole. But the world they are going back to is the same evil, corrupt world that lured them to this prison in the first place. I'm here to tell you, that if you accept Jesus as your savior, the world you will parole to is a world without temptation or accusation. A world of perfection with no wants, no needs, no worries or danger for yourself or your loved ones. You will be paroled to a world full of love and peace."

By the time I'd finished, the men were on their feet. Some of the biggest and strongest were crying. Everyone else was cheering. Me? I was in the clouds. After 20 something years of full time ministry to the lost and homeless, I was looking at another bunch of guys who were lost and homeless. Tears threatened to fall as I looked out on the prisoners. They were all ages, all colors, men of every heritage imaginable. It was so clear to me; this was where I belonged. This was where I was created to serve.

ACKNOWLEDGEMENTS

ELIZABETH "PAIGE" EVANS
For the gazillions hours of editing, re-editing and helping me correct everything that spellcheck mis-corrected
(if that's a word).
For the seemingly endless meals, warm bunks and the seren-
ity of the early morning call from dozens of Longhorn cattle
during our countless working sessions in Kiowa Colorado.
You will never really know how much your dedication to this
project means to me.
Raylene and I love you and Greg. You are family.

SAM SPITZER
He spent many hours designing the cover as I grumbled that
it wasn't quite what I wanted. But instead of complaining, he
simply kept working. Thanks a bunch Sam, you rock.
Cover Art Director: John Swanger
Cover Art Layout: Sam Spitzer

PRE READERS & PROOF READERS
Bo - Betty - Paul & Aileen - Michael - Tammy - Leanor -
Mike & Mary
Craig - Sarah - Leif - Mary - Traci - Sheri - Steve - Walter -
Diedre - Randa

FALL 1984

Raylene: "Mom, I think God has sent me the man I'm
supposed to marry."
Maxine: "Oh?"
Raylene: "He's a musician."
Maxine: "And?"
Raylene: "And he's a biker."
Maxine: "And?"
Raylene: "And . . . and he used to rob banks."
Maxine: "Well in the natural, you wouldn't think it's right. But
once you get into the spirit . . ."

MAXINE

Thank you for listening to God and trusting me with your
daughter.
This side of salvation, she's been the greatest gift.

SUGAR RAY

Thank you, Raylene, for being my love, my compass, and my
inspiration.
You have been my adventure partner on this amazing jour-
ney that God has brought us through.
You have corrected our course, and navigated our way.
You are my gift, and I will forever treasure you.

PRISON VOCABULARY

A BUSTER: A fake or imitation

A WAKE UP: Refers to the day of an inmate's release

ACADEMY: Jail

AD SEG: Administrative Segregation

ALL DAY: A life sentence, as in "He's doing all day"

APARTMENT: Cell

ATTORNEY GENERAL: The authorities

B & W: Bread and water

BABY RAPER: A child molester

BACKING: Support or protection provided by other inmates

BAG: A large quantity of drugs

BALLOON: a balloon full of drugs smuggled in through visits and Keester stashed

BARGIN: A reduction of an original sentence

BEATING THE GUMS: Talking; screaming; shouting

BEEF: Crime; infraction; a problem the inmate faces in prison

BEING MADE: The process of being discovered, identified or found out

BIG BITCH: Third conviction under the habitual criminal act which carries a mandatory life sentence. See also Little Bitch

BITCH-MARK: A slash across the face made with a razor; intended to let other prisoners know that the individual wearing the scar is on the hit list

BLADE: Sharpened instrument; knife, shive, shank

BLIND: Area where correctional officers cannot see, as in "Let's go to the blind."

BOMB: Paper rolled tightly together that is lit and used to heat items

BONA ROO: One's best clothes. Comes from the French words Bona (good) and Roo (street) because they are said to be good enough for the streets. "I've got my bona roos on, ready for my next visit"

BOOGIE MAN: Guard, hack, turnkey, screw

BOOKS: Trust fund account, "on the books." All money received by a prisoner is placed into a trust account and may be withdrawn for canteen purchases, special orders, postage, and other expenses

BOX: A carton of cigarettes

BOXCARS: Consecutive sentences

BULLET: One year in custody

BUM BEEF: A conviction for a crime for which the person is innocent

BUM RAP: A conviction for a crime for which the person is innocent

BUSH PAROLE: Escape

BUTCHER: Captain of the guards

CALL IT A DAY: A prison phrase used to indicate that someone entered protective custody

CANTEEN: Prison Stores

CAT WALK: Walkway on a tier where officers patrol. Or officers are in the area, as in "cat walk front to back."

CHAINS IN THE HOLE: Transport Bus has arrived

CHECK IN: To voluntarily be placed into protective custody

COFFEE AND A WAKE UP: Out in just over a day

COMMISARY: Anything bought at the Canteen

CON: A prisoner who has gained respect

COUNT: The institutional count, repeated at different times in the day. Everything stops while prison staff make sure no one is missing. May be referred to as the "count time."

CRANK: Amphetamines

CROAKER: A prison medical officer

CUT ME A SKID: give me a break

DADDY: Dominant in a homosexual relationship

DANCING: Fighting

DIME: A 10-year sentence

DIME BAG: $10 worth of drugs

DOWN & OUT: Report to the office (or bars)

DROP A DIME ON: Snitch

DRY SNITCH: To provide incriminating information in a criminal matter to law enforcement, but refuse to testify

DUCKIT: A pass issued in prison allowing an inmate to go from point A to point B

DUST: Kill

FELL DOWN: Got stabbed

FINK: An informer

FISH: A new inmate

FIT: Short for outfit a home-made contrivance for injecting drugs Intravenously

FIX: To inject drugs intravenously. Or a Syringe

FLAT TIME: To serve one's time without parole

FLAT: A prison shank made from flat metal stock

FLIP: A slang phrase that denotes an individual cooperating with law enforcement

FOG DOWN: The suspension of routine prison activities due to heavy fog

GALLO: Spanish for "rooster." Pressure Artist. Dominant role in a forced homosexual relationship

GEN POP: General Population

GET AT: To contact

GET DOWN: To fight with fists or weapons

GLOBO: Spanish for balloon. This word is often used to describe a balloon full of drugs

GOOD TIME: Credits earned toward one's sentence

GOON SQUAD: A tactical team sent to control an inmate or a group of inmates

GREEN: Cash, folding money

GREEN LIGHT: To authorize the murder of an inmate

GROWING DAISIES: Dead

GUNS: Powerful Arms

HACK: A prison correctional officer

HARD CANDY: A phrase to describe an assault with intent to kill

HARD RULES: Rule that if broken are punishable by death

HAT ON TIGHT: Going home

HAVE A TAIL: To be on parole or probation

HIT LIST: A list of individuals to be murdered

HOLE: Solitary confinement, segregation, disciplinary detention cells

HOMIE, HOMEBOY: Another prisoner from one's hometown or neighborhood.

HOOP: To secret contraband in the rectum

HORN: To inhale drugs through the nostrils

HOT SHOT: An intentional overdose of intravenous drugs or lacing the drugs to be injected with a poisonous substance

HOUSE: Cell

HUMPS: Prison slang term for Camel non-filter cigarettes

INK: Tattoo

INMATE: A term used in prison to describe prisoners who have yet to earn respect

JACK: Home-made alcoholic beverage

JACKET: Central File. Label. To be marked as a snitch, informant, or other identifying label

JOINT: Prison

JONES: Drug habit (or any other habit) Addiction, or an urge

JOTO: Spanish for homosexual

JUICE: Influence or power within the organization

JUNGLE: Recreation yard

KEISTER STASH: To secret contraband into the rectum

KICKING: To withdraw from an addictive substance

KITE: A message sent from one prisoner to another in a different cell block or prison

LA RAZA: Spanish for the People

LAY OVER: To stay at a jail facility for a short period of time while in transit to another jail

LETTING YOUR EAGLE MOUTH OVERLOAD YOUR HUM-MINGBIRD ASS: Making threats you can't back up

LIP: To stash contraband under the lip

LITTLE BITCH: Second conviction under the habitual criminal act which carries a mandatory 20 year sentence. See also Big Bitch

LOCK DOWN: To suspend normal prison operations

LOCK UP: To enter into protective custody

LOP: Loss of privileges

MAIN STREET: General population

MULE: A person who smuggles drugs or contraband into a prison

NADA: Spanish for nothing

OUT COUNT: To count an inmate whose whereabouts are accounted for but not in his cell

PAROLE DUST: Fog

PC: Protective Custody

PC UP: To enter into protective custody

PLAN: A tube for hiding things in and keister stashing

POPPED: Arrested

PRUNO: Prison manufactured alcoholic beverages

PUNK: A term used to describe a coward or homosexual

PUTO: A term used to describe a coward or homosexual

PUT OFF: Parole date set back

RACK: To open or close cell doors

READY ROLLS: A term used in prison to describe store bought cigarettes

RIG: Syringe

ROLLED IT UP: A phrase used to describe an inmate who has entered into protective custody

RUN A MAKE: To locate and check the credentials of an inmate

RUNNER: A person who does favors for prisoners, such as, smuggle drugs into the institution and relaying messages, etc

RUSH: The euphoric feeling after injecting drugs intravenously

SALLYPORT: The secured area where officers and other individuals pass into the institution or enter particular areas of the prison

SANCHO: The person who takes up a relationship with a prisoner's wife while he is serving a time

SANDWICH: To stab an individual using two or more assailants thereby sandwiching the target

SAW BONES: Doctor

SCHOOL: To educate or teach an inmate the ways of jail

SCREW: A correctional officer

SHAKEDOWN: A search of a cell, work area, or person

SHANK: Knife

SHORT TIMER: Close to a parole date

SHORTS: Cigarette Butt

SHOT: Disciplinary write up

SKIN POP: To inject drugs subcutaneously

SLAM: To inject drugs intravenously

SNITCH JACKET: Reputation as an informant

SOFTIE: A term utilized to describe a weak individual

SPOON: A dose of heroin

STANDING COUNT: A counting of inmates in which standing is required to ensure that all inmates are alive

STASH: To hide something

STRAIGHTS: A term used in prison to describe store bought cigarettes

STREETS: The free world

TAILOR MADE: A term used in prison to describe store bought cigarettes

TAKE OUT: To kill

TALK IT A WALKING: I don't want to hear it. Go tell it to someone else

TALKING OUT THE SIDE OF THE NECK: Disbelief in what a prisoner is saying. From past practices when prisoners were not allowed to speak to each other and learned to talk to the person next to them while standing and looking straight ahead

THE GREY GOOSE: The prison transportation bus

THE KEYS ARE WALKING: Courtesy call that a guard is heading your way

THE WALK: A long corridor between cell blocks or Units

THROUGH: To be marked for death

TIE OFF: To place a tourniquet on the arm for intravenous drug use

TIER: Rows of cells, each row rising above another

TO HAVE THE KEYS: To be in a position of leadership

TURF: Gang territory

TURN: To cooperate with law enforcement

TURN OUT: To force an individual into homosexual activity

UNIT: Cell block

WACKED: High on drugs

WALK THE LINE: To be an inmate in the general prison population

WALKING PAPERS: Release papers

YARD: The exercise area. In segregation, the yard may be nothing more than a concrete "dog run" with no equipment. Other units may have a basketball court, recreation equipment, or grassy areas